W9-ACY-560

JANE AUSTEN

Literary Lives
General Editor: Richard Dutton, Senior Lecturer in English,
University of Lancaster

This series offers stimulating accounts of the literary careers of the most widely read British and Irish authors. Volumes follow the outline of writers' working lives, not in the spirit of traditional biography, but aiming to trace the professional, publishing and social contexts which shaped their writing. The role and status of 'the author' as the creator of literary texts is a vexed issue in current critical theory, where a variety of social, linguistic and psychological approaches have challenged the old concentration on writers as specially-gifted individuals. Yet reports on 'the death of the author' in literary studies are (as Mark Twain said of a premature obituary) an exaggeration. This series aims to demonstrate how an understanding of writers' careers can promote, for students and general readers alike, a more informed historical reading of their works.

Jane Austen

A Literary Life

Jan Fergus

Professor of English
Lehigh University

St. Martin's Press   New York

First published in the United States of America in 1991

Printed in Hong Kong

ISBN 0–312–05712–1

Library of Congress Cataloguing-in-Publication Data
Jane Austen : a literary life / Jan Fergus.
    p.   cm.
ISBN 0–312–05712–1
1. Austen, Jane, 1775–1817   2. Novelists, English—19th century—
Biography.   I. Title.
PR4036.F47   1991
823'.7—dc20
[B]   90–47976
                                                               CIP

For Ruth and Gerry Portner
Many Jaunts

Contents

Preface
and Acknowledgements

> You will be glad to hear that every Copy of S[ense] & S[ensibility]
> is sold & that it has brought me £140 besides the Copyright, if
> that sh^d ever be of any value. – I have now therefore written
> myself into £250 – which only makes me long for more.

These words of Jane Austen to her brother Frank, written on 3
July 1813, after she had published two novels, are those of a
professional author who is acutely conscious of her sales and
eager to increase her profits. Most biographies have set Austen
within her social context. This biography places her firmly within
her professional context as one of an increasing number of women
who published novels between 1790 and 1820. Being a professional
writer was, apart from her family, more important to Austen than
anything else in her life.

Austen wrote when opportunities for women to publish had
never been greater, and from her childhood her aim was to see
her works in print. Her literary career depended to some extent
upon the other women novelists of her time, who created and
sustained a market for domestic fiction by women, and whose
attitudes toward writing, like Austen's own, became increasingly
professional. To discover the effect of the literary profession on
Austen's life, I have studied the remaining publishing records of
the period. Some of these are familiar, like the Archives of John
Murray, publisher of *Emma, Northanger Abbey, Persuasion*, and the
second edition of *Mansfield Park*. Others are less well known:
the records of the House of Longman and of Hookham and
Carpenter, firms that published more novels than Murray, and
far more by women. Chapter 1 uses these sources, among others,
to depict what it meant to be a woman writer during Austen's
lifetime, and Chapter 5 draws upon them to offer new insight into
Austen's options, choices and earnings as a professional writer.

Once Austen is placed within her professional context, not only
her life but her works take on new meaning. Acutely conscious of
other women's writing and of women's subordinate and marginal

position within society, Austen began by writing burlesques that offer comic images of female power and possibility. Her unconventional portraits of women in the juvenilia reflect her scepticism about contemporary notions of what women were like – and what they should be like. When she began to write novels, she necessarily addressed a wider audience than her like-minded family and friends. She therefore transformed the images of female power that pervade the juvenilia, giving them more conventionally acceptable dress. From picturing women who literally get away with murder in her burlesques, Austen went on to portray women who figuratively do so in her earliest realistic fiction – women who confront and reject conventional behaviour. In her later novels, she managed to convey an increasing sense of women's insecure and even threatened position within their social worlds without destroying a comic tone. Austen's comedy remains secure, however serious its implications.

Those who are interested in reading more about Austen's life can refer to the list of primary and secondary sources heading the Notes. Almost all the available biographical information on Austen and her family is conveniently and impressively collected in Deirdre Le Faye's recent revision of the 1913 *Life and Letters*, but the less familiar works by Constance Hill and Mary Augusta Austen-Leigh still repay reading; all these works are cited before the Notes. J.M.S. Tompkins' entertaining and scholarly work, *The Popular Novel in England, 1770–1800*, originally published in 1932, still remains the best introduction to the minor writers of Austen's period, although Jane Spencer's *The Rise of the Woman Novelist* (1986) and Nancy Armstrong's *Desire and Domestic Fiction* (1987) provide modern feminist perspectives. Roy Porter's *English Society in the Eighteenth Century* (1982) offers a fine social history of the world that Austen was born into. For visual images of the distance between the freedom of her world and the confinement of Victorian women, see *Mrs Hurst Dancing & Other Scenes from Regency Life 1812–1823*, a book of watercolours by a Regency woman, Diana Sperling, who portrays young Regency women (and men) leading active lives despite their elegant costumes – riding on trunks of trees, slipping on grass, planting and digging, fishing and so on (text by Gordon Mingay, 1981). Literary criticism of Austen's novels is extensive, as David Gilson's impeccable *Bibliography* (1982) attests. The classic works by Mary Lascelles (*Jane Austen and Her*

Art, 1939), A. Walton Litz (*Jane Austen and Her Artistic Development*, 1965) and Stuart Tave (*Some Words of Jane Austen*, 1973) remain valuable and very readable.

I am grateful to the Oxford University Press, by whose kind permission all citations of Austen's fiction are drawn from the editions of R.W. Chapman, 5 vols, 3rd edn (1933) and *Minor Works*, vol. 6 (1954). Page references are inserted directly into the text, with the following abbreviations whenever any ambiguity may occur: *NA Northanger Abbey*; *SS Sense and Sensibility*; *PP Pride and Prejudice*; *MP Mansfield Park*; *E Emma*; *P Persuasion*; *MW Minor Works*. The Oxford University Press has also permitted quotations from Austen's letters to be drawn from Chapman's edition of *Jane Austen's Letters to her Sister Cassandra and Others*, 2nd edn (1952). Citations from this edition will be inserted directly into the text, using the abbreviation *L* followed by the page number and date of the letter.

Some part of the research for this book was made possible by a Travel to Collections grant from the National Endowment for the Humanities. I am grateful to the present representatives of the firm of John Murray and especially to Mrs Virginia Murray, archivist, for permission to examine their archives and for much assistance in doing so. My department chair, Professor Edward J. Gallagher, the Dean of the College of Arts and Sciences, James Gunton, and Provost David Sanchez of Lehigh University, Bethlehem, Pennsylvania, very generously provided time for me to write the book. I am grateful also to the editor for the series, Dr Richard Dutton, who has been helpful, encouraging and patient to an exemplary degree. I would especially like to thank my friends Dr Anne Beidler, Dr Antonia Forster and Geoffrey Holt for looking over much of the typescript, and particularly Dr Virginia Hjelmaa, Hazel Holt, Dr Ruth Portner and Dr Janice Farrar Thaddeus for their careful readings, excellent advice and absolutely indispensable conversation, ideas and encouragement at every stage. I offer gratitude tinged with shame to Ruth Portner; without her astonishing willingness to listen to and comment upon immense blocks of text over the telephone, this book would never have been begun, far less completed.

1
Conditions of Authorship for Women, 1775-1817

Many biographers have written social lives of Jane Austen, and for good reason. Material for a biography of Austen's life is scanty. Apart from her works themselves and the letters that were selected by her sister to be as unrevealing as possible, for information about her we have to rely on family records and traditions along with a few comments from other contemporaries. The family sources tend to stress Austen's ordinariness, indeed to seem proud of it. They considered the decorous absence of 'very important, very recordable events' in her life as appropriate for an unmarried woman as it was for the ball at the Crown in *Emma* (326). In short, although Austen's genius, her brilliant wit, and her consummate art confront us in all her writing, she herself must always elude us in what is written about her.

In these circumstances, biographers have chosen to place what they know about Austen in context, generally by describing the family and the social world she grew up in. This choice, evident in the earliest accounts by her brother Henry Austen (1818)[1] and her nephew James Edward Austen-Leigh (1870), as well as in the most recent studies, makes good sense. Her family was clearly central. All sources agree that family life took up most of her time, energy and affection; social life occupied a good deal of the rest; and literary life had to be crammed into what remained.

But a clear distinction between these three 'lives' is not really possible. When Austen lived, the term 'social' had a much broader meaning than it does now. Social life included both private and public life: in the pre-romantic world Austen was born into, private satisfaction and individual fulfillment grew out of a properly enacted public role. Duties and obligations to others constrained but also enriched the self. In this world, the realities of class, gender, estate, money and manners dictated relationships to family, friends and neighbours; and one's life, especially

1

as a woman, was firmly grounded in these relationships. Austen's novels sharply mirror this world, and literary critics as well as biographers have devoted much effort to rendering it and defining Austen's own place within it. Their work has firmly established the importance of seeing her life and work in context. The need to do so has become in fact a truth universally acknowledged.

One context, however, has not yet been fully explored: the literary or professional. This 'literary life' of Austen will focus on how the conditions of being a writer at the turn of the nineteenth century affected her life and work. These conditions were quite different from those we know. For instance, writers could much more readily publish, though their chances of supporting themselves by writing were as slim. To focus on the literary context, on what it meant to be a writer between 1775 and 1817, does not mean ignoring other contexts. It does mean that Austen's most familiar words and actions, those reiterated by biographers and exhaustively mined by critics, will gain fresh immediacy when they are seen as part of her professional life.   For example, most commentators have not fully understood the frequently quoted advice Austen sent to her niece Anna, who was herself attempting a novel. Austen wrote:

> You are now collecting your People delightfully, getting them exactly into such a spot as is the delight of my life; – 3 or 4 Families in a Country Village is the very thing to work on – & I hope you will write a great deal more, & make full use of them while they are so very favourably arranged. You are but *now* coming to the heart & beauty of your book; till the heroine grows up, the fun must be imperfect.
>
> (*L* 401; 9 Sep. 1814)

The phrase '3 or 4 Families in a Country Village' is usually taken as a definition of Austen's own deliberately limited territory, chosen with delight. But in fact, this phrase applies to the action of only parts of her novels – except *Emma*, which she had been working on for seven months when she wrote this letter to her niece on 9 September 1814. *Emma* does in fact focus on '3 or 4 families' in Highbury, and Austen is probably expressing in part her pleasure in working on the novel. But she is also advising her niece to refrain from introducing more characters until she develops those she has already assembled. In the previous letter to Anna, written one month earlier, we hear of more than 15 characters belonging to at least five different families and appearing in five settings (London, Bath, Lyme, Dawlish and Ireland), all before the heroine has grown up. In that letter too, Austen had mentioned her sister Cassandra's fear that 'there will be too frequent a change from one set of people to another', but added that she herself thinks that 'Nature and Spirit cover many sins of a wandering story – and People in general do not care so much about it – for your comfort' (*L* 395-96; 10 Aug. 1814).

Evidently in the month between this remark and the next, Anna's story wandered too far, so that in context '3 or 4 Families in a Country Village' is less a statement of Austen's own territory than advice on technique of characterisation: concentrate, dramatise, develop your characters, permit them to interact with one another, 'make full use of them'. A country village is one place where those interactions might occur, but so is Bath, so is Portsmouth, so is Rosings. This technique of concentrating characters, permitting them to interact among themselves, to talk about their relationships at the same time that they dramatise them, is an art that Austen brought to perfection, although in the novels she certainly did not confine it to village settings.

Equally striking in Austen's advice is that she was thinking firmly in terms of publication: she comforts her niece by referring to her likely audience ('People' do not mind a wandering story). That is, her advice is geared to the market; it is professional as well as aesthetic. She tells Anna in addition that six of her 48-page booklets 'will make a very good sized volume', and she corrects a detail because it will *'appear* unnatural in a book' (*L* 394; 10 Aug. 1814). Although Anna burnt the uncompleted novel some time after her aunt's death, Austen herself assumed that she would not only finish but publish it. She took the same stance toward Anna's brother Edward's novel-in-progress, telling her sister Cassandra that it will be 'in a style, I think, to be popular' (*L* 462; 4 Sep. 1816).

Anna was 21 and Edward 17 when Austen made these comments; clearly, in her view, youth was no bar to publication. Although today few would be likely to encourage young unpublished writers to expect to see their novels in print, Austen does not hesitate. She takes printing for granted in a way that reflects the greater availability of publication in her lifetime. We know too that she herself began to write very early. She told her twelve-year-old niece Caroline that she wished she had '*read* more and written *less*' when she was her age.[2] Publishing probably *always* formed some part of Austen's idea of authorship even when she was a child, certainly because her family encouraged it, but also in part because the conditions that prevailed in her youth were favourable to such ideas.

During the last quarter of the eighteenth century, increasing numbers of novels were being published, especially by women. Until recently, literary curricula have treated Austen's lifetime as a vast novelistic wasteland, occupied only by herself and perhaps Frances Burney or Ann Radcliffe. Many of her contemporaries, however, including Radcliffe and Burney, Charlotte Smith, Elizabeth Inchbald, Maria Edgeworth and Amelia Opie, among others, received much greater fame and fortune as novelists in their own time than Austen did. Current interest in women's writing has brought scholarly attention to such writers, modern reprints of their works, and their inclusion in course reading lists at universities. But these novelists are only the most visible of a large mass of women who rushed into print at the end of the eighteenth century. The number of women writers increased dramatically throughout the century, as Judith Phillips Stanton's research has shown, but exploded at the end, rising by 'around 50 per cent *every decade* starting in the 1760s'.[3] What conditions of authorship made this publishing explosion possible for women?

This question raises others. What problems did authorship create for women as they entered a profession that men had dominated? What was a literary property and how was it published? How was a book actually produced, advertised, reviewed and distributed (by sale or loan) to readers? What audience was available? Frances Burney's first novel *Evelina, or a Young Lady's Entrance into the World*, published in January 1778 (when Austen was two years old), offers a revealing case study in relation to most of these questions. The case is also particularly relevant to Austen, who admired Burney and may have modelled her career to some extent on hers.

PROBLEMS OF AUTHORSHIP

Like Austen and many other women, Burney insisted on anonymity when she published her first novel. Anonymity addressed a major problem: for a woman in this period, the fame of any kind of authorship could become infamy, and novels were particularly reprehensible, as their famous defence in *Northanger Abbey* indicates (37-8). Proper women were modest, retiring, essentially domestic and private. Authorship of any kind entailed publicity, thrusting oneself before the public eye - thus loss of femininity. Matthew Gregory Lewis, author of the notorious *The Monk* (1796), was outraged when he learned in 1804 that his mother intended to publish a novel. He forbade publication; she yielded but tried to argue with him. His reply pronounced that 'I always consider a female author as a sort of half-man'.[4] Just as 'notoriety' for a woman meant becoming de-sexed, it also involved loss of caste, possibly even loss of marriageability, if one's social position were high enough. In 1815, Lady Louisa Stuart (whose works circulated only in manuscript during her lifetime) told Lady Hood, who was being urged to publish her journal from India, that to do so would be 'losing caste'. The journal remained unpublished, Lady Hood remarried, and Lady Louisa adds a cautionary tale:

> she has told me since, she once said to her present husband [Mr Mackenzie], "Do you know I was on the very point of publishing a book." "I am sure" answered he, "I would never have married you if you had."[5]

Perhaps Mrs Mackenzie had twinges of regret, or a fleeting vision of what might have been, at this provocative dictum from her spouse – or perhaps not. Few questioned that 'for well-educated young women of small fortune, . . . [marriage] must be their pleasantest preservative from want' (*PP*, 122-3). Conservatives like Stuart certainly endorsed this notion as well as the late eighteenth-century prejudice that authorship vitiated female modesty and sacrificed gentility. They were fighting a rear-guard action against authorship, however; such attitudes were in retreat – or at least they were ineffective in preventing women of all classes from venturing to publish.

Predictably, amassing money through print was in some ways

even more compromising than seeking fame, and not just to women. In the eighteenth century, literature became firmly fixed in the marketplace, to the dismay of many. Before the invention of the printing press in the fifteenth century, it had been an aristocratic amusement: Geoffrey Chaucer in the act of reading a Canterbury Tale to a courtly audience or writing a begging poem to his patron presents us with the most familiar images of 'polite letters' before print. An élite audience and a patron would yield court appointments or pensions, not direct payment for writing. Eventually, the new technology was accompanied by changed attitudes towards literature, changes that Alvin Kernan has succinctly summarised:

> An older system of polite or courtly letters – primarily oral, aristocratic, amateur, authoritarian, court-centered – was swept away at this time and gradually replaced by a new print-based, market-centered, democratic literary system.[6]

The public replaced the patron as a source of income. But the older aristocratic attitudes that saw print and payment as vulgar were surprisingly persistent. As late as 1751, Thomas Gray was circulating his 'Elegy in a Country Church-Yard' in manuscript, just as Sir Philip Sidney had done his *Arcadia* or Lady Mary Wroth her *Urania* one or two hundred years earlier. Gray agreed to print his poem only to forestall a pirated version: a periodical was planning to include an unauthorised text. He accepted no money for the poem, but in this respect Gray was exceptional. Most male writers of all classes in the eighteenth century were happy to be paid for their writing, and many unabashedly obtained the best terms – like Alexander Pope, generally said to be the first poet who truly gained his living by his pen.

Not surprisingly, as literary men made themselves at home in the marketplace, they preferred it to be rather exclusive. Much of the old aristocratic disdain for all print was transferred with renewed energy to hack writers – the notorious denizens of Grub Street – and to women who wrote. Only desperate financial need, preferably to support aged parents, a sick husband or destitute children, could excuse a woman's exposing herself in print to obtain money. Accordingly, women's prefaces often apologise for writing by alluding to distresses of this kind, causing reviewers frequently to condescend kindly to their work, though increasingly they bemoaned the number and grammar of 'female scribblers'. Antonia Forster cites a 'small masterpiece of a review of *The Trinket. A Novel, by a Lady* in 1774' which manages to patronise and criticise at once:

> As this Novel is said to be written by a lady, and really appears to come from a female hand, we are too polite to point our critical cannon against her. Could we believe it to be the composition of a man, we should not scruple to say that it contains a crude and indigested heap of characters, incidents, and adventures, tossed and thrown together without much meaning, and less moral.[7]

A woman who managed to overcome all these prejudices might also face legal obstacles to authorship if she were married. Married women had no legal existence. They could not own property or sign contracts. Although Charlotte Smith began to publish in order to support herself and her children after her feckless husband was imprisoned for debt, a contract for her novel *Desmond* (1792) survives signed not by her but by Benjamin Smith, who was at the time residing in Scotland under an alias.[8] The publishing records for Ann Radcliffe's *The Romance of the Forest* (1791) list William Radcliffe, her husband, as the work's author; he apparently received £40 for the second edition (1792).[9] Comparable restrictions survived in France within living memory: 'it was not until 1965 that married women were legally permitted to publish a work or to engage in any profession without the consent of their husbands'.[10]

A single woman with no matrimonial millstones, Frances Burney wrote three increasingly equivocal prefaces to the anonymously published *Evelina*. In them, she apparently accepts but actually rejects the prejudices against female authorship. She apologises for possible faults in the work itself but not really for writing it. Later in life, she asserted that she wrote *Evelina* for 'private recreation' and 'printed it for a frolic, to see how a production of her own would figure in that author-like form'.[11] So far, she sounds conventionally diffident: her writing was amateur, her printing a 'frolic'. The term 'author-like' also suggests proper diffidence. Burney wished to try out for the role of author, not to be known as one, and the three prefaces, addressed to her father, to the reviewers and to readers, witness how problematic the role was for her. All three allege incapacity for authorship and take comfort in concealment and obscurity – anonymity. Yet the subtext in each case is increasing assertion of power. In addressing her readers, for example, she evokes the great names that have preceded her – Rousseau, Johnson, Marivaux, Fielding, Richardson and Smollett – associating herself with them and yet claiming originality too. Significantly, as she becomes more assertive, she adopts a male persona: 'no man need blush at starting from the same post' as the six writers she cites.[12] Implicitly, she rejects the condescension usually bestowed on novels and on women's writing. She asks to be judged by the highest standards.[13]

If women were increasingly able, like Burney, to confront or disregard prejudices against their writing, other hindrances were less easy to set aside. Women's lives usually made authorship difficult. Although a few lower-class women and men took up the pen for profit in the eighteenth century, most were debarred by lack of leisure and education from doing so. Women of the 'middling' classes – wives and daughters of artisans, tradesmen, farmers, and the like – were apt to find themselves engaged in sewing, cooking, shopkeeping, housekeeping and above all child-raising, all the forms of women's work that have proved so tenacious over time and sometimes so hostile to writing. And even women of the professional classes or on the fringes of the gentry, like Burney or Austen, devoted themselves to serving and nurturing in the traditional ways. When Austen was left in charge of housekeeping, she wrote jokingly to her sister:

> I often wonder how *you* can find time for what you do, in addition to the care of the House; – and how good Mrs. West c^d have written such Books & collected so many hard words, with all her family cares, is still more a matter of astonishment! Composition seems to me Impossible, with a head full of Joints of Mutton & doses of rhubarb.
>
> (*L* 466; 8 Sep. 1816)

Burney, as her father's regular scribe, had more family duties than Austen, who occasionally did copy a sermon for her father or brother, but as a rule was responsible only for breakfast and the charge of tea, sugar, and wine stores.[14] Burney copied her father's works for the press from her sixteenth year.[15] Her hand was so well known to publishers that when she desired anonymity for *Evelina*, she was forced to disguise her writing in making her own fair copy.

Burney never complained of her unpaid secretarial work for her father, but Laetitia Hawkins, another contemporary novelist, did, even though her father Sir John Hawkins sometimes paid her: 'I was, I will not say *educated*, but *broke*, to the drudgery of my father's pursuits'.[16] But Hawkins goes on to describe quite remarkable activity, considering the demands that her parents made on her:

> I had no time but what I could *purloin* from my incessant task of copying, or writing from dictation – writing six hours a day for my father, and reading nearly as long to my mother. But two thousand pages never daunted me. I learnt Italian, and extracted from every book that came in my way; I made as large a part of my clothes as could be made at home; I worked muslin; I learnt botany; and I was my mother's storekeeper. Air and exercise were little thought on. I aired indeed with Lady H. in the carriage, but I read or worked.[17]

And what Hawkins means by 'work' is the needlework that all conventionally proper women engaged in, not the work that she was actually paid for.

THE PROCESS OF PUBLISHING

The obstacles to women's writing make their success in publishing all the more remarkable. They were assisted by a rising demand for print, certainly, and by a somewhat more open market than the one we know. For instance, anyone could submit short pieces of fiction or poetry to dozens of magazines – such as the *Lady's Magazine* or the *Gentleman's* – that printed selected readers' submissions without payment; Thomas Chatterton's poems first appeared in several periodicals, particularly the *Town and Country Magazine*. Quite decent payment was offered to regular contributors to the review journals, from about two pounds to four guineas a 'sheet' (sixteen pages), and it was possible for an unknown to obtain such work, but more frequently writers were recommended by other writers, that is, they already had some literary connections.[18] All writers, known or unknown, who wished to obtain payment for a longer work had four options for publishing: by subscription, by profit-sharing, by selling copyright, and lastly on 'commission', a system whereby the author was responsible for paying all the expenses of publication while the publisher distributed the copies and took a commission on all sold.[19]

The parallel stories of how Burney and Hawkins, in particular, managed to publish their first novels by the third method, selling copyright, are instructive. The difficulty for these women, whose employment made them fairly familiar with the publishing world, lay not so much in finding a publisher – at that time called a bookseller – as in preserving secrecy. Hawkins writes with an interesting combination of coy apology for her own youthful efforts and irony at the expense of the whole process:[20]

> Some few years previous to this time [Johnson's death in 1784], being in want of a sum of money for a whim of girlish patronage, and having no *honest* means of raising it, I wrote a downright novel. . . . It was done in the secrecy of a coiner, my only confidential friend being my younger brother. Not at all foreseeing the open contact into which I might be called with any bookseller, I had written to Cadell on the subject of publishing my manuscript – he had declined it, unless he might know the writer. I was not ignorant of the sagacious scent of these agents between authors and the public; and when called on to write what Mr Cadell was to see, I dreaded his recognition of my handwriting, and his incautiously betraying me; but the matter, I suppose, had slipped out of his mind, and I escaped harmless.
>
> On this subject, may I be allowed to say a few words more? The manuscript was published for me by Hookham, who, as I have elsewhere stated, was content to remain in ignorance, and who most honourably sent me for it, twice as much as I needed, and most kindly encouraged me to proceed.[21]

Hawkins suggests that she anonymously published other novels also: 'though I wrote many subsequent volumes, I still preserved my *incognito*.'[22] Neither her first work nor its possible successors have been identified.[23] If the first novel was published a few years before Johnson's death in 1784, Hawkins was probably in her teens when she wrote it. After her father's death in 1789, she eventually did publish five novels under her own name, including one that Austen herself read, *Roseanne, or a Father's Labour Lost* (5 vols, 1814).

The little details that Hawkins discloses in her anecdote of a first publishing venture are revealing. She wanted the money for someone else, the conventional feminine disclaimer: 'for a whim of girlish patronage'. She knew whom to approach. Not having completed the work, she submitted only part of the manuscript: she mentions that she was 'called on to write what Mr. Cadell was to see' and that Hookham 'encouraged me to proceed', as if the work were incomplete. Finally, a respectable publisher like Cadell was unwilling to consider an anonymous manuscript. She herself seems baffled by the secrecy that she preserved in writing and publishing her first novel – 'I scarcely know why I acted thus clandestinely'[24] – but her experience in having to find a second publisher who would tolerate her anonymity was duplicated by Burney, who first approached Robert Dodsley when she wished to publish *Evelina*. Just like Cadell, Dodsley declined to consider an anonymous work; the novel was therefore offered to Thomas Lowndes. And like Hawkins, Burney submitted an incomplete manuscript (first a sample, then two of three volumes, delivered by her brother in disguise). When Lowndes accepted the work but refused to print it until she had finished the third volume – which seems quite a reasonable stipulation – Burney was offended and wrote in her journal:

> Now, this man, knowing nothing of my situation, supposed, in all probability, that I could seat myself quietly at my bureau, and write on with all expedition and ease, till the work was finished. But so different was the case, that I had hardly time to write half a page in a day; and neither my health nor inclination would allow me to continue my *nocturnal* scribbling for so long a time, as to write first, and then copy, a whole volume. I was therefore obliged to give the attempt and affair entirely over for the present. [25]

Burney's writing for herself was 'nocturnal' partly because she spent her days copying for her father and partly because she desired secrecy from her family. Only when she managed to get away from home, on visits to Mr Crisp, could she finish the work. Although preparing their fathers' works for the press certainly gave Burney and Hawkins less time to write, it may have felt like an apprenticeship and made publishing their own works more conceivable. It produced a familiarity with the publishing world in any case that made them able to approach and negotiate with publishers successfully. It did not, however, make representing themselves as fellow authors to their fathers any easier. Burney eventually asked for and received her father's permission to print something anonymously but revealed *Evelina* as her own only after its success; Hawkins never acknowledged her writing to Sir John.

Austen did not negotiate with publishers for herself until late in her career, but she had a completely different relationship with her father than did Burney or Hawkins. He tried to help her publish an early version of *Pride and Prejudice*. His offer of *First Impressions* to the publishers Cadell and Davies, dated 1 November 1797, reveals a reasonable knowledge of options and conditions for publication, but perhaps not as much as that of Burney and Hawkins:

Sirs

I have in my possession a Manuscript Novel, comprised in three Vols. about the length of Miss Burney's Evelina. As I am well aware of what consequence it is that a work of this sort should make its' first appearance under a respectable name I apply to you. Shall be much obliged therefore if you will inform me whether you chuse to be concerned in it; what will be the expense of publishing at the Author's risk; & what you will advance for the Property of it, if on a perusal it is approved of?

Should your answer give me encouragement I will send you the work.

I am, Sirs, Yr. obt. hble. Servt:

Geo Austen[26]

George Austen seems to have known that answers to his enquiries would depend to some extent on the length of the novel and the number of volumes, for he has carefully indicated both. A publisher estimating the expenses of publishing a work at the author's risk would need to know its length. The information that *First Impressions* was about as long as *Evelina* would make it easy to estimate costs for an edition of, say, 500 or 750 copies, which was usual for a first novel in the 1790s and earlier. Similarly, a publisher's offer for the copyright of a novel frequently depended on the number of volumes. During the 1790s, the cheap Minerva Press was offering authors perhaps five pounds per volume; the more reputable Cadell and Davies offered Charlotte Smith fifty pounds a volume.[27] No doubt it was their association with Smith, whose *Emmeline, the Orphan of the Castle* (1788) and *Ethelinde, or the Recluse of the Lake* (1789) Austen had enjoyed, that prompted George Austen to approach Cadell and Davies.

Despite George Austen's evocation of the successful *Evelina*, Cadell and Davies rejected the manuscript of *First Impressions* sight unseen. Possibly, as Burney and Hawkins had found, these respectable booksellers simply would not consider an anonymous manuscript. If they said so in their reply, which does not survive, Austen may have decided that anonymity was too essential to sacrifice. She may not have understood that another publisher might tolerate anonymity – as Hookham and Carpenter would, for they brought out at least one novel at this time whose author they have not recorded, the pseudonymous *Joan!!!* (1796). Austen seems not to have tried again to publish until she sold the copyright of *Susan*, the early version of *Northanger Abbey* that was never published, to B. Crosby and Company in 1803, and at that time she did remain strictly anonymous.

R.W. Chapman has conjectured that Cadell and Davies 'declined by Return of Post' (for so George Austen's letter was marked by them)[28] because they found the query unbusinesslike: 'for the alternatives – that the publisher should be paid or should pay – are not clearly stated as such'.[29] But in fact, the alternatives seem clear enough: publishing on commission ('at the Author's risk', not quite the same as Chapman's 'the publisher should be paid') and sale of copyright. These are the only options among the four available methods of publishing a book that Austen herself ever exercised. She sold the copyright of *Pride and Prejudice* as well as *Susan*, and published *Sense and Sensibility*, *Mansfield Park* and *Emma* on commission. Publishers differed on which of the four available methods they preferred to offer, and the money an author was likely to receive varied with each one, so that an author's choice of publisher was very important.

LITERARY PROPERTY AND SALE OF COPYRIGHT

Although sale of copyright was extremely common, what was actually being bought and sold – a literary property – remained something of a vexed question throughout the century. According to sixteenth-century law, the right to print works was originally vested in the Crown, primarily to enforce censorship. But printer-booksellers gradually came to view a license to print a work as a property right. Once they had purchased this property, called a 'copy', they believed that they owned it exclusively and perpetually until sold or transferred, like any other piece of property. In practice they did enjoy perpetual copyright until 1774, when the House of Lords struck it down; a blanket fee for limited copyright (14 or 28 years) then became possible. Thus over several centuries what had been thought to be the immaterial product of a human mind inspired by God materialised as property owned for a limited time by an individual author. In France, the National Convention recognised this development by passing a law on literary property in 1793. As Carla Hesse has summarised it:

> This law, proclaimed as nothing less than a "declaration of the rights of genius" by the revolutionary legislators, recognized the author, rather than God, as the sole originator of his work, and as a consequence, consecrated his authority to determine the fate of his work as an "inviolable property right" rather than a "privilege" granted by the "grace of the King".[30]

Hesse goes on to note that historians and literary critics have linked the notions of individuality, rights and property to the emergence of a new definition of 'authority':

> Whether liberals celebrating the rise of individualism, Marxists diagnosing the commercialization and alienation of bourgeois literary production, or post-structuralists aimed at the deconstruction of the unified authorial subject, all the divergent

critical schools exhibit a striking consensus on one point: the author as the individual proprietor of truth emerged sometime between 1650 and 1850 as either a cause or a consequence of something we call modernity.[31]

To most eighteenth-century British authors eager to dispose of their property, sale of limited copyright for a fee was by far the most prestigious and desirable option available, if they could find a purchaser. The fee offered a clear sum of money, generally payable within a year of publication, and it removed the writer comfortably and decorously from the marketplace as none of the other options did, for the publisher was obliged to pay the sum agreed upon however poorly the work sold. If sales were good and further editions were printed, a publisher who had purchased copyright might send the author an additional payment, as Lowndes did Burney: she eventually received £30 for *Evelina*, instead of the twenty guineas originally offered, but not until Lowndes had printed a first edition of 800 copies (an unusual number), a second of 500 and a third of 1000.[32] By 1800, unwilling to leave themselves at the mercy of such limited generosity, established authors might contract for additional payments once a specified number of copies or editions were printed or sold. Radcliffe probably had done so when she sold the copyright of *The Romance of the Forest* for an unnamed sum to Hookham and Carpenter. Burney herself made such arrangements for her last two novels, *Camilla, or a Picture of Youth* (1796) and *The Wanderer, or Female Difficulties* (1814). Although she earned only £280 altogether for her first two novels, she managed to collect £4000 for the two last.[33]

Austen was either too new to authorship or too ignorant to demand that the bookseller Thomas Egerton make her additional payments if *Pride and Prejudice* (1813) were successful. It went into three editions, but Egerton contented himself with paying the copyright fee of £110 that he had originally offered. Having made £140 on *Sense and Sensibility*, Austen was disappointed with this offer, but as she wrote to her friend Martha Lloyd, 'I would rather have had £150, but we could not both be pleased, & I am not at all surprised that he should not chuse to hazard so much' (*L* 501; 29 Nov. 1812). The offer was rather niggardly. Longman, publisher of many women novelists, was paying £50 per volume for novels at this time; Austen's wish for £150 for the three-volume *Pride and Prejudice* was very reasonable. Still, £110 was considerably better than the £10 Austen had accepted nine years earlier for *Susan*. In the meantime, retail prices for novels had nearly doubled: from about three shillings and sixpence per volume to six (eighteen shillings for the three-volume *Pride and Prejudice*), so that publishers were prepared to pay higher fees. Nonetheless, Austen never sold a copyright again.

PUBLISHING ON COMMISSION

Austen's preferred mode of publication was at her own risk, or 'on commission' as it was called. The author was ultimately responsible for the cost of paper, printing and advertising; the publisher kept accounts, distributed the books to the trade, and charged to a 10 per cent commission on each copy sold - a kind of royalty in reverse. If not enough copies were sold to cover costs, the author had to make up the difference. Austen herself assumed that this method required an initial outlay of capital: she wrote to her sister on the appearance of the second edition of *Sense and Sensibility* that 'I suppose in the meantime I shall owe dear Henry [her brother] a great deal of Money for Printing &c' (*L* 368; 3 Nov. 1813). But surviving publishers' records indicate that as a rule the publisher seems to have paid for production of a book, charging the expenses off against receipts some months later, after the work had sold. A letter from the House of Longman describes this procedure:

> The Publisher gets the W[or]k Printed at the trade price, purchases the Paper at the best market, superintends the general interests of the W[or]k & takes upon himself the risk of Bad Debts for which he charges a commission of 10 per cent on the Sales.[34]

Even Hookham and Carpenter, fashionable booksellers but a relatively small publishing firm, operated this way. When Miss Mary Barker published 750 copies of her three-volume novel *A Welsh Story* in June 1798, Hookham carried the cost of almost £120. But less than half the copies were disposed of by the end of September, so that the author owed the firm over £48.

Similarly, printing 500 copies of *Calaf, a Persian Tale* (2 vols) cost £53 in February, 1798, 335 remained to be sold in May, and the author, Mrs Margaret Holford, thus owed Hookham nearly £20. Two other works of hers were also being sold, *Gresford Vale, and Other Poems* and *Selima*; all lost money, and in May 1800, she settled the combined debts [G/138, 145].

This mode of publication could be more remunerative to an author than selling copyright, but clearly the risks were great – to publishers also, if they financed the outlay. Hookham and Carpenter may never have recovered the money owed them by Mary Barker. Her debt of £48 includes the commission gained on selling 180 copies, only about £5. If the work had sold out, their total profit on commission would have been less than £25. This seems a small reward for which to risk £120, and perhaps a series of similar losses helps to account for the dissolution of the partnership between Hookham and Carpenter in 1799. Records of the larger firms of John Murray and the House of Longman generally show fewer losses on commission. They were perhaps warier of offering this risky mode of publication and better judges of the market.

Austen generally did well by publishing on commission. Only the second edition of *Mansfield Park*, brought out by Murray, lost money. The closest equivalent we have to this method is to employ a 'vanity press' – that is, to pay for printing one's own works. This form of publication, not respected now, means that books will be neither reviewed by the public press nor sold in shops; authors frequently distribute them free of charge. By contrast, in Austen's lifetime a book published on commission was perfectly respectable, as likely as any other book to be reviewed and sold.

OTHER FORMS OF PUBLICATION

The two options that George Austen ignores, publishing by subscription and by profit-sharing, were not particularly attractive in the 1790s. Subscription was declining somewhat, for it was a cumbersome and demeaning business, and not always remunerative. Subscribers paid for a projected book, preferably in advance. A list of their names would be printed in the work when it appeared. An author solicited subscribers (usually by publishing proposals), kept records and collected money – or asked friends to do so, rather a heavy tax on friendship because subscribers generally were reluctant to part with cash. Booksellers would also agree to keep lists but would collect a 10 per cent commission on all money received. Although subscription could be the most lucrative method of publication for an author, the pickings might be slim. Subscribers too may have become wary over the century: many authors, like Samuel Johnson for his edition of Shakespeare, collected subscriptions and produced no book for years. In some cases, subscription payments were a form of charity – resented, perhaps, on both sides – rather than a sign of genuine desire for a book.

Admittedly, Frances Burney made £1000 – a tremendous sum – by selling subscriptions to *Camilla, or a Picture of Youth* (1796); 'Miss J. Austen, Steventon' is listed as a subscriber in the first volume. Burney also received £1000 in copyright money.[35] But her success in combining these two forms of publication was possible only because her reputation was pre-eminent. The Hookham records show how unlikely such rewards were for other women. A Mrs Clutterbuck attempted to get subscribers through Hookham and Carpenter for a projected 'Beauties of St Pierre' in June and July 1798; she got five and had Hookham return the money. Miss Hutchinson paid two guineas to print five hundred proposals for 'Exhibition of the Heart' in February 1798; she got only four subscribers through Hookham at a guinea each between April and July 1798 (G/127, 135).

If subscription was declining, profit-sharing had yet to flourish. Some instances are known before 1800, but not until 1807 did the House of Longman decide that it shared profits frequently enough to justify keeping such 'divide' records separate from copyright and commission records. Publishers who chose this form of publication paid for printing and advertising, repaid themselves as the books were sold, and shared any profit realised over and above the costs. If the sale did not cover expenses, the firm absorbed the loss. Publishers generally offered profit-sharing to untried authors whose market they could not predict. The first volume of Edward Gibbon's *Decline and Fall of the Roman Empire* (1776) was brought out in this way by Thomas Cadell, bookseller, and printed by William Strahan. They assumed the risk and shared the profits with

Gibbon; he rightly wrote in his *Memoirs* of the 'very easy terms' offered him.[36]

In some cases, sharing profits could be more remunerative than publishing for oneself or selling copyright. Amelia Opie made less money per volume by selling copyright to Longman than by profit-sharing with the firm. And if Austen had published all the editions of her works that appeared during her lifetime by profit-sharing, she would have made more money than she actually did.[37] Obviously, an author who published for himself took all the profits, not just half, but in practice this meant only about 50 per cent more money. When Lady Impey inquired of Longman in 1811 about publishing her son's work, he explained that profit-sharing would yield about £22 for the author if the edition sold out; if her son took the risk and the entire edition was sold, he would gain only about £33.[38] These figures assume identical expenses, however – not always the case. When their own profits were at stake, publishers were likely to shave costs.

BOOK PRODUCTION AND DISTRIBUTION

From inception to issue, producing a book was extremely laborious during Austen's lifetime. Considerable drudgery was necessary. As Burney and Hawkins knew too well, authors had to write out fair copies of their works for their publishers entirely by hand, using a quill pen, handmade paper, and ink that they may have mixed for themselves from cakes purchased at a stationer's shop. Furthermore, Austen's lifetime occurred at the very end of the hand press period, when every stage of book production was performed by hand. Although powered printing machinery was being used in England before Austen's death in 1817, all her novels were printed in the traditional way, on hand presses similar in principle to those used by Gutenberg more than 300 years earlier.

Having accepted a manuscript, a publisher would send it to a printer. Individual volumes might be sent to different printers if speed were necessary (the second edition of *Mansfield Park* was so divided). The printer would 'cast off' the manuscript, that is, estimate how many sheets of paper would be required to print it. Paper was handmade, bought in reams from a papermaker and very expensive, usually more so than any other item in producing a book. Although printing itself required much skill, particularly among compositors who set type by hand but even from those who operated the press, labour was cheap enough to keep costs down. The paper for printing the 750 copies of Mary Barker's *Welsh Story* in 1798 cost about £61; the composing, printing and correcting came to a little less than £50; and advertising took almost another £6 (G/138). The high price of paper made small editions more economical than large ones, unless a strong and steady demand were assured. It was much cheaper to print a small edition of 750 copies and to recompose and reprint if it sold out than to risk a large edition of 2000 or 3000 that might ultimately be sold as waste paper. But this advantage could disappear if very expensive paper were used. Ordering cheaper grades of paper considerably increased profits. The archives of John Murray show that paper for *Emma* cost 37 shillings per ream and for *Mansfield Park* 35, while the posthumous 1818 edition of *Northanger Abbey* together with *Persuasion* was produced on much cheaper stock, 23s 6d a ream.[39] Austen's heirs had evidently learned something about expenses. Austen herself would have made at least £150 more profit had similarly cheap paper been used for Murray's editions of *Emma* and *Mansfield Park*.

These traditional methods of printing served the small novel-reading public of Austen's day quite well. Composing by hand was surprisingly efficient. Most modern authors would be amazed at receiving proof sheets of a work as long as *Evelina* only two months after it was accepted by the publisher, as Burney did. Distribution was also efficient. By the time Austen published her first novel in 1811, a London publisher would 'subscribe' an edition to other booksellers before it was issued, offering a slightly deeper discount than would be available after the work was actually published. Heavy pre-publication subscriptions could cause an increase in the size of an edition. London booksellers took or 'subscribed' 351 copies of *Emma* in advance, which boded reasonably well for the edition, but only 36 of the second edition of *Mansfield Park* were subscribed, pointing accurately to poor sales.[40]

London booksellers in turn had efficient arrangements to ship books quickly to the provinces by carriages that made regular runs, but demand there and in the metropolis was stimulated to a great extent by advertising in local and London newspapers. These papers were very short, perhaps four or six pages, of which two-thirds or more were devoted to advertising, little to news. Thus when Austen describes Edmund Bertram taking up a newspaper to give Henry Crawford the opportunity to court Fanny Price, she mentions that he read not news but 'the various advertisements of "a most desirable estate in South Wales" – "To Parents and Guardians" – and a "Capital season'd Hunter"' (*MP*, 342). Advertisements for books usually began 'This Day is Published' (not always true), and placing them became an increasing expense in bookselling. Murray debited Austen's account more than £50 for advertising *Emma* within the first nine months of publication. Some of that money found its way back to Murray himself, who charged for listing her books in his own printed trade catalogues – a practice that would outrage modern authors, but seems to have been usual then.

Of course, hand production of paper and books did sometimes cause delays that sound quite familiar to present-day writers. Austen herself was 'very much disappointed and vexed' by the delay in printing *Emma* (*L* 432; 23 Nov. 1815), and at least one other writer of her acquaintance, her cousin Mrs Cassandra Cooke, was thoroughly disgusted with the publisher of her 'Historical Tale, Founded on Facts', *Battleridge*: 'she is so little satisfied with Cawthorn's dilatoriness that she never means to employ him again' (*L* 24; 27 Oct. 1798). Strained relations between authors and publishers are probably inevitable. Austen's joking remark on Murray suggests these tensions: 'He is a rogue of course, but a civil one' (*L* 425, 17 Oct. 1815). To writers, a publisher never seems fast enough in producing a work or energetic enough in promoting it. Publishers feel that writers never understand the market or the way the trade operates. Modern authors often complain that their books are not in bookstores, not advertised enough, not reviewed enough, as though they find the publisher personally responsible for a slow sale and meagre profit, and similar complaints are frequently voiced by Austen's contemporaries.[41]

THE AUDIENCE FOR FICTION

As Dr Johnson notoriously proclaimed, no one but a blockhead ever wrote except for money – and he might have added, nor wrote without an audience in mind. From the beginning of her career as a writer, Austen wrote to and for family and friends. She always had an audience in mind, an intimate one, composed of like-minded members of her own social group – members of the professional classes and the gentry. These were readers who traditionally would buy expensive books like novels, though increasingly members of the 'middling classes' bought such works, and all classes were prepared to borrow them. Nonetheless, the market for domestic fiction like Austen's remained small throughout her publishing lifetime. As we have seen, novels by unknown writers would be published in editions of just 500, 750 or 1000 copies, while proven novelists might sell 2000 or 3000 in one or more editions. The largest known edition for an Austen novel was 2000, for *Emma* (1816), and it failed to sell out. It took Walter Scott's novels to enlarge the novel-reading public, beginning with the publication of *Waverley* in 1814.

These editions are small not just by our standards but by contemporary ones. Then as now, most novels were far outsold by non-fictional works. At the end of the eighteenth century, bestsellers were Bibles, common prayer books, devotional works, school books, guides and other reference works, 'classics' (tried and true works by established authors) and ephemera (cheap almanacks, magazines and so forth). Controversial works in politics or divinity occasionally sold well, though not spectacularly. Admittedly, in the politically unstable 1790s, some writers did succeed in reaching what we would call a mass audience: Thomas Paine's revolutionary *Rights of Man* (part 2, 1792) sold more than 100 000 copies and probably these were lent to many more readers, while Hannah More's reactionary Cheap Repository Tracts were distributed in at least equal numbers. But as a rule readers prepared to purchase any books at all were relatively few, and individual purchasers of fiction even fewer.

Thus, although the eighteenth century is generally praised for giving birth to the English novel, it was far more prolifically the mother of the digest – selections of short entertaining pieces, generally reprinted from other sources at no copyright cost to the publisher, and welcomed by the public. These digests or reprints were to be found in many forms, from fat books like the *Elegant Extracts in Prose* (or *Verse*) to sixpenny monthly magazines, the latter composed of squibs from newspapers, extracts from books, letters from correspondents and the like. Some of the most popular digests were the collections entitled 'Beauties of', with an admired author's name following – Goldsmith, Johnson or Sterne, among others. Mrs Clutterbuck had hoped to exploit this genre with her projected 'Beauties of St Pierre'. The *Beauties of Sterne*, for instance, sold rather better among provincial readers than his novels. The *Elegant Extracts* could appear in editions of 5000 or 6000 every few years and be snapped up by such readers as the Martins of Abbey Mill Farm in *Emma*: Harriet Smith tells us that Robert Martin 'sometimes of an evening, . . . would read something aloud of the Elegant Extracts – very entertaining' (E 29).

The success and respectability of such collections and the relative failure and disrepute of many novels underlie Austen's famous ironic attack in *Northanger Abbey*:

> And while the abilities of the nine-hundredth abridger of the History of England, or of the man who collects and publishes in a volume some dozen lines of Milton, Pope, and Prior, with a paper from the Spectator, and a chapter from Sterne, are eulogized by a thousand pens, – there seems almost a general wish of decrying the capacity and undervaluing the labour of the novelist, and of slighting the performances which have only genius, wit, and taste to recommend them.
>
> (*NA* 37)

Austen clearly exemplifies here the 'modern' attitude that a real author must be original, not a plagiarist, not a borrower. It was an attitude voiced earlier by the poet Edward Young in his *Conjectures on Original Composition*: he adjures a writer 'to prefer the native growth of thy own mind to the richest import from abroad; such borrowed riches make us poor'.[42] But the eighteenth-century reading public apparently adopted this view only gradually. Even at the end of the century, individual readers generally preferred to buy cheap ephemera like magazines and to confine their expensive purchasing to reprints of classics and abridgements.

Probably the most reliable portion of the market was supplied by book clubs or societies and circulating libraries throughout the country, which could be depended on to take many new works of fiction. They operated rather like the Boots lending libraries in Britain in the 1950s, whose guaranteed orders made small editions of so-called women's novels economical. As the numbers and prices of books shot up during Austen's lifetime, readers seem to have depended more and more on obtaining books cheaply through libraries, societies and friends. Provincial readers were especially fond of the clubs, which allowed a number of readers to pool their resources, order books jointly, circulate them for a year or so, then divide them among themselves. It was through a local book society that Austen read Hawkins' *Roseanne* (1814). Her comments to her niece Anna are amusing:

> We have got 'Rosanne' in our Society, and find it much as you describe it; very good and clever, but tedious. Mrs. Hawkins' great excellence is on serious subjects. There are some very delightful conversations and reflections on religion: but on lighter topics I think she falls into many absurdities; and, as to love, her heroine has very comical feelings. There are a thousand improbabilities in the story. Do you remember the two Miss Ormesdens, introduced just at last? Very flat and unnatural. - Mlle Cossart is rather my passion.
>
> (*L* 422; 24 Nov. 1814)[43]

Earlier, in 1813, Austen had mentioned with mocking triumph no less than three local societies, her own at Chawton, an older one serving Steventon and Manydown (where she had lived 12 years earlier) and a projected society:

> The Miss Sibleys want to establish a Book Society in their side of the country, like ours. What can be a stronger proof of that superiority in ours over the Steventon & Manydown society, which I have always foreseen & felt? No emulation of the kind was ever inspired by *their* proceedings. No such wish of the Miss Sibleys was ever   heard in the course of the many years of that Society's existence.
>
> (*L* 294; 24 Jan. 1813)

Borrowing books from small circulating libraries was even cheaper than sharing them through a society. They were consequently almost as ubiquitous. Probably almost every provincial bookseller in England within a hundred miles of London had a small collection of books to lend; certainly all those whose records have survived did so.[44] The proliferation of such sources of inexpensive entertainment should not surprise us, for the way books were circulated in Austen's day closely parallels the way we obtain videotapes of new films now. Almost no one will pay the full price for a new video when it comes out (excepting those aimed at children, who enjoy watching the same film over and over again). But most people who own a videocassette recorder are willing to rent tapes. As a result, small video rental shops have sprung up in most neighbourhoods in England and the United States, just as circulating libraries proliferated in England in the last half of the eighteenth century.

Of course, the cheapest way to obtain books then as now was to borrow them from friends. The most interesting evidence of this widespread practice comes from a reading list kept by Miss Mary Orlebar, a gentlewoman of Ecton in Northampton-shire, who read several hundred volumes between 1789, when she began her list at the age of 59, and 1820, a year before she died, aged 91. She evidently liked novels, which comprise most of her reading. *Pride and Prejudice* appears twice on her list, once in 1813 (borrowed from a Mrs Isted), and again in 1815, when she also read *Mansfield Park* (both borrowed from a Mrs Sotheby); in 1816 she read her sister-in-law's copy of *Emma*. Like herself, all the owners belonged to the local gentry. The list unfortunately almost never records a comment on the reading. Miss Orlebar did describe seven works as 'clever' or 'very clever', but although these included five novels, none were Austen's.[45]

The Orlebar reading list tells us typically little. We can seldom acquire solid information about who actually read Austen's novels (or those of any other writer of the period), let alone how they were read. Reviews, letters, anecdotes and above all the 'Opinions' Austen compiled of *Mansfield Park* and *Emma* offer our only clues. On the whole, Austen received few reviews – during her lifetime, two for *Sense and Sensibility*, three for *Pride and Prejudice*, none for *Mansfield Park* and ten for *Emma* (although two of these were written in German). Most were short and reasonably favourable. The longest, on *Emma*, was written by Walter Scott at Murray's urging:

Have you any fancy to dash off an article on 'Emma'? It wants incident and romance, does it not? None of the author's other novels have been noticed [by Murray's own periodical, the

Quarterly Review] and surely 'Pride and Prejudice' merits high commendation.[46]

Reviews were thought to increase sales; there is evidence that book societies paid particular attention to reviews in the last decades of the eighteenth century.[47] Scott's review of *Emma* took a hint from Murray's remark that the novel lacked 'incident and romance': he argued that a new species of novel, one that dealt with ordinary life, was emerging, and that Austen had mastered this form in *Sense and Sensibility* and *Pride and Prejudice* as well as *Emma*. Murray sent Austen a copy of the review, and her response survives – a surprising one:

> I return you the Quarterly Review with many Thanks. The Authoress of *Emma* has no reason I think to complain of her treatment in it, except in the total omission of Mansfield Park – I cannot but be sorry that so clever a man as the Reviewer of *Emma* should consider it as unworthy of being noticed.
>
> (*L* 453; 1 Apr. 1816)[48]

There seems no trace of irony or comedy here. Like Burney addressing her publishers in 1817, Austen takes refuge in the third person ('the Authoress'), something she almost never does. And she honestly and vainly – in both senses – seems to regret Scott's failure to mention *Mansfield Park*, perhaps because the novel had never been reviewed, but possibly because she knew that sales of the second edition had already stalled by the time she wrote.

We probably should be grateful that no review mentioned *Mansfield Park* when it first came out in 1814, for Austen's decision to record all the opinions she could gather of the novel may have arisen from that omission. Her lists of 'Opinions' of *Emma* and *Mansfield Park* are wonderfully comic – and offer fascinating insights into the way her contemporaries read and misread her works, as will be seen. But the most egregiously silly comments in the 'Opinions' bear no comparison to one reported by Austen's brother Henry in the 'Memoir' he wrote for the 1833 edition of her novels. It serves to close this discussion of the conditions of authorship for women with appropriate irony:

> When 'Pride and Prejudice' made its appearance, a gentleman, celebrated for his literary attainments, advised a friend of the

authoress to read it, adding, with more point than gallantry, 'I should like to know who is the author, for it is much too clever to have been written by a woman.'[49]

2

Background and Literary Apprenticeship, 1775-1793

Leo Tolstoy's opening line for *Anna Karenina*, that all happy families are alike, cannot apply to Jane Austen's family. She is unique, and her family must be so too. But the particular quality of happiness in the large, lively, healthy, intelligent Austen family may surprise modern readers, used to stories of separation, divorce, drug and alcohol abuse, and all the other taxes upon contemporary life. Like Elizabeth Bennet, the Austens seem to have made it their family business to be satisfied, and it was their temper to be happy (*PP*, 239). Most of them were resilient and united in adversity when it came, affectionate and cheerful in prosperity. No other writer's childhood comes to mind that can bear comparison to hers for love, warmth, encouragement, security and sanity.

It seems too good to be true, and some modern biographers have tried to destroy the legend of family harmony that began with Austen's brother Henry's biographical notice in 1818, a legend confirmed and amplified by every other family account. Jane Aiken Hodge saw most of the family, particularly Austen's mother, as unpleasant, while John Halperin made Austen herself into a soured, disappointed, nasty woman within a somewhat less nasty family.[1] But little evidence supports such readings, as recent biographers George Holbert Tucker, Park Honan, and Deirdre Le Faye have found, re-emphasising the family's wholesomeness, its good nature, its unique ability to nurture Austen's talent.[2] While the Austen children were not precisely 'born to struggle and endure' like the Prices of *Mansfield Park*, they did have to make their way in the world. In doing so, they experienced, along with some failure, much of the Prices' impressive 'well-doing and success . . . all assisting to advance each other' (473).

FAMILY

Austen grew up in the beauty and liberty of the Hampshire countryside, at Steventon rectory, as far from the Prices' squalid Portsmouth home as can be imagined. The term 'liberty' is her own, taken from *Mansfield Park*: Henry Crawford asserts that Fanny 'ought never to be long banished from the free air, and liberty of the country' (411). In her childhood, outdoor air and exercise were as available for Austen as for Catherine Morland, who 'loved nothing so well in the world as rolling down the green slope at the back of the house' (*NA*, 14): at the back of Steventon parsonage too was a 'garden which sloped up to the terrace "walk"'.[3] Austen loved country pleasures; a family manuscript asserted that she 'loved the country and her delight in natural scenery was such that she would sometimes say she thought it must form one of the joys of heaven'.[4] Country pleasures are, however, not simply scenic but also physical – the refreshing air, the freedom of movement. Her niece Anna's first memories of Austen all focus on her being out of doors. She recalls 'the frequent visits of my two Aunts [Jane and Cassandra], & how they walked in winter through the sloppy lane between Steventon & Dean in their pattens' – iron rings with platforms above that were slipped over shoes for walking in bad weather. Anna adds that later, when she was 'perhaps 7 or 10 years old I recollect thinking it so *odd* of Grand Papa [George Austen] to speak of them as the *girls* – "Where are the Girls? Are the Girls gone out?"'[5]

Clearly, the 'girls' went out as often as they pleased. We sometimes tend to think of Austen as at her desk, writing, or in the parlour, sewing or reading or talking, but neither as child nor adult was she content to be desk-bound. Nor did Austen's upbringing restrict her knowledge and her activity to a 'ladylike' sphere. She did not suffer the sort of mental and physical confinement imposed on Victorian little girls like M. Vivian Hughes, who was never permitted to go with her brothers on outings into the country, and whose father's slogan was 'that boys should go everywhere and know everything, and that a girl should stay at home and know nothing'.[6] Many readers have been struck by Austen's jokes about mistresses, illegitimate children, drunkenness and the like in her youthful writing, jokes that her family clearly relished and encouraged. It was probably this eighteenth-century freedom of action and expression that prompted Austen's favourite niece Fanny Knight to write so disparagingly of her aunt's lack of refinement long after her death: 'it is very true that Aunt Jane from various circumstances was not so *refined* as she ought to have been from her *talent*, & if she had lived 50 years later she would have been in many respects more suitable to *our* more refined tastes'.[7]

Austen was fortunate in missing Victorian notions of refinement and even more fortunate in both her parents. They seem to have been able to enjoy loving and nurturing their children, delighting in their different natures rather than viewing them as mere extensions of themselves. Austen's father George was a country parson who spent almost all of his time at home; she probably had more time with her father than many children brought up in the 1950s and 60s. Though the Manor House of Steventon was rented by the Digweed family, Mr Austen served to some degree as the representative of its owner, his second cousin Thomas Knight, who had presented him to the livings of Steventon (1761) and nearby Deane (1773), together valued at £210.[8] George Austen supplemented this income by farming Cheesedown (a 200-acre property, which Mr Knight had agreed to let his cousin use for extra income)[9] and by teaching. He was a good scholar, and prepared two of his sons for Oxford and two for the naval academy at Portsmouth. Between 1773 and 1796, he also took in pupils to increase his income.[10]

Cassandra Leigh, whom George Austen married in 1764 when he was 33 and she 24, was a good countrywoman, managing her poultry and dairy with energy and success, though her family connections were aristocratic. They had eight children, most of whom were at home when Austen, the seventh, was born on 16 December 1775: James (ten years old), Edward (eight), Henry (four), Cassandra (almost three) and Frank (21 months). Charles, the youngest, was born three and a half years later. Another brother, George, a year younger than James, was probably retarded or epileptic; he did not live at home.

Mr Austen was especially affectionate, to both his wife and children. As Austen wrote when he died, 'His tenderness as a Father, who can do justice to?' (*L* 146; 22 Jan. 1805). Some evidence of that tenderness survives in letters written to his sister-in-law Susanna Walter when his children were very young:

My James . . . and his brothers are both well, and what will surprise you, bear their mother's absence [to assist her sister in a first childbirth] with great philosophy: as I doubt not they would mine and turn all their little affections towards those who were about them and good to them; this may not be a pleasing reflection to a fond parent, but is certainly wisely designed by Providence for the happiness of the child.

(8 July 1770).[11]

George Austen's fondness seems to have permitted him to enter imaginatively but not possessively into his children's feelings. The 'happiness of the child' is paramount, not parental authority. His account to Mrs Walter of Austen's birth is characteristically affectionate and perceptive:

You have doubtless been for some time in expectation of hearing from Hampshire, and perhaps wondered a little we were in our old age grown such bad reckoners but so it was, for Cassey certainly expected to have been brought to bed a month ago: however last night the time came, and without a great deal of warning, everything was soon happily over. We have now another girl, a present plaything for her sister Cassy and a future companion. She is to be Jenny, and seems to me as if she would be as like Henry, as Cassy is to Neddy.

(17 Dec. 1775).[12]

He knew his children remarkably well, almost prophetically. Jane was in fact to have an especially close relationship to Henry, her favourite brother, as Cassandra had with the more staid and solid Edward; and the companionship of Jane and her sister Cassandra was lifelong. The nicknames reinforce the picture of family intimacy and affection.

The letters of Austen's mother Cassandra Leigh display comparable affection for her children and a keener observation of their development. Like George Austen, she displays a wonderful combination of closeness and distance in observing her children, along with quite remarkable energy and good nature, given her quick succession of pregnancies – and probable miscarriage in the more than three and a half years between Edward's birth and Henry's.[13] After Henry was born, she wrote to Mrs Walter, 'Thank

God I am got quite stout again, had an extraordinary good time and Lying in, and am Bless'd with as fine a Boy as perhaps you ever saw, he is much the largest I ever had, and thrives very fast' (21 July 1771).[14] All the Austen children, after being weaned, were put out 'to be nursed in a cottage in the village' for about a year: 'The infant was daily visited by one or both of its parents, and frequently brought to them at the parsonage, but the cottage was its home'.[15] Of this practice, Mrs Austen writes to Mrs Walter:

> I want to shew you my Henry and my Cassy [the two whom Mrs Walter had never seen], who are both reckoned fine children. I suckled my little girl [now five months old] thro' the first quarter; she has been weaned and settled at a good woman's at Deane just eight weeks; she is very healthy and lively, and puts on her short petticoats today.
>
> (6 June 1773).[16]

Children seem to have been weaned early. At 11 months, Cassandra was 'almost ready to run away' and we hear of her once more, aged two and a half, after the birth of Frank, when Mrs Austen is five months pregnant with Jane:

> I am more nimble and active than I was last time, expect to be confined some time in November. My last boy [Frank] is very stout, and has run alone these two months, and he is not yet sixteen months old. My little girl talks all day long, and in my opinion is a very entertaining companion. Henry [four years old] has been in breeches some months and thinks himself near as good as a man as his brother Neddy, indeed no one would judge by their looks that there was above three years and a half difference in their ages, one is so little and the other so great.
>
> (20 Aug. 1775).[17]

Clearly, putting her children out to nurse after having suckled them herself did not interrupt Mrs Austen's affectionate interest in their growth and development. She seems in fact to have enjoyed the benefit of an early and quite sensible form of day care, one that permitted her to see her child every day but to exercise her considerable responsibilities at the parsonage without having to look after an infant as well. James Edward Austen-Leigh, who first wrote about this custom, asserted that it was 'not unusual in those days', although I have come across no other recorded instance within the family or outside it.[18] The custom does testify strongly that Austen grew up in 'the world we have lost', to use Peter Laslett's evocative phrase. A world in which children can be shared between the cottage and the parsonage is a 'face-to-face society', as social historians call it,[19] not the one we know – or even that of the Victorians, who wrenched nurses and nannies away from their families to minister to richer children.

In any event, George and Cassandra Austen's sons were on the whole remarkably successful, doing credit to their upbringing. The eldest, James, became a good scholar, prosperous clergyman and decent essayist and versifier, devoted to his second wife Mary Lloyd and his two children by her; Anna, the child of the first marriage, was neglected and understandably rebellious. His literary leanings along with Austen's publications probably account for the fact that all three of his children attempted novels, though only Anna published one, a novella in 1833. James was treated as the heir of Mrs Austen's wealthy but childless brother James Leigh Perrot, who supplemented his nephew's income. But James also eventually succeeded to his father's livings, occupying the parish adjoining Steventon as a curate from 1792, and Steventon itself from 1801. George, the invalid, was looked after, probably in Monk Sherborne, a few miles from Steventon.[20] The reliable and responsible Edward was adopted by Thomas Knight and his wife, took the grand tour, married very happily into a county family, fathered 11 children and inherited extremely rich estates in Kent and Hampshire. Mary Russell Mitford tells us that his income from the estate in Kent was 'five thousand a year' and that the Hampshire estate was 'nearly double the value'.[21] Austen and especially Cassandra often visited Edward at Godmersham, the Kentish property. Henry, of whom Austen wrote, 'he cannot help being amusing', was the least successful Austen (*L*, 152; 8 Apr. 1805). He prepared for the church, but became by turns a captain in the militia, a banker, a receiver for taxes, a bankrupt and at last a clergyman; he married twice but remained childless. In the 1790s his duties as a soldier took him to various camps all over England, but by the 1800s he was settled in London, where Austen frequently visited him. Henry did not leave London until his bankruptcy forced him to return to Hampshire – to Chawton, as a curate. Frank and Charles became captains and eventually admirals in the Navy, working their way to promotion and (in Frank's case) some fortune. Both married twice and had large families. Frank and his wife shared a home with Mrs Austen and her daughters in Southampton for about two years after George Austen's death; once Mrs Austen removed to Chawton, Frank and Mary with their children spent a good deal of time nearby, at Chawton Manor and in neighbouring Alton. Frank was on duty some of this time; Charles was more steadily but less prosperously employed in the Navy. As a result, Austen saw him less frequently than her other brothers. He and his wife and children saved money, for instance, by living on board his ship, the Namur, in 1813-14.

EDUCATION AND READING

We are reminded in *Emma* that it was the usual destiny of sons to go away to school, and daughters to remain at home. Emma complacently reflects that Anna Weston's birth means that Mr Weston's 'fireside' will be 'enlivened by the sports and the non-sense, the freaks and the fancies of a child never banished from home', a child that Mrs Weston would instruct (461). But in the Austen household it was otherwise. The boys remained at home to be instructed by their father, and the girls by their mother, until Cassandra and Jane were sent to school themselves, perhaps because neither parent had time to tutor them. They had about two years of formal schooling. They first went to Mrs Cawley's Oxford boarding-school in the spring of 1783, when Cassandra was ten and Jane seven, a venture that ended badly.[22] Mrs Cawley was a 'connection' – sister of their uncle Dr Edward Cooper, the husband of Jane Leigh, Mrs Austen's sister. Their daughter Jane Cooper was 12 years old and had been enrolled with her cousins at the school, which moved to Southampton in the summer of 1783. Typhus broke out, both Austens caught it, and Jane Cooper wrote a letter that brought her mother and Mrs Austen to Southampton to remove their children. Austen nearly died, and Mrs Cooper became ill and died in October, 1783.[23] Jane Cooper remained close to her cousins after her mother's death and apparently joined Cassandra and Jane when they were again sent away, early in 1785, to the rather casual Abbey School in Reading. On this occasion, Mrs Austen is supposed to have made the notorious remark that 'if Cassandra were going to have her head cut off, Jane would insist on sharing her fate'.[24] Mrs Austen's choice of imaginary fate possibly had something to do with Austen's early passion for Mary Queen of Scots, whose execution is mockingly (and seriously) lamented in Austen's 'The History of England' (1791). Park Honan, drawing on contemporary accounts of the Abbey School, describes a very relaxed regime: 'after tea or cocoa in the mornings they sat "an hour or two" at lessons in needlework, English and French with some Italian and history'.[25] Perhaps Austen studied music there and Cassandra drawing; those were their only conventional accomplishments.[26]

Although we can't know what it meant to Austen to be sent from home so early, certainly it was a great advantage to her to have a beloved and protective older sister with her at school – someone to hide behind – and an older cousin as well. In later life, Austen described herself as rather an awkward child: she speaks of 'all the ready civility which one sees in the best Children in the present day; – so unlike anything that I was myself at her age, that I am often all astonishment & shame' (*L* 179; 8 Feb. 1807). It is hard to know whether Austen refers to youthful shyness here or something else – perhaps youthful silliness. Austen's cousin Philadelphia Walter described her as 'not at all pretty & very prim' as well as 'whimsical & affected' (23 July 1788).[27] Possibly the staid Philadelphia saw too much of the 'sports and the nonsense, the freaks and the fancies' of her twelve-year-old cousin. Austen's niece Caroline Austen remembered her in later life as raising laughter:

> by imagining for her neighbours impossible contingencies – by relating in prose or verse some trifling incident coloured to her own fancy, or in writing a history of what they had said or done, that *could* deceive nobody – As an instance I would give her description of the pursuits of Miss Mills and Miss Yates – two young ladies of whom she knew next to nothing – they were only on a visit to a near neighbour but their names tempted her into rhyme – and so *on* she went.[28]

If Austen as an adult could enjoy such fooling, we can readily imagine her as a child going on and *on* similarly, seeming whimsical, affected and silly at one moment, awkward and prim at another, to those who didn't know her – such as schoolmates, if she ever revealed herself to them. For it is clear that, whoever may have heard these performances, they were aimed (like Austen's early writing) at a family audience who loved entertainment and found her highly entertaining – and who took versifying and writing for granted. By the time Austen was through with school in late 1786, when she had just reached her eleventh birthday, her brothers had written and recited prologues to plays given at family theatricals from 1782 on. Rhymed charades were a continual family amusement, and Mrs Austen even wrote verses to amuse Mr Austen's pupils who were boarded with them.[29]

The instruction that Austen picked up at the Abbey School must have been considerably less than she got at home, from her mother, father, sister and brothers. Religious teaching began at home as the foundation for everything else – as it was not for Maria and Julia Bertram in *Mansfield Park*: 'They had been instructed theoretically in their religion, but never required to bring it into daily practice . . . and of the necessity of self-denial and humility [Sir Thomas] feared they had never heard from any lips that could profit them' (463). For Austen, religion was an essential part of daily life. The prayers she composed ask for charity and forbearance in dealing with 'fellow-creatures' and for self-knowledge: 'save us from deceiving ourselves by pride or vanity' (*MW*, 453-7). Her works are deeply religious in this sense, although she deliberately avoided overt religious instruction. A clergyman who knew 'a lady who had known Jane Austen well', a Mrs Barrett, recorded her recollections of Austen's religious attitudes, dwelling on:

> the tribute of my old friend to the real and true spring of religion which was always present though never obtruded. Miss Austen, [Mrs Barrett] used to say, had on all the subjects of enduring religious feeling the deepest and strongest convictions, but a contact with loud and noisy exponents of the then popular religious phase [Evangelicalism] made her reticent almost to a fault. She had to suffer something in the way of reproach from those who believed she might have used her genius to greater effect. But her old friend used to say, "I think I see her now defending what she thought was the real province of a delineator of life and manners and declaring her belief that example, and not 'direct preaching', was all that a novelist could afford properly to exhibit."[30]

As for other home instruction, Mrs Austen probably taught her sons and daughters to read, leaving higher education to her husband. We have no record of when Austen learned to read or write, but she certainly could read before being sent away to school at seven. Even her rather difficult niece Cassandra, daughter of Charles, read before she was five: according to her mother, she 'begins now to read very prettily, but I have had an amazing deal of trouble with her not owing to a dulness of comprehension but a dislike to learning (4 Oct. 1813).'[31] Austen probably also took in something of her brothers' lessons in Latin from their father, as did many women, from Lady Mary Wortley Montagu to Laetitia Hawkins.

Learning through recitation was essential to eighteenth-century pedagogy, particularly in teaching reading. Reading and writing were taught separately during the eighteenth century. Reading came first. Children were made to recognise and recite lists of two-letter combinations, such as ba, be, bi, and so forth, printed out in hornbooks, battledores or small books. They then proceeded to read aloud words of one syllable, then two syllables and up, combined in improving texts – for example: 'Pa-rents, mas-ters, and mis-tres-ses' often reward the unworthy and slight the worthy, but they are punished when their favourites are ungrateful, showing 'ir-re-gu-la-ri-ty and dis-o-be-di-ence', said to be a 'just re-tri-bu-ti-on'.[32]

To hear young children sounding out such words must have been a kind of retribution in itself to parents and schoolmasters. This particular text comes from one of more than 100 eighteenth-century editions of Thomas Dyche's *A Guide to the English Tongue*, first published in (1707), which also included lines for children to copy out. It was in this way that children learned to write. Copying does tend to fix words in the memory. Austen alludes to one of Dyche's two-line copy-texts in *Northanger Abbey* when she writes of Mrs Allen's repeated wish for acquaintance in Bath, that 'we are told to "despair of nothing we would attain", as "unwearied diligence our point would gain"; and the unwearied diligence with which she had every day wished for the same thing was at length to have its just reward' – the appearance of the Thorpes (31). The lines as printed in Dyche's work emphasise learning to make a capital D and are very appropriate to the Drudgery of writing upper- and lower-case letters with a quill pen: 'Despair of nothing that you would attain: / Unwearied Diligence your point will gain'.[33]

Austen's clear, elegant handwriting even as a child indicates that she profited from this sort of instruction. She apparently had none of the difficulties recorded by Frances Burney (in the third person): 'At eight years of age she was ignorant of the letters of the alphabet; though at ten, she began scribbling, almost incessantly, little works of invention; but always in private; and in scrawling characters, illegible, save to herself'.[34] Burney may mean that she was backward in learning to write, not read. But in any event, the secrecy and privacy of her writing reminds us of the Brontë children's juvenilia, 'meant for themselves alone, and . . . kept a strict secret not only from their later friends and acquaintances, but even from the other members of their household: hence the tiny size of the books and their famous microscopic print.'[35]

Such accounts contrast remarkably with the openness of Austen's early writing. Her juvenile works began as stories to amuse her younger brother Charles and were copied in a good round hand into three volumes for family entertainment – and for safekeeping. Her father, in fact, gave her the book she labelled Volume the Second: she inscribed 'Ex dono mei Patris' on the end-leaf.[36] (By contrast, again, Burney destroyed everything she wrote before she was 15). What is most important about Austen's education at home is that she was surrounded by encouragement and approval. Her writing was valued and appreciated by a family that evidently shared and enriched her sense of the ridiculous. Her early writing is, then, a form of social play, begun perhaps to amuse a younger child but continued for the entertainment of her elders. It was not a solitary spinning-out of unsanctioned fantasies and dreams. Austen's juvenilia arise from a deeply-felt sense of security and acceptance, a certainty of being valued and understood, a freedom that her family gave her to relax into freaks and fancies, sports and nonsense.

The extent of Austen's reading is also evident in all her early writing.[37] Amusingly, what appear to be her earliest written words were scribbled in a school book, *Fables Choisis*, in which an adult hand wrote 'Miss Jane Austen, 5th Dec. 1783', and where Austen herself seems to have written, along with her own name, two sentences: 'I wish I had done' and 'Mothers angry fathers gone out'.[38] Although the first of these is not remarkable (it probably means that she wished she had finished her French lessons), the second is quite unlike the sort of egoistic scrawling one usually sees in children's books - endless signings of one's own name, for example, as Frank Austen has done on the same page. This sentence suggests that at eight, Austen was already an observer, a slyly humorous one: she implies that her father's exit is owing to her mother's anger (or perhaps the reverse – that her mother is angry because her father has gone out). Although we should not make too much of five words, their detachment suggests an already developed, secure sense of self.

In the next writing we have, Volume the First, Volume the Second and Volume the Third, whose dates are usually given as 1788-93, Austen draws on her early reading in complex ways. These include direct allusion to at least 16 works or writers, from Hugh Blair's *Sermons* to the *Arabian Nights* and Goethe's *Sorrows of Werther*.[39] She had acquired a few books: mostly children's books like *Goody Two-Shoes* and a few little texts in French, but probably also by this time copies of Samuel Richardson's *Sir Charles Grandison*, Samuel Johnson's *Rasselas* and the *Spectator*.[40] Cassandra too owned books; their niece Anna described bookshelves over a press in the room that the sisters shared.[41] Furthermore, Austen had access to many other books as well, not only those in her father's library (which contained more than 500 volumes by 1801 [*L* 111; 14 Jan. 1801]) but probably in friends' libraries and local circulating libraries as well. Certainly in a family of 'great Novel-readers & not ashamed of being so' (*L* 38; 18 Dec. 1798), classics like Burney's *Evelina* and *Cecilia*, Fielding's *Joseph Andrews* and *Tom Jones*, Richardson's *Pamela* and *Clarissa*, would have been made available, if they weren't owned. Austen had access to *Evelina* at least in later life. Her niece Caroline Austen, who was 12 when Austen died, remembers that 'She was considered to read aloud remarkably well. I did not often hear her but *once* I knew her take up a volume of Evelina and read a few pages of Mr Smith and the Brangtons and I thought it was like a play.'[42]

The Austens also enjoyed performing plays among themselves in private theatricals. Many editions must have been lying about, and not merely of those plays actually performed: in 1782, Dr Thomas Francklin's tragedy *Matilda*; in 1784, Richard Brinsley Sheridan's *The Rivals*; in 1787, Susannah Centlivre's *The Wonder; or, a Woman Keeps a Secret*; in January 1788, *The Chances* (probably by Garrick) and in March, *The Tragedy of Tom Thumb* (perhaps Fielding's); and in January 1790, *The Sultan* (attributed to Isaac Bickerstaffe) and James Townley's *High Life Below Stairs*. For most of these performances James wrote prologues in verse, and for some of them epilogues also.[43]

Although Austen said just before her death that she wished she had read more and written less before she was sixteen, her reading clearly was not stinted.[44] She seems to have read with great eagerness. Books came alive in her imagination. Her nephew tells us that 'every circumstance narrated in [Richardson's] Sir Charles Grandison, all that was ever said or done in the cedar parlour, was familiar to her; and the wedding days of Lady L. and Lady G. were as well remembered as if they had been living friends.'[45] That books truly lived for her is probably one of the reasons that she read aloud so well, as so many of her contemporaries insist. Her pro-Stuart marginalia in her copy of Goldsmith's *History of England* demonstrate the energy and intensity she was capable of in reacting to her reading. Mary Augusta Austen-Leigh has given the following account of them:

> It was the History of the Rebellion that stirred her loyal soul to its depths. At first she contents herself with these short interjections on the behaviour of Cromwell's party –
>
> *'Oh! Oh! The Wretches!'*
>
> but she grows eloquent when Goldsmith delivers his verdict against the whole family of Stuart, and cries out in answer –
>
> *'A family who were always ill-used, BETRAYED OR NEGLECTED, whose virtues are seldom allowed, while their errors are never forgotten.'*
>
> It is perhaps fortunate – in case some destructive critic should arise in the future to declare the impossibility of Jane Austen having written any such words – that a postscript has been added to this note by a sympathetic young nephew, into whose possession the book afterwards passed: 'Bravo, Aunt Jane! Just my opinion of the case.'
>
> At the conclusion of Walpole's speech her remark is slightly ironical –
>
> *'Nobly said! Spoken like a Tory!'*
>
> And, again, when Goldsmith refers to the King as a Master unworthy of faithful followers, come these words –
>
> *'Unworthy, because he was a Stuart, I suppose – unhappy family!'*
>
> Lord Balmerino's execution in 1745 is thus lamented –
>
> *'Dear Balmerino! I cannot express what I feel for you!'*
>
> On the subsequent change in the dress of the Highlanders

she writes –

'*I do not like this. Every ancient custom ought to be Sacred, unless it is prejudicial to Happiness.*'

Next comes a very sapient announcement. Goldsmith having condemned those who were 'Stunning mankind with a cry of Freedom,' Jane thus addresses him –

'*My Dear Mr. G – , I have lived long enough in the world to know that it is always so.*'

Here she was probably thinking of the French Revolution, in which all at Steventon had a special reason for taking very deep interest.

She did not approve of Anne leaving her father's cause to side with her brother-in-law, and, being unwilling to blame any Stuart, finds her own way out of the dilemma –

'*Anne should not have done so, indeed I do not believe she did.*'

In writing of James II's obstinate adherence to his own policy, Goldsmith refers it to this King's conviction that 'nothing could injure schemes calculated to promote the cause of heaven,' on which Jane observes –

'*Since he acted upon such motives he ought not to be blamed.*'
. . .

Goldsmith . . . described the extreme destitution of the poorer classes after the Revolution, in consequence of which a man and his wife committed suicide. On this her comment is ready –

'*How much are the poor to be pitied, and the Rich to be Blamed!*'[46]

These statements illuminate one of the most remarkable aspects of Austen's youthful sense of herself: her ability to laugh at her most cherished feelings, to view them ironically without relinquishing them. In the comment here on Queen Anne's behaviour, we see some evidence of this double vision: '*Anne should not have done so, indeed I do not believe she did.*' But it is most evident in Austen's brilliant treatment of the Stuarts in Volume the Second of her juvenilia: 'The History of England . . . by a partial, prejudiced, and ignorant Historian' (finished 26 November 1791). Her absurd defences of the Stuarts in this work show her ironically examining and exposing her own prejudices while maintaining them nonetheless. The heroine of the piece is Mary Queen of Scots, the villain Elizabeth, and as Austen begins to describe Mary's execution, her ironic voice becomes briefly serious:

Oh! what must this bewitching Princess whose only freind
was then the Duke of Norfolk, and whose only ones are now Mr
Whitaker, Mrs Lefroy, Mrs Knight & myself, who was abandoned by her son, confined by her Cousin, Abused, reproached
& vilified by all, what must not her most noble mind have
suffered when informed that Elizabeth had given orders for her
Death! Yet she bore it with a most unshaken fortitude; firm in
her Mind; Constant in her Religion; & prepared herself to meet
the cruel fate to which she was doomed, with a magnanimity
that could alone proceed from conscious Innocence.

(*MW* 145)

Mrs Lefroy and Mrs Knight are older women who befriended
Austen; Mr Whitaker is the author of a passionate and poorly
argued *Vindication of Mary Queen of Scots* – and for Austen to
incorporate him in her ironic list of Mary's friends offers further
evidence of how intimate reading was to her, how vivid books
were. The serious intentions of Austen's 'History' are revisionist.
She is revising conventional views of Elizabeth's and Mary's
characters. But more important, in offering these unconventional
images of two powerful women, and in making them central to
her narrative, she is revising history itself, which (as Catherine
Morland laments) has 'hardly any women at all' (*NA* 108). And
Cassandra's amusing portraits of various monarchs underscore
Austen's version of history: the men appear foolish, the portrait
of Mary is by far the most attractive, that of Elizabeth the least.

Another line in 'The History of England' discloses more of
Austen's early double vision: she was able to laugh at and to
cherish at the same time not merely her own prejudices but her
own infatuations. Concerning the Duke of Somerset, Protector
during the reign of Edward VI, Austen writes, 'This Man was
on the whole of a very amiable Character, & is somewhat of a
favourite with me, tho' I would by no means pretend to affirm that
he was equal to those first of Men Robert Earl of Essex, Delamere,
or Gilpin' (143). What all three 'first of Men' have in common is
eagerness and energy – Austen's own youthful qualities – and
William Gilpin's energies show themselves in his books, his style.
Again, for Austen, books were very much alive. When Henry
Austen's 'Memoir' (1818) informs us that 'At a very early age she
was enamoured of Gilpin on the Picturesque; and she seldom
changed her opinions either on books or men' (*NA* 7), the word

'enamoured' is revealing. Gilpin was apparently one of Austen's literary infatuations, like Frederick Delamere, the flawed hero of Smith's *Emmeline*, and certainly the funniest and most interesting character in it. Austen's readiness to poke fun at her own delight in these figures is typical.

EARLY FRIENDSHIPS

Apart from her family and her reading, probably the greatest influences on Austen's juvenilia were provided by her friends. Austen's preference as a child for much older people is striking. Before she wrote the 'History of England', she knew Mrs Knight, more than 20 years her senior, well enough to praise Mary and abuse Elizabeth with her. Mrs Knight counted as a friend, then, before Austen was 16. Mrs Lefroy, a neighbour who was 26 years older, was an even earlier friend; with her husband George, she came to reside at Ashe rectory, close to Steventon, in May 1783. Martha Lloyd and her sister Mary were ten and four years older than Austen when they met and befriended her in 1789, aged 13; and Eliza de Feuillide, her cousin, had fourteen years' advantage. Even her cousin Jane Cooper was four years older. Possibly it was Austen's closeness to Cassandra, born three years earlier, that drew her to other people older than herself. She is said always to have looked to Cassandra as her superior. In their niece Caroline Austen's words:

> Aunt Cassandra was the older by 3 or 4 years, and the habit of looking up to her begun in childhood, seemed always to continue – When I was a little girl, she would frequently say to me, if opportunity offered, that Aunt Cassandra could teach everything much better than *she* could – Aunt Cass. *knew* more – Aunt Cass. could tell me better whatever I wanted to know – all which, I ever received in respectful silence – Perhaps she thought *my* mind wanted a turn in *that* direction, but I truly beleive she did always *really* think of her sister, as the superior to herself.[47]

Austen apparently enjoyed the safety of looking up to those around her, and of being herself something of a pet. The division of chores between her and Cassandra when their mother gave up running the household indicates that Austen continued to be babied within the family: while she had charge of breakfast and the stores of wine, tea, and sugar, Cassandra took care of the rest.[48] More importantly, for a child of Austen's powerful critical intelligence, the privilege of *not* feeling superior to those around her but being greatly appreciated by them must have been invaluable. If others are superior but loving, one is secure and protected – free to relax, to poke fun at oneself, at them, and particularly at others outside the enclave. Certainly, that so many older women found Austen worthy of friendship when she was a child testifies to her liveliness, her lack of self-absorption, her responsiveness.

The most fashionable of these older friends, Eliza de Feuillide, was charming and fascinating to almost all who knew her. Her story is worthy of a heroine and must have been known to her cousin. She had been born in India, the daughter of George Austen's sister Philadelphia, who had been sent there to marry. The husband she found in 1753 was Tysoe Saul Hancock, 20 years older than she. So far, her fate sounds very like that of Cecilia Wynne, a character Austen created in 'Catharine, or the Bower', the work in which Austen most conspicuously began to abandon burlesque (*MW* 194). But unlike Cecilia's husband, Hancock was not rich. It was his sometime partner, Warren Hastings, Governor-General of India from 1773-1785, who provided for Eliza, settling £10 000 on her when it became clear that her father could not. Hastings' generosity made it possible for Eliza to marry in 1781 a French captain who inaccurately claimed to be a Count – a marriage that she describes as a love match on his side if not on hers.[49]

Eliza first met Austen in 1786 when she visited Steventon with her mother and her six-month-old son, saw her again in London in 1788, and four years later wrote her first direct description of both Austen cousins:

> Cassandra & Jane are both very much grown (the latter is now taller than myself) and greatly improved as well in manners as in person, both of which are now much more formed than when you saw them. They are I think equally sensible, and both so to a degree seldom met with, but still my heart gives the preference to Jane, whose kind partiality to me indeed requires a return of the same nature.

(26 Oct. 1792)[50]

Eliza's husband remained in France and finally was guillotined on 22 February 1794; she married Austen's brother Henry about four years later. It has frequently been conjectured that Eliza's witty and flirtatious personality, particularly in force when she took part in the Steventon theatricals in 1787, and her dislike of a clergyman as a husband, was a source for Mary Crawford in *Mansfield Park*. If so, it can only be in the most subliminal, unconscious way. Austen composed *Mansfield Park* between February 1811 and the summer of 1813; Eliza became ill shortly after April 1811, and died (perhaps of cancer) in April 1813. It is inconceivable that Austen, who in any event strenuously rejected the notion that she drew her characters from life,[51] would have consciously chosen to dissect a dying sister-in-law. Nor, as Deirdre Le Faye points out, would she have been so 'cruel as to write and show to Henry a novel which pilloried his recently deceased wife'.[52]

Anne Lefroy, the wife of the rector of Ashe, only about a mile away from Steventon, was an equally vivid but perhaps more beloved friend. Her death in 1804 on Austen's birthday inspired her to write her only piece of serious verse four years later, 'To the Memory of Mrs Lefroy'. The poem praises her worth, grace, 'looks of eager love', 'voice and countenance almost divine', sense, 'genius, taste, and tenderness of soul', 'genuine warmth of heart without pretence', 'purity of mind', eloquence, 'Christian spirit', and then asks:

> Can aught enhance such goodness? yes, to me
>   Her partial favour from my earliest years
> Consummates all: ah! give me but to see
>   Her smile of love! The vision disappears.

(MW 440-1)

A two-page obituary of Mrs Lefroy appeared in the *Gentleman's Magazine* for December 1804, probably written by her brother, Samuel Egerton Brydges, a writer of bad novels and slightly more respectable antiquarian works. Like Austen, he praises Anne Lefroy's 'lively and enchanting manners' and the 'overflowing benevolence of her disposition', revealing that Mrs Lefroy had published poetry when quite young.[53] But Austen never dedicated any of her juvenilia to Mrs Lefroy, although almost all her other friends – the Lloyds, Eliza and her cousin Jane Cooper – as well as everyone in her family had at least one dedication. Presumably Austen did not acknowledge authorship to Mrs Lefroy. Among all her many recorded virtues, humour is conspicuously absent. She may have been all the more valuable as a friend for that lack. At home, Austen was surrounded by wits, by minds who inspired her own wit. With this older, loving, sensible yet enthusiastic friend, Austen could perhaps discuss the virtues of Mary Queen of Scots without immediately laughing at her own enthusiasm; one feels that this might not have been possible at Steventon.

The Lloyds were another clerical family, composed of two daughters, Martha and Mary, and their mother; a third sister had married her own cousin, Fulwar Craven Fowle. The Fowle, Lloyd and Austen families became closely connected. George Austen had known Fulwar Craven Fowle's father at Oxford and tutored both Fulwar and his younger brother Thomas at Steventon.[54] Probably his pupil Fulwar's marriage to Eliza Lloyd acquainted Mr Austen with the Lloyd family. In any event, when Mr Lloyd died in 1789, Mr Austen invited the mother and daughters to become tenants of Deane parsonage, only a mile and a half from Steventon.[55] Eventually Mary Lloyd was to become James's second wife; Cassandra was to become engaged to Thomas Fowle, who died before they could marry; Martha joined the household of Mrs Austen and her two daughters after Mr Austen's death; and finally Martha aged 62 would marry Francis. Martha also became one of Austen's closest friends apart from Cassandra. She seems to have been the only person outside the family who was allowed to read *First Impressions*, the early version of *Pride and Prejudice*, in manuscript – several times (*L* 67; 11 June 1799). And the first tale in Volume the First of the juvenilia, 'Frederic & Elfrida', was dedicated to her.

MONEY AND CLASS

The Austens' 'class' is rather hard to identify. David Spring has proposed that we call it the 'pseudo-gentry', borrowing the term from Alan Everitt. Spring argues that Austen's family belongs to the unlanded classes who 'sought strenuously to be taken for gentry', that is, the landed classes:[56]

This group comprised the nonlanded: the professional and rentier families, first and foremost the Anglican clergy; second, other professions like the law – preferably barristers rather than solicitors – and the fighting services; and last, the rentiers recently or long retired from business.[57]

This group, Spring goes on to say, 'is the one most likely to be described by Jane Austen interpreters as bourgeois', and he is certainly right to reject that term. He is also right to say that the class Austen belongs to:

> had a sharp eye for the social escalators, were skilled in getting on them, and (what was more important) no less skilled in staying on them. They were adept at acquiring what the economist Fred Hirsch has aptly called "positional goods" – those scarce services, jobs, and goods which announce social success.[58]

In other words, advancement in the professions Spring cites – law, the Army, the Navy, and the clergy – required patronage, the exertion of 'interest', connection with the establishment. Advancement in these professions provided non-landed income without compromising one's status as a gentleman. To apply the term 'pseudo-gentry' to such professionals, however, carries too many connotations of fraudulence to be accurate. A more correct description for the position of a clerical family like Austen's is to say that they were located on the fringes of the gentry.[59] This marginal position was built into the élite social structure; it was not an arriviste creation. Thanks to the practice of primogeniture, the landed gentry in England were always producing unlanded younger sons and daughters who nevertheless retained gentry status for a generation or two, and for whom their richer relatives would solicit whatever pensions, places, offices, livings or other sources of income they could obtain through their 'interest'. A kind of guide to the country's holders of interest and privilege was published every year during Austen's life in the form of inexpensive 'Court Calendars' – lists of placeholders at court, of all aristocrats and baronets, of members of parliament, Army and Navy officers, and endless office holders (sometimes with their salaries) from Lords of the Admiralty to directors of hospitals and commissioners of sewers, lamps and pavements. In Austen's world, nearly everything was a property right or privilege, even the right to name an inmate to a vacant place in an asylum. The diary of John Morley, a Warwickshire clergyman, shows the efforts that he made to get a place in Guy's Hospital for his insane sister through Sir Richard Neave, whom he did not know personally but who was known to a fellow clergyman. He seems to have been successful after years of trying only because in 1801 he noticed in a newspaper that a female inmate of Guy's had died, and he immediately got his friend to beg the place.[60] This sort of waiting on dead men's shoes was common. After his bankruptcy, Henry Austen wrote to ask a landed relative for his brother James's living of Cubbington two years before James died – letting the relative know that James was in ill health.[61]

Clergymen had at best only a life interest in the incomes of their livings, which were generally given them by relatives; the fees of curates who substituted for an absent rector or vicar were even less secure. After George Austen retired to Bath in 1801, his total income had been nearly £600 a year (*L* 103; 3 Jan. 1801), but when he died, the tithes and rents from his livings and his farming passed to his son James. Mrs Austen was left with what little property had been settled on her, which produced only £140 a year by one account, £122 by another more reliable one.[62] This meagre property had made it impossible for the Austens to dower their daughters. Their sons could be established in life only by drawing upon the resources of the gentry network. This network included not merely richer relatives, but friends, friends of friends and even more remote connections – anyone who had 'interest'. For example, George Austen asked his friend Warren Hastings to use his influence with a member of the Admiralty Board to secure Frank's promotion to commander. But Frank was promoted only when Admiral James Gambier, a remote family connection, exerted his interest four years later. Even so remote a patron had vanished for Frank shortly after 1814, as his own memorandum (written in 1844) makes clear: 'That I have not served at sea since 1814 is not from want of inclination or application, but have had no influence of a political or family description to back my pretensions'.[63]

On the whole, the network that the Austens drew on most effectively was composed of their rich relatives. One had given George Austen his early education at Tonbridge School, which in turn enabled him to take a degree at Oxford. As already indicated, Thomas Knight, another relative, gave him his two livings and adopted his third son, leaving Edward large landed estates in Kent and Hampshire. Mrs Austen's ancestry qualified her sons James and Henry for places at St John's College, Oxford, as Founders' Kin. Her connection the Hon. Mary Leigh presented James with the living of Cubbington on his marriage, valued at £269 a year. Her brother James Leigh Perrot supplemented James's income for many years and made him his heir; the extensive Leigh Perrot property eventually went to James's oldest son James Edward. Less fortunately, James Leigh Perrot stood surety for Henry Austen in the amount of £10 000 when he became Deputy-Receiver of Taxes for Oxfordshire; Henry's brother Edward guaranteed another £20 000; and all this money was lost in the failure of Henry's bank in 1816. Despite this loss, Edward allowed Henry to hold the living of Steventon after James's death in 1819, until his own son was old enough to take it.[64]

The Austens were thus well-connected to the landed gentry, particularly through Mrs Austen's Leigh relatives, although their own income was small. But the lower a family's income, the more marginal its status on the fringes of the gentry, and the less likely it was to associate with the landed gentry, always the measure of position. Austen's niece Fanny Knight, Lady Knatchbull, makes this point clear in the analysis of her aunt's class and manners already quoted in part:

> They were not rich & the people around with whom they chiefly mixed, were not at all high bred, or in short anything more than *mediocre* & *they* of course tho' superior in *mental powers* & *cultivation* were on the same level as far as *refinement* goes – but I think in later life their intercourse with Mrs Knight (who was very fond of & kind to them) improved them both & Aunt Jane was too clever not to put aside all possible signs of 'common-ness' (if such an expression is allowable) & teach herself to be more refined, at least in intercourse with people in general. Both the Aunts (Cassandra & Jane) were brought up in the most complete ignorance of the World & its ways (I mean as to fashion &c) & if it had not been for Papa's marriage which brought them into Kent, & the kindness of Mrs Knight, who used often to have one or the other of the sisters staying with her, they would have been, tho' not less clever and agreeable

in themselves, very much below par as to good Society and its ways. If you hate all this I beg yr. pardon, but I felt it at my *pen's end* & it chose to come along & speak the truth.[65]

If we remember that the common, unrefined, unfashionable behaviour mentioned here probably alludes to the robust humour and unstylish clothes of Steventon rectory, we can accept this account. Although Austen visited and dined occasionally with some of the neighbourhood at Steventon, and went to balls as well, reciprocal dinners were seldom offered at the rectory.[66] The ways of so-called 'good society'– dining with county families and offering them dinners in return – were something Austen experienced with frequency only when she stayed in Kent. But that is precisely the sort of 'good society' that Mr Elliot approves and Anne Elliot deprecates in *Persuasion*. It requires only 'birth, education and manners, and with regard to education is not very nice', as Mr Elliot admits; it does not necessarily provide what Anne calls for, 'clever, well-informed people, who have a great deal of conversation' (150). We can be certain that Anne's definition, not Mr Elliot's, is in Austen's mind when she writes of finally feeling equal, at 32, to Mrs Knight: 'I cannot help regretting that now, when I feel enough her equal to relish her society, I see so little of the latter' (*L* 202; 26 June 1808). But she must also have been aware that others would view her as far from Mrs Knight's equal in Mr Elliot's sense – as her own niece did in retrospect.

As Austen grew up, then, she enjoyed a strong sense of mutual support and security within her family and among her friends, but the family's actual position in their world was somewhat marginal. The tensions that this conflict between security and marginality created are visible in Austen's own juvenilia. Learning the rules of society and the 'rules' of literature is of great significance in the early novels as well as the juvenilia: Catherine Morland, 'from fifteen to seventeen . . . in training for a heroine', is equally ignorant of both literary and social convention (*NA* 15). 'In training' for a writer from before age fifteen, Austen very early chose to burlesque both the rules of fiction and the rules of her social world – particularly the rules governing women's behaviour. Her treatment of literary and social convention in the juvenilia offers a revealing perspective on both her own social world and the distorted view of it presented by much contemporary fiction.

LITERARY APPRENTICESHIP

What made Austen begin to write? The easy answer to that question is provided by Cassandra's note in Volume the First, which she gave at her death to her brother Charles: 'For my brother Charles. I think I recollect that a few of the trifles in this Vol: were written expressly for his amusement'.[67] We can readily imagine Austen at a very early age telling stories to her brother like those that Anna Austen Lefroy remembered:

> Aunt Jane was the general favorite with children – as well she might be – her manners were so playful, & her long circum-stantial stories, continued from time to time & invented for the occasion were so delightful – I would give any thing now to have the power of recalling them.[68]

Her sister Caroline, whose memory was better, gives us more details:

> she would tell us the most delightful stories chiefly of Fairyland, and her Fairies had all characters of their own . . . She amused us in various ways – *once* I remember in giving a conversation as between myself and my two cousins, supposed to be grown up, the day after a Ball.[69]

Austen's 'invention', to use the eighteenth-century term, was clearly inexhaustible. She was a born storyteller. But most of the tales in Volume the First were probably not originally meant simply to amuse Charles. They are full of nonsense, but they are also full of literary parody (particularly of sentimental novels), unconventional portraits of women, violence and family jokes. Why did she write them?

The answer of two of Austen's best critics, Mary Lascelles and A. Walton Litz, is probably as good as we can expect: she was staking out her essentially realistic territory, by making fun of the 'world of illusion' or the 'land of fiction', showing those to be not only absurd but undesirable – embodying corrupt representations of real virtues like genuine feeling.[70] But contemporary fiction also embodied unrealistic and ridiculous portraits of women. Some of the 'illusions' that Austen undermines in her earliest work include the images of women enshrined in both social and literary convention. Even as a teenager, Austen is sceptical of her contemporaries' notions of what women are like and what they should be like. The unconventional portraits of women in the juvenilia comically reflect this scepticism. That is, Austen always subjects conventional notions of women to two tests: first, that of reality (do women act this way?), and second, that of reason (should they act this way?). Thus, the early juvenilia present in bolder, more outrageous terms the unconventional behaviour and the critique of conventional notions of women that are embodied more subtly and realistically in the novels. Austen goes from picturing women who literally get away with murder in the juvenilia, to women who figuratively do so in the novels – who confront and reject conventional behaviour. In addition, the early fictions show that Austen is already engaged – however comically – in a critical scrutiny of money and class, of security and marginality, from a woman's perspective.

If Austen began to write partly because she was interested in laughing at conventional notions of women, she soon became equally interested in publication. That is, it is one thing to write down ideas or tales on scraps of paper, as Austen seems always to have done, another to copy them into volumes in order to preserve them. I would argue that Austen began to write out her works in Volume the First as a way to 'publish' them privately. From the beginning, she decided to make her written copy resemble a printed book as much as possible. The quarto book in which she wrote may have been a present from someone in the family, just as the (more expensive) book that she labelled Volume the Second was a present from her father. Or she may have purchased it herself. In any case, she follows as many of the contemporary conventions of printing as she can in her 184 pages. She supplies not only a table of contents, page numbers, titles and chapter divisions in many tales, but also features that are characterisitic of some books printed in the last quarter of the eighteenth century: printers' lines above and below chapter numbers and above and below the 'Finis' with which she usually ends each tale, headings like 'Letter the first' and so forth in the epistolary fiction, and in the earliest tales, quotation marks at the beginning of each line of quoted material.[71] Most interestingly, however, from about 1789 she adds dedications to family and friends. In thus creating something very like a printed book, but for family circulation, Austen was typically having it both ways:

treating her writing both privately, as a family entertainment, and yet seriously, 'publishing' her own collected works in a form that has allowed them to come down to us. The authorial confidence that allowed her to write her comic dedications – and even to go back to and dedicate her very earliest works – is impressive.[72]

Except for the few pieces that Austen herself dated, we do not know when she composed her works or copied them into the three Volumes. Most critics believe that the earliest entries in Volume the First date from 1787 or 1788, although they may have been composed earlier; she is clearly making fair copies of work already completed. The latest datable entries are short pieces dedicated to two new-born nieces: the 'Scraps' for Fanny Catherine Austen (later Fanny Knight), born 23 January 1793, are entered at the end of Volume the Second; the 'Detached Pieces' for Anna are dated June 2, 1793, and occupy some of the last pages in Volume the First. These works too may have been composed earlier. They resemble the earliest burlesques much more than they do the later, longer, more complex works: 'The Three Sisters', from Volume the First (1790?); 'Love and Freindship' (13 June 1790), 'Lesley Castle' (1791?),[73] 'The History of England' (26 November 1791) and 'Collection of Letters', from Volume the Second; and 'Evelyn' (between 6 May and August 1792) and 'Catharine' (August, 1792), the only works in Volume the Third, which bears a date on the first leaf of 6 May 1792.[74]

WOMEN AND THE JUVENILIA

The longer works, together with some of the early tales in Volume the First, are the most interesting. As many critics have pointed out, they show Austen in the process of developing her criticism of current fiction through parody and burlesque; they also show her developing her sense of what fiction should be. But these works are also surprisingly, though hilariously, violent – full of women who pursue men, knock them down and are 'carried home, Dead Drunk' (*MW* 14). Women loom large in these tales – they generally outnumber the men and outmanoeuvre them also.They are on the whole more powerful, more assertive, more successful. They challenge contemporary notions of what women are and what they ought to be.

In Volume the First, 'Frederic & Elfrida', the opening tale, is full of hilarious behaviour that would be unimaginable in conduct books and other contemporary accounts of female manners. The families of Fitzroy, Drummond and Falknor (almost entirely female) 'did not scruple to kick one another out of the window on the slightest provocation' (*MW* 6). The marriage of Rebecca Fitzroy to Captain Roger is brought about by a threat and a promise: Mrs Fitzroy's consent will bring her a 'smelling Bottle', but if she refuses, 'this dagger which I enclose in my left [hand] shall be steeped in your hearts blood' (10). Who is this dagger-wielding 'I'? – Rebecca, Elfrida, Frederic and Captain Roger jointly kneeling at Mrs Fitzroy's feet. And Elfrida herself brings about her own marriage when 'she flew to Frederic & in a manner truly heroick, spluttered out to him her intention of being married the next Day' (11).

In 'Jack & Alice', men and women reverse roles more clearly than in the earlier tale. The hero, Charles Adams, is a splendid parody of Samuel Richardson's perfect hero Sir Charles Grandison, whose dazzling merit subdues all: Charles Adams 'was an amiable, accomplished & bewitching young Man, of so dazzling a Beauty that none but Eagles could look him in the Face' (13). Accordingly, he is pursued by Alice Johnson, who is addicted to the bottle and dice, and by Lucy, a tailor's daughter of Wales. Alice sends her father to ask for Charles's hand in marriage (in vain), but Lucy writes him 'a very kind letter, offering him with great tenderness my hand & heart. To this I received an angry & peremptory refusal, but thinking it might be rather the effect of his modesty than any thing else, I pressed him again' (21). Lucy resembles the determined male suitors of fiction, who will not take no for an answer, or who interpret 'no' as 'yes', just as 'the lovely, the lively, but insensible Charles Adams' (15) resembles a disdainful beauty. Lady Williams sends Lucy to Bath where she forgets Charles, becomes engaged to a duke, and is in danger from the envious Sukey Simpson: 'often has she threatened, & sometimes endeavoured to cut my throat' (27). She is poisoned by Sukey, who is hung for her crime; another Simpson consoles the duke, and a third goes off in pursuit of higher rank, becoming 'the favourite Sultana of the great Mogul' (29). Lady Williams marries Charles. The envious Sukey's fate seems rather harsh compared to that of Anna Parker in 'Letter from a Young Lady . . . ', who manages to murder her father and mother with impunity, and is about to 'murder my Sister' (*MW* 175).

Assertion and power are natural to the women of the earliest juvenilia. Even the extremely susceptible Emma, of 'Edgar & Emma', who 'continued in tears the remainder of her Life' when she found that her beloved Edgar was away from home, learned of his residence at college by demanding 'in a resolute manner': 'Mrs Willmot, you do not stir from this House till you let me know how all the rest of your family do, particularly your eldest son' (32–3). Eliza, of 'Henry & Eliza' robs her adoptive parents of £50, flees to France with the fiancé of a Duchess's daughter, returns to England on her husband's death 'in a man of War of 55 Guns, which they had built in their more prosperous Days', but the Duchess's officers take her 'to a snug little Newgate of their Lady's' (36). In vain; she escapes, is reconciled to her parents when Lady Harcourt remembers that Eliza is her real daughter, not simply adopted, and:

> No sooner was she reinstated in her accustomed power at Harcourt Hall, than she raised an Army, with which she entirely demolished the Dutchess's Newgate, snug as it was, and by that act, gained the Blessings of thousands, & the Applause of her own Heart. (39)

In the playlet 'The Visit', women are completely in control. A deceased grandmother is responsible for the presence of short beds, gooseberry wine and only six chairs in the drawing room when eight people are present. As a result, Miss Fitzgerald suggests, 'if your ladyship will but take Sir Arthur in your Lap, & Sophy my Brother in hers, I beleive we shall do pretty well' (52). Lady Hampton never allows her spouse Sir Arthur to speak, eat or drink. Sophy finds Lord Fitzgerald 'very light' in her lap, tosses off a bumper of 'warm ale', agrees to circulate the bottle at dinner, and is asked in marriage by Lord Fitzgerald. And Miss Fitzgerald concludes the play by saying, 'Since you Willoughby are the only one left, I cannot refuse your earnest solicitations – There is my Hand' (54). A Steventon performance of this play must have been very funny.

The most assertive and entertaining woman in these early tales is certainly 'The Beautifull Cassandra', the daughter of 'a celebrated Millener in Bond Street. Her father was of noble Birth, being the near relation of the Dutchess of ————'s Butler'. Having taken a bonnet made for a Countess, Cassandra 'walked from her Mother's shop to make her Fortune'. In seven 'well spent' hours, she curtseys to a Viscount but otherwise ignores him; devours 'six ices, refused to pay for them, knocked down the Pastry Cook, & walked away'; takes a hackney coach to Hampstead and back, bestowing a bonnet on the driver instead of money and running away; encounters and passes Maria 'in a mutual silence' after both have 'trembled, blushed, turned pale'; curtseys to her friend the Widow; and embraces her mother. Cassandra, more than a match for the pastry cook and the driver, takes no interest in the Viscount, 'a young Man, no less celebrated for his Accomplishments & Virtues, than for his Elegance & Beauty'. Once again, roles are reversed. The Viscount is described in terms appropriate to an eligible young lady, not a gentleman (*MW* 44-7). This tale is very properly dedicated to Austen's sister Cassandra: 'Madam You are a Phoenix" (44). Such characterisations allow Austen her typical ironic stance. The outrageous humour permits those who think women ought to resemble conduct-book models to see Austen's aggressors as amusing comic monsters. Those whose attitude is more sceptical can enjoy the free play of images of power and possibility.[75]

Austen's early interest in reversing sexual roles does not disappear in the later juvenilia or in the novels. It is no accident that Mary and Elizabeth are the major figures in the 'History of England'; indeed, Austen shapes her history so that all characters, all sovereigns, are measured by the part they played in the catastrophe of Mary's execution. Throughout her literary career, not just in the juvenilia, Austen is sceptical of conventional notions of male and female behaviour. As one of her first critics noted, with great relief, Austen's women are not taken from a conduct book, a guide for proper young women, but from life:

As liable to 'fall in love first,' as anxious to attract the attention of agreeable men, as much taken with a striking manner, or a handsome face, as unequally gifted with constancy and firmness, as liable to have their affections biased by convenience or fashion, as we, on our part, will admit men to be.[76]

Although Austen always subjects the behaviour of women in her novels to the test of reality, so that she may portray women as they are, she seldom does so in the early juvenilia. The crude reversals of sex roles and the incursions of violence in the earliest juvenilia, although they are irresistibly funny, are not consistent with the aims of Austen's later fiction: her wish to create fully developed characters and her commitment to realism. But they do register even more forcibly than do the novels, her early and stringent criticism of conventional notions of what women should be. Claudia L. Johnson has rightly pointed out that in 'Frederic & Elfrida', the behaviour of Charlotte Drummond (who is so obliging that she agrees to marry two men and then commits suicide in consternation):

> has only slightly exaggerated what passes for standard behavior every day. So little are proper young ladies ever trained or expected to disoblige others, particularly suitors, by saying "no", that heroines as unlike as Elizabeth Bennet and Fanny Price both find it impossible to refuse marriage proposals and be believed.[77]

Charlotte Drummond takes the obligingness and submissiveness enjoined by conduct books to such an absurd extreme that she effaces herself utterly; self-murder is the logical consequence of her actions.

Austen soon lost interest in the relatively simple strategies of the early juvenilia. Instead of turning conventional expectations of women and of fiction upside down, the later juvenilia engage in more sustained criticism of contemporary sentimental fiction – its language, its values – and of contemporary notions of gender. The quality, the incisiveness of Austen's criticism is astonishing. Many writers, some almost equally youthful, were engaged in parodying the sentimental novel, but their efforts only underscore Austen's achievement – as is evident in comparing a passage from Matthew G. Lewis's parody, 'The Effusions of Sensibility', written in his 'sixteenth year',[78] to a similar one from 'Love and Freindship', also a novel-in-letters and written when Austen was 14. In both passages, the heroine suffers a shock to her sensibility. Lewis's heroine, Lady Honoria Harrowheart, busy lamenting her departure from home, has just been told by her father to eat buttered toast:

Judge what must have been my feelings, when the luxury of tender grief was disturbed by so vulgar an invitation! 'Eat some buttered toast!' My sensibility could not sustain the shock – I sunk beneath it. 'Cruel, cruel father!' said I; and concealing my tears with my white cambric handkerchief, I hurried out of the apartment, having heard Lord Dunderhead say, as I left him, 'Plague take the girl! She's always a whimpering.' Yes, my beloved Sophonisba! So little idea has my father of sentiment, he called the streams which the softest sensations demanded from my tender heart, 'a whimpering!' But if sentiment must bear that odious name, often, very often, may the same emotions I then felt engage myself, and you, and all my friends, and the whole of my acquaintance, in one general, one heart-alleviating whimper![79]

Austen's heroine Laura reports on the decline of Sophia's and Augustus's stolen funds when she and her husband are their guests:

By our arrival their Expenses were considerably encreased tho' their means for supplying them were then nearly exhausted. But they, Exalted Creatures! scorned to reflect a moment on their pecuniary Distresses & would have blushed at the idea of paying their Debts, – Alas! what was their Reward for such disinterested Behaviour. The beautifull Augustus was arrested and we were all undone. Such perfidious Treachery in the merciless perpetrators of the Deed will shock your gentle nature Dearest Marianne as much as it then affected the Delicate Sensibility of Edward, Sophia, your Laura, & of Augustus himself. To compleat such unparalelled Barbarity we were informed that an Execution in the House would shortly take place. Ah! what could we do but what we did! We sighed & fainted on the sofa. (88)

In both passages, the characters are overcome, in heightened, absurd language, by the intrusion of a prosaic world, but Austen's prosaic world bears some resemblance to that world of causes and effects, getting and spending, that the devotees of sensibility wish to circumvent. Austen ironically conveys both sets of values – those of sensibility, above monetary concerns, and those of the world, which exacts payment. Her irony turns on the word 'disinterested', for of course the delicate sensibility of Laura and her companions is extremely self-interested; the barbarous, treacherous, merciless, perfidious world owes them a living. By contrast, Lewis's parody is crude. Though he does capture parental boredom with teenage enthusiasm, Lewis opposes quite simple values: for one character, weeping is sentiment; for the other, whimpering; and Honoria makes herself more ridiculous by temporarily accepting and using the term 'whimpering'. There is nothing in Lewis's passage either of the hilarious and slightly wicked image at the end of Austen's – the four piled together on the sofa.

At this stage of Austen's literary development, sensible, rational women tend to be pushed aside, as is Augusta Lindsay, Edward's sister in 'Love and Freindship'. Even when she creates the reasonable and witty Georgiana Stanhope, in 'The Three Sisters', Austen uses her primarily to report the unreasonable and foolish behaviour of her mother, her sister Mary and Mary's suitor Mr Watts. Her most sustained and effective treatment of a sensible woman in the juvenilia is the portrait of Maria Williams in the third of 'A Collection of Letters'. Maria's mother requires that her daughter associate with the snobbish and autocratic Lady Greville, who victimises her, but Maria manages to repel some of Lady Greville's snobbish attacks with impertinence. Just as Anna Parker literally gets away with murder in 'Letter from a Young Lady', Maria is figuratively getting away with murder, as Elizabeth Bennet does in her encounters with Lady Catherine de Bourgh in *Pride and Prejudice*.

These early fictions also show Austen to be extremely concerned – however comically – with a critical scrutiny of money and class. These concerns are even more evident in her brother's publication of 1789-90, *The Loiterer*. It establishes a revealing social and literary context for Austen's works – primarily for the juvenilia but also the novels – and as a result many Austen scholars have read it. Like A. Walton Litz, most critics connect its satiric attitudes, its increasing focus on short tales of love and marriage, with Austen's own concerns.[80] These connections are valuable, and worth pursuing: the importance of her brothers' youthful periodical to Austen can scarcely be exaggerated. But Litz is certainly right to say that the *Loiterer* is most important for what it tells us about the context of Austen's early writing: 'as a record of the ideas and opinions which prevailed in Jane Austen's early environment'.[81]

THE LOITERER

While Austen was compiling the first of her Volumes, her brothers were becoming published authors. On Saturday, 31 January 1789, shortly after Austen's 13th birthday and Cassandra's 16th, James Austen, then 23, launched his weekly periodical *The Loiterer*, printed and sold by C.S. Rann for threepence in Oxford. The next issue was sold in London and Birmingham as well, and eventually booksellers in Bath and Reading also carried the work. *The Loiterer* ceased publication with the 60th number, on 20 March 1790, and was issued shortly afterward in two volumes by Prince and Cooke (Oxford, 1790), who had taken over the printing from Rann on 24 October 1789 (the 39th number). James wrote the first seven numbers, and his much younger brother Henry wrote the eighth, which appeared on 21 March when he was 17: 'Disadvantages arising from misconduct at Oxford'.

The Loiterer declared itself to be written by friends at Oxford, not only James and Henry but Benjamin Portal (known to Austen as a relative of some Hampshire neighbours) as well as some anonymous contributors. We might be surprised that these young men would think such a project might have any chance of success, but in fact *The Loiterer* immediately followed two well-received periodical publications by schoolboys and university men. Its predecessors were, first, *The Microcosm*, written by boys at Eton and published as a book in 1787, and the 48 numbers of the *Olla Podrida*, published in book form in 1788 and (like *The Loiterer*) sold by Rann at Oxford. The *Olla Podrida* was edited by Thomas Monro of Magdalen College, Oxford, though others aided him. Both these works were noticed very favourably by the major review journals, the *Monthly* and the *Critical*, and were reprinted more than once.

James's periodical was not so fortunate. It received a courteous but rather lukewarm reception from the *Critical Review*, and the *Monthly* ignored it; it was not reprinted except in a pirated Irish edition. The *Critical*'s estimate is worth quoting, for in many respects it anticipates both the praise and the objections that Austen's novels met with from contemporary reviewers:

> if [the author] does not strike the fancy by the brilliancy of his wit, if he does not amuse by the fictions of a fertile imagination, if he does not conquer worlds and 'then imagine more', he conciliates our esteem by faithful descriptions of life

and manners, he instructs by judicious precepts and apposite examples, and he promotes the cause of virtue by the purest dictates of religion and morality.[82]

Austen herself was always praised in reviews that appeared during her lifetime for faithful descriptions of life and manners and for pure or useful morality, even by reviewers who conceded her 'want of *newness*' – that is, want of imagination.[83]

Perhaps most important to Austen, *The Loiterer* conclusively demonstrated that publication was a real, available goal for a writer – perhaps even an inevitable one. After all, the first *Loiterer* asserted that a 'small Society of Friends' began by reading together, writing 'extracts, remarks, and criticisms', and finally:

> in a little time a number of Essays on various subjects were produced. But if from reading to writing it is but one step, from writing to publishing it is less – and finding in course of time our works swell upon our hands, after a decent struggle between fear and vanity, we at length agreed that to keep our Talent any longer wrapt in the Napkin would be equal injustice to our writings, the world, and ourselves. (*Loit* 1, p. 7)

James's phrase is powerful and surprising to us, who generally do not think of publication as quite so easy: 'if from reading to writing it is but one step, from writing to publishing it is less'. Perhaps Austen took these words as a challenge. Some readers think that she herself first ventured into print by these apparently easy steps from reading to writing to publishing in the week after Henry's debut. But if she wrote the letter signed 'Sophia Sentiment' and published on 28 March 1789, in *Loiterer* 9, objecting to the absence of stories, love and women from the first eight numbers, she used a style very different from that employed in other writing from this period. The letter is discursive, lacking the incisiveness of Austen's juvenilia. And no family tradition of her authorship has come down to us. If Austen was the author, which I am inclined to doubt, her brother James probably edited the letter extensively. Nothing in its style is inconsistent with James's burlesque writing in *The Loiterer*, and much is inconsistent with Austen's.[84]

But whether or not *The Loiterer* includes Austen's first publication, it does provide important clues to attitudes toward money, class and education in the juvenilia. When they began their periodical, both James and Henry were supported by their father and by their status as founders' kin at St John's College, Oxford, and both were intended to support themselves as clergymen. As a result, they naturally had two sources of concern: money and class, that is, their expenses as students and their incomes as clergymen after taking orders, incomes which would determine what position they held on the fringes of the gentry. Students' expenses could be heavy, ranging from £80 to £200 a year, although the expenses of tuition were minimal.[85] Even prosperous parents could have difficulty keeping sons at the universities.[86] James and Henry Austen were excused tuition fees as founder's kin but must have lived very cheaply, for their father could not possibly have supported two sons at Oxford at what appears to be the usual rate.

Accordingly, James and Henry make problems of money and class central to many of their essays in *The Loiterer*. Interest in money takes many forms, among them specifying parents' incomes, students' extravagant expenses at Oxford or the emoluments of a clerical living to be obtained afterward. They address several times in their papers the horrible fate of being a curate on £50 a year or less – a fate that temporarily overlook both, James immediately and Henry after the failure in 1816 of his bank.[87] Concern with class appears in several satiric accounts of tradesmen's sons at Oxford who attempt to ape the gentry, and in generally approving discussions of family pride. On the whole, *The Loiterer* aligns itself firmly on the side of social hierarchy, although it values good education and is somewhat sympathetic to the notion that education might improve one's social position.

The social context that *The Loiterer* establishes is, interestingly, one of threat. Oxford is a place where the sons (not children) of men of moderate fortune can qualify themselves for orders. But the consequence may be (as Henry puts it) 'sinking into Country Curates, [growing] old on fifty pounds a year' or (as James has it) 'starving on a country Curacy of forty pounds a year' (*Loit.* 8; *Loit.* 7). In short, poverty and dispossession, the possible loss of position, are present to James's and Henry's imaginations in *The Loiterer*, even though their prospects looked fair. James was ordained in June 1789 at Oxford and had the curacy of Stoke Charity in hand, and as the eldest son, he had his father's family living to look forward to since it was in the gift of the Knights and his brother Edward was their heir. But even Henry might suppose too that a family living would be found for him eventually.[88] Not surprisingly, then, the emphasis on money and class in *The Loiterer* is ambivalent: a sense of both threat and security is present. Security is conveyed by distancing: those facing starvation on poor curacies are sons of tradesmen or graziers, with no connections to the landed gentry like those of the Austens. That is, the Austen brothers tend to focus their criticism on the circumstances of the class below them, the sons of prosperous or near-prosperous tradesmen, a stance that reinforces their own sense of belonging to the gentry. At the same time, this choice also betrays the insecurities of marginality: extreme awareness or ridicule of the class below one is the hallmark of the arriviste, as Mrs Elton's attitude to the Tupmans from Birmingham amply demonstrates (*E*, 310). Both James and Henry clearly entertained some anxieties about their future as members of the gentry, anxiety that eventually became fully justified in Henry's case.

This ambivalent sense that one's class and income are both secure and threatened is visible too in Austen's juvenilia, although she explores the issue from a woman's perspective. As an undowered woman, Austen's place on the fringes of the gentry was more marginal than her brothers'. Unless she married, she would have an assured home and social position only during her father's lifetime, and perhaps not even then: if he resigned his living or if he retired early, the home would be lost. It was lost, in fact, in 1801, when George Austen turned the rectory and the work of the parish over to his son James and took his wife and daughters to Bath; Austen is reported to have fainted when she heard of the move.[89]

Just as the juvenilia explore discrepancies between what women actually are and what they are supposed to be, they comically express tensions between security and marginality, principally by portraying women who find themselves thrown onto the world. In the earlier juvenilia, they are comically ejected as thieves: Eliza of 'Henry & Eliza' is 'turned out of doors' when she steals £50; Sophia of 'Love and Freindship' suffers a similar fate when discovered at Macdonald-Hall 'majestically removing the 5th Bank-note from the Drawer to her own purse' (34, 96). In the later juvenilia, women's marginality derives from more complex circumstances. Louisa Burton, the defaulting wife of Margaret Lesley's brother in 'Lesley Castle', was left a penniless orphan at 'about eighteen to the protection of any . . . Relations who would protect her'. She had been taught dissimulation 'by a father who but too well knew, that to be married, would be the only chance she would have of not being starved' (117). The marginal position of Miss Jane, in 'Letter the Second' of 'A Collection of Letters', is indicated by her name. She has been married but concealed her marriage from her father, Admiral Annesley:

> 'As I could not prevail upon myself to take the name of Dashwood (a name which after my [husband] Henry's death I could never hear without emotion) and as I was conscious of having no right to that of Annesley, I dropt all thoughts of either, & have made it a point of bearing only my Christian one since my Father's death.' (154–5).

And Miss Grenville's melancholy at leaving Suffolk in 'Letter the Fourth' is finally explained: she has been dispossessed because both her parents have died. Austen treats dispossession more thoroughly and even less comically in 'Catharine'.

In pursuit of their interest in marginality, the juvenilia exploit some of the anomalies of class that Austen perceives in both life and literature. Edward Copeland has noted that 'Nothing is funnier to the youthful Austen than finding the lower ranks in fiction',[90] citing Lucy the highly accomplished tailor's daughter in 'Jack & Alice', Cassandra the daughter of a near relation of a duchess's butler, Laura in 'Love and Freindship' whose mother 'was the natural Daughter of a Scotch Peer by an italian Opera-girl' (*MW* 77). These instances and others all suggest that like her brothers, Austen was amused by attempts to appropriate the status of a higher class. But she can be equally amused by imagining the reverse, a willful sacrifice of class. In 'Edgar & Emma', Sir George and Lady Marlow have been living for two years 'in a paltry Market-town, while we have 3 good Houses of our own situated in some of the finest parts of England, & perfectly ready to receive us!' (*MW* 29-30).

'CATHARINE, OR THE BOWER'

Austen's real interest in allowing different classes to mix lies in exploring what happens when members of one class falsely assume superiority to another – when they perceive others as marginal. Austen treats this assumption of superiority ironically but seriously in the juvenilia. The two works that dwell on it are the third of the 'Collection of Letters', which portrays Maria Williams' conflict with Lady Greville, and 'Catharine, or the Bower', the most interesting of all the juvenilia. It was completed in August 1792, when Austen was 16. It is generally felt (wrongly, I believe) to be unsuccessful in its attempt to incorporate seriousness with comedy, though it does seem closest of all the juvenilia in style and substance to the early novels.

In general I think it mistaken to look to Austen's family and friends as immediate sources for her plots and characters, but it is possible that one event in 1792 may have suggested the subplot of 'Catharine': the fate of the heroine's friends the Wynnes. Austen had been reminded of the marginality of wives or daughters of clergymen in 1789, for her friend Martha Lloyd experienced it in that year. Her father had died, and she with her sister and mother had been forced to leave his parish in Shropshire. They rented Deane parsonage from George Austen, and lived there only a mile away from the rectory at Steventon for three years – until once again they were dispossessed. When James Austen married in March 1792, he obtained the curacy of Deane and the parsonage from his father. The Lloyds moved 15 miles away, a loss to Austen that may account for some of the uneven tone of 'Catharine',[91] copied into Volume the Third only a few months later. Catharine Percival's friends the Wynnes, daughters of a clergyman, joined with her before the novel opens to create the bower of the title. Their father's death has forced them to leave the neighbourhood and to depend upon rich, fashionable, selfish and uncaring relatives. Cecilia and Mary Wynne's fate is presented in a sombre, even melancholy style that quarrels with the exuberant comedy of Catharine's subsequent encounters with the Stanleys, and the fragment ends with a threat to destroy the bower that is Catharine's solace for the loss of the Wynnes.

The Wynnes' deprivation is more severe than Catharine's in losing them, for Cecilia and Mary lose their independence, not simply their friend. Cecilia is sent by her relative Sir George Fitzgibbon to India to seek a rich husband, just as Austen's aunt Philadelphia was sent (*MW* 203). She marries 'Splendidly, yet unhappily' in Bengal (194). Her sister Mary is a companion in the family of Lady Halifax, who apparently grudges her clothes and considers her fortunate (203). Discussion of the Wynnes' fate comprises only a minor part of the concern with class in 'Catharine', however. The heroine compares the well-educated but impoverished Wynnes to Miss Dudley, whose mother is 'an ill-educated, untaught woman of ancient family' and who 'inherited the ignorance, the insolence, & pride of her parents' (195), and to Camilla Stanley, whose 12 years of education,

> which ought to have been spent in the attainment of useful knowledge and Mental Improvement, had been all bestowed in learning Drawing, Italian and Music, more especially the latter, and she now united to these Accomplishments, an Understanding unimproved by reading and a Mind totally devoid either of Taste or Judgment. (198)

Both the Dudleys and the Stanleys despise or condescend to the Percivals' family. The Dudleys are especially poisonous. 'They at once despised the Percivals as people of mean family, and envied them as people of fortune. They . . . were continually seeking to lessen them in the opinion of the Neighbourhood by Scandalous & Malicious reports' (196). But even the Stanleys, distantly related to the Percivals, look down on them. Much is made of Camilla Stanley's indignation when her brother makes Catharine begin a dance at the Dudley's ball. It is a *faux pas* for Catharine very like those of the heroine of *Evelina*: 'As an heiress she was certainly of consequence, but her Birth gave her no other claim to it, for her Father had been a Merchant' (223-4). When Camilla makes her indignation known in ridiculously self-contradictory statements like, 'I am sure I am not at all offended, and should not care if all the World were to stand above me, but still it is extremely abominable, & what I cannot put up with', Catharine has no trouble understanding her and offers 'a very submissive apology, for she had too much good Sense to be proud of her family, and too much good Nature to live at variance with any one' (226).

Having money and education but no family, Catharine occupies an ambiguous social position. She is not marginal, precisely, because no one with enough money can be, but she is not secure either. Her sexual position – as a young women within her social world – is also made difficult by her aunt's horror of sexual misconduct. Mrs Percival fears that Catharine will marry imprudently if allowed to choose, and deplores her 'open and unreserved' disposition with young men. She therefore refuses to mix more with her neighbourhood lest Catharine encounter sexual opportunity (196). When Mrs Percival sees the mischievous Edward Stanley kiss Catharine's hand in her bower, she draws the worst conclusions:

> Well; *this* is beyond anything I could have supposed. *Profligate* as I *knew* you to be, I was not prepared for such a sight. This is beyond any thing you ever did *before*; beyond any thing I ever heard of in my Life! Such Impudence, I never witnessed before in such a Girl! . . . the welfare of every Nation depends upon the virtue of it's individuals, and any one who offends in so gross a manner against decorum & propriety is certainly hastening it's ruin. (*MW* 232-3)

Claudia L. Johnson has drawn some important inferences from this passage in its entirety. She asserts that debates on female manners have political content in the 1790s: 'as recent research into women's conduct literature has shown, "agreeableness" is not a politically neutral female grace but . . . one thing needful to guarantee paternal authority without unseemly confrontations'. Reaction to the French Revolution tended to link:

> political survival with the private and domestic virtue of English subjects . . . and women, accordingly, found themselves and every aspect of their behavior – their learning, their chastity, their exercise, their housewifery – at the center of arguments about national security itself.[92]

Feminist critics like Johnson find in Austen's sceptical treatments of conventional female behaviour, and in Austen's ironic portraits of upholders of decorum and propriety like Mrs Percival, evidence that Austen is not as politically 'conservative' as some critics have contended, and they are certainly correct.[93] Austen's political sympathies may be fundamentally conservative, but her mind is critical and her vision ironic. Accordingly, she will sometimes seem to adopt the 'reformist' and 'progressive' stances that Johnson identifies.[94] At other times, she will with equal plausibility seem to adopt a 'conservative' position.

Austen's critical, double vision creates in Catharine a comic heroine whose social position is marginal and whose sexuality is threatened, and this already not intrinsically very amusing picture is darkened by Catharine's sense of dispossession and deprivation. The first sentence powerfully establishes the deprivation of love that Catharine suffers:

> Catharine had the misfortune, as many heroines have had before her, of losing her Parents when she was very young, and of being brought up under the care of a Maiden Aunt, who while she tenderly loved her, watched over her conduct with so scrutinizing a severity, as to make it very doubtful to many people, and to Catharine amongst the rest, whether she loved her or not. (192)

No wonder comedy is difficult in this work. Catharine is caged, deprived of experience, deprived of love, deprived of friendship; and her aunt even wishes to dispossess her of the bower that she romantically clings to as 'sacred', the one relic of her friends' love (195). But despite her need for affection – which makes her respond at first more favourably to Camilla and Edward Stanley than they deserve – Catharine can judge them rightly after her initial confusion. Her need, however, does make her vulnerable to Camilla's later assertion that Edward is in love with her. The fragment ends with Catharine in the throes of an infatuation quite like Elizabeth Bennet's attraction to Wickham or Emma's to Frank Churchill, but we have less assurance that Catharine will be able to extricate herself safely despite her good spirits and 'fund of vivacity and good humour' (193).

The juvenilia reveal, then, a very young artist of extraordinary intelligence and mastery of language, for whom criticism of literature and of life coincide. We see in a work like 'Catharine' some hints of the mature artist who will emerge, despite its uncertain mixture of hilarious comedy (in the Stanleys' behaviour) with more painful perceptions about women, class, and society – material which formed part of Austen's consciousness from her first juvenile writings and which is assimilated brilliantly into the successful comedy of her novels.

3

The Idea of Authorship, 1794-1800

During the period that Austen drafted *Lady Susan* and early versions of *Sense and Sensibility*, *Pride and Prejudice* and *Northanger Abbey*, she was also engaged in the public courtship rituals of her world – attending local balls as well as more distant ones when she visited relatives in Bath and Kent. She was writing about courtship while to some degree taking part in it herself and observing it in her brothers Henry and James (after his wife's death in 1795), in Cassandra and her fiancé Tom Fowle, and among friends like Elizabeth Bigg and William Heathcote.

Early accounts of what Austen was like during this period differ. We have only two first-hand descriptions of her youth. They have been already quoted: Philadelphia Walter called her at 12 not at all pretty, very prim and affected; and Eliza de Feuillide found her sensible and improved in person and manners at 16, as was Cassandra at 19. Other versions are written much later or are based on hearsay. For example, her niece Caroline Austen tells us that, 'She was not, I beleive, an absolute beauty, but before she left Steventon she was established as a very pretty girl, in the opinion of most of her neighbours – as I learned afterwards from some of those who still remained'.[1] No doubt she was, as Mary Crawford says of Fanny Price, 'pretty enough' (*MP* 230), but with an energy and eagerness that Fanny lacks.

For what Austen's conduct was like when she was young, we have to return to the contradictory views of Philadelphia and Eliza – and to the only other contemporary account. Mary Russell Mitford has notoriously reported that her mother was acquainted with the family before her marriage, and said 'that she [Austen] was *then* the prettiest, silliest, most affected, husband-hunting butterfly she ever remembers'.[2] Although earlier biographers tended to dismiss this report, arguing that Mrs Mitford left

Ashe, near Steventon, when Austen was 10, more recent ones prefer to believe it in part, primarily because Austen's earliest letters reveal a delight in balls and flirtation.[3] Unquestionably she did enjoy both. But by the time she composed 'Catharine, or the Bower' in 1792, she could portray an attractive, careless, casual flirt like Edward Stanley and an ingenuous but sensible girl like Catharine, who is partly taken in by him and partly sees through him. That is, Austen was at 16 already a critic of the deceits of courtship rituals, already amused by the delusions of infatuation – the reverse of most sixteen-year-olds, who take their infatuations for a modern version of *Romeo and Juliet*. In short, Mrs Mitford's report sounds suspiciously like one that Mrs Percival, Catharine's censorious aunt, might have issued after watching her niece at the ball with Edward Stanley. The young Austen understood that reports of this kind tell us most about the observer, little about the person observed. Catharine is not silly, affected, nor husband-hunting, though she is not fully able to resist Stanley.

Catharine's story was dedicated to Cassandra, whose importance in Austen's life and literary career cannot be exaggerated. Every source indicates that Cassandra was closer to Austen than anyone else. The most revealing statement is also the least well known – provided by a great-niece, Fanny Caroline Lefroy, who was born after Austen's death but knew Cassandra:

> In addition to the natural affections which in their case was [sic] very strong, they were wedded to each other by the resemblance of their circumstances, and in truth there was an exclusiveness in their love such as only exists between husband and wife.[4]

Austen's letters to Cassandra do suggest that, especially after the death in 1797 of Cassandra's fiancé Tom Fowle, they were married in mind. The allusiveness and the elliptical quality of the letters, noticed by all readers, indicate how closely the sisters' intelligences were attuned to each other, and the letters' concern with everyday life paradoxically witnesses the depth of their intimacy. When Austen died, Cassandra's response was anguished:

> I *have* lost a treasure, such a Sister, such a friend as never can have been surpassed, – she was the sun of my life, the gilder

of every pleasure, the soother of every sorrow, I had not a thought concealed from her, & it is as if I had lost a part of myself. (*L* 513-4; July 1817)

Fanny Caroline Lefroy, visiting Cassandra at Chawton in 1837, 20 years after Austen's death, was 'greatly struck and impressed by the way in which she [Cassandra] spoke of her sister, there was such an accent of *living* love in her voice'.[5] During Austen's lifetime, Cassandra was also her sister's best audience and critic. Although after writing the three Volumes of the juvenilia, Austen did not dedicate her works to friends or family, everything that she wrote was probably presented first to Cassandra for her delight and her judgement – particularly after 1791, when all their brothers had left home (in that year, Charles, the youngest, went to the naval academy at Portsmouth).

Austen's life between the completion of the juvenilia and the first of her letters in 1796 is known only indirectly, by events that happened within the family. She must have been horrified when news reached her that her cousin's husband, Jean François Capot de Feuillide, had died on the guillotine in February 1794; many have noted that she expresses only distaste for France afterward. In October of the same year, Thomas Knight, Edward's benefactor, died, leaving Austen and her sister £50 apiece. In April 1795, after a trial that began in 1788, the family's friend Warren Hastings was acquitted of the charges brought against him in Parliament for corruption and cruelty in his administration in India, certainly good news to all the Austens. Henry apparently proposed to Hastings' goddaughter Eliza de Feuillide sometime in 1795, and his brother James was pursuing her as well after his wife's death in May. James's daughter Anna, two years old when her mother died, was sent to Steventon at some point, to be looked after by her aunts and grandmother. Anna must have moved back to Deane parsonage after James's marriage to Mary Lloyd in January 1797, for she heard Austen read *First Impressions* there when she was thought too young to take notice:

I have been told that her earliest Novels, certainly P. & P were read aloud in the Parsonage at Dean when I was in the room – & not expected to listen – that I did listen with all my might, was so much interested & talked so much afterwards about Jane &

Elizabeth that it was resolved for prudence sake to read no more of the story aloud in my hearing – This was related to me a long time afterwards when the Novel had been published & when it was thought that the names would recall to my recollection that early interest, – It was not so, I remembered nothing of the sort.[6]

LADY SUSAN

We know of two works that Austen composed at this time. Most scholars assign the epistolary *Lady Susan* to 1794–95, although Austen made a fair copy no earlier than 1805.[7] This work shows how well Austen could orchestrate and structure the novel-in-letters and how brilliantly she could portray a female rake. *Lady Susan* brings to their fullest development those aims characteristic of Austen's earlier juvenilia: to reverse gender roles, to offer unconventional portraits of women who seem to get away with murder. Lady Susan herself, conducting an affair with a married man, manages to become engaged to Reginald De Courcy, a much younger man who was initially prejudiced against her. A comic denouement reveals the lover to Reginald, and Lady Susan is forced to make do by marrying a rich fool whom she can cuckold without difficulty. In creating her heroines, it is always Austen's impulse to go from one extreme to another; we need not be surprised to find the invulnerable Lady Susan succeed the vulnerable Catharine Percival.

Lady Susan Vernon, one of Austen's few aristocrats, is evidently a sustained rendering of Richardson's aristocratic rake Lovelace as a woman. The echoes of *Clarissa* are pervasive and suggest conscious parody of Richardson's most powerful epistolary novel. For example, Lady Susan's second letter declares that, in the Manwaring household, 'We are now in a sad state; no house was ever more altered; the whole family are at war' (*MW* 245; Let. 2), recalling Clarissa's first letter to Anna Howe, 'Our family has indeed been strangely discomposed. – *Discomposed!* – It has been in *tumults* ever since the unhappy transaction'.[8] Admittedly, Lady Susan does not kidnap Reginald De Courcy, install him in a brothel, drug and rape him, as Lovelace does Clarissa. But Richardson portrays the rape as caused by a drive to dominate and humiliate, not by sexual passion. One of Lovelace's typical meditations, addressed to himself, accuses Clarissa of rebellion against his power:

> View her, even *now*, wrapped up in reserve and mystery; meditating plots, as far as thou knowest, against the sovereignty thou hast, by right of conquest, obtained over her. Remember, in short, all thou has *threatened* to remember against this insolent beauty, who is a rebel to the power she has listed under.[9]

Lady Susan shares this drive for conquest with Richardson's hero:

> There is exquisite pleasure in subduing an insolent spirit, in making a person pre-determined to dislike, acknowledge one's superiority. I have disconcerted him [Reginald] already by my calm reserve; & it shall be my endeavour to humble the Pride of these self-important De Courcies still lower.
>
> (254; Let.7)

We hear the voice of Lovelace throughout, in Lady Susan's determination to dominate every scene, every person; in her emphasis on triumph and defeat; in her dedication to imposing her will:

> I call on you, dear Alicia, for congratulations. I am again myself; – gay and triumphant. When I wrote to you the other day, I was in truth in high irritation, and with ample cause. Nay, I know not whether I ought to be quite tranquil now, for I have had more trouble in restoring peace than I ever intended to submit to. This Reginald has a proud spirit of his own! – a spirit too, resulting from a fancied sense of superior Integrity which is peculiarly insolent. I shall not easily forgive him I assure you.
>
> (291-2; Let. 25)
>
> . . .
>
> When my own will is effected, contrary to his, I shall have some credit in being on good terms with Reginald, which at present in fact I have not, for tho' he is still in my power, I have given up the very article by which our quarrel was produced, & at best, the honour of victory is doubtful.
>
> (294; Let. 25)

Like Lovelace, Lady Susan is an accountant in relationships, keeping track of 'credit' and loss. And like him too, she is wonderful at manipulating others through language. She has no fear that her daughter Frederica's tale of being forced to marry Sir James Martin will inconvenience her:

> I trust I shall be able to make my story as good as her's. If I am vain of anything, it is of my eloquence. Consideration & Esteem as surely follow command of Language, as Admiration waits on Beauty.
>
> (268; Let. 16)

In short, Lady Susan is an astonishing creation for a young woman of 19 but not so surprising from the author of the juvenilia, who delighted in images of female power and whose own 'command of language' was extraordinary.

Most critics believe that Austen did not write the conclusion of *Lady Susan* until she made the fair copy, probably in 1805. The conclusion indicates almost as much disillusionment with the form as leaving the work unfinished would have done: 'This Correspondence . . . could not, to the great detriment of the Post office Revenue, be continued longer' (311). At this point, Austen had scarcely ever finished anything she wrote. Many of her dedications to the juvenilia take notice of the unfinished state of her works. Only 'Love and Freindship' and 'The History of England' among the longer pieces actually reach completion. 'Love and Freindship' is a novel-in-letters and 'The History of England' is composed of short pieces on 13 monarchs. Burlesque and parody flourish best in quick bursts, as the formula worked out by Monty Python's Flying Circus attests: brief sequences without punch lines, that is, without structured endings. Clearly, Austen found it difficult to sustain interest in longer works, and epistolary fiction may have been attractive to her because it was possible to finish individual letters, even though (as in the case of *Lady Susan*) the whole might remain incomplete. In any event, her next fiction was also a novel-in-letters: 'Elinor and Marianne'. According to Cassandra, this work was a precursor to *Sense and Sensibility* and written about 1795. Judging by Austen's earlier work, we can assume that she left 'Elinor and Marianne' unfinished when she turned to *First Impressions* in October 1796. As far as we know, she never attempted epistolary fiction again.

FLIRTATION

From the year 1796, biographers can refer to Austen's own letters. Most of what we know about Austen's life is, in fact, provided by the surviving letters, though in many respects they almost require a translator. The depth of the sisters' intimacy is what makes the letters to Cassandra disappointingly mundane to some critics, frighteningly harsh to others. The most famous statements of both objections come from E.M. Forster's review. For him, the letters were written by Lydia Bennet, infatuated with 'balls, officers, giggling, dresses, officers, balls'. He also professes to hear the 'whinnying of harpies' in such remarks as:

> Mrs. Hall, of Sherborne, was brought to bed yesterday of a dead child, some weeks before she expected, owing to a fright. I suppose she happened unawares to look at her husband.
> (*L* 24; 27 Oct. 1798)[10]

Forster was wrong, however, not only about the letters' content but about their tone. Austen treats the subjects of sex, infatuation, dances and even dress with brilliant comedy. She writes this wonderful line about Mrs Hall in absolute security that Cassandra will relish it and will understand all the assumptions behind it: that wives can unfortunately scarcely avoid looking at husbands, particularly if they are to produce children; and that a dead child and a frightful husband are not logically connected, although comedy will yoke the two. As Austen wrote in *Persuasion*, 'fair or not fair, there are unbecoming conjunctions, which reason will patronize in vain, – which taste cannot tolerate, – which ridicule will seize' (68).

Perhaps it is the female sexuality implicit in the remark on Mr and Mrs Hall that offends male readers like Forster. Modern readers might better appreciate the quality of Austen's irony in these letters through a line that implicates them less, one that may seem less complex. On a trip to Bath, Austen must part from her luggage. How does she express this anxious state to Cassandra? Not in the ordinary ways, with irritation ('As usual, my baggage caused trouble') or with fear ('With luck, my baggage will arrive'). She writes, from much deeper sources, 'I have some hopes of being plagued about my trunk' (*L* 60; 17 May 1799). Her remark undercuts superficial irritation and fear to arrive at our profound love of a grievance. And her style is splendidly precise in elucidating this contradictory motive: it juxtaposes 'hopes' and 'plagued', all issuing in the prosaic thump of 'trunk'.

To be rightly understood, most of Austen's letters to Cassandra require this sort of analysis. They all assume a reader who fully shares Austen's ironic view of the human comedy as well as her love of language, and they all depend upon the complex context that is created by the depth of her relationship to Cassandra. A good example of the difficulty is provided by the first relationship that Austen's letters present, her flirtation with Tom Lefroy. The Irish nephew of her friend Mrs Lefroy, he met and became infatuated with Austen on a visit in the winter of 1795-96. In his old age, he 'told a young relation that "he had been in love with Jane Austen, but it was a boy's love"'. [11] He married an Irish woman three years after leaving Ashe. All of Austen's references to Tom in her letters of January 1796, are highly comic and suggest that whatever attraction she felt to this 'very gentlemanlike, good-looking, pleasant young man', was accompanied by a sense of how ridiculous it was (L 2; 9 Jan. 1796). After all, she writes, 'as to our having ever met, except at the three last balls, I cannot say much; for he is so excessively laughed at about me at Ashe, that he is ashamed of coming to Steventon, and ran away when we called on Mrs. Lefroy a few days ago' (L 2; 9 Jan. 1796). At all three balls, however, she and Tom had flirted with great spirit, giving instruction to the acknowledged lovers Elizabeth Bigg and William Heathcote:

> *they* do not know how *to be particular*. I flatter myself, however, that they will profit by the three successive lessons which I have given them.
>
> You scold me so much in the nice long letter which I have this moment received from you, that I am almost afraid to tell you how my Irish friend and I behaved. Imagine to yourself everything most profligate and shocking in the way of dancing and sitting down together. I *can* expose myself, however, only *once more*, because he leaves the country soon after next Friday, on which day we *are* to have a dance at Ashe after all.
>
> (L 1-2; 9 Jan. 1796)

When the day of the ball arrives, she writes:

Friday.– At length the day is come on which I am to flirt my last with Tom Lefroy, and when you receive this it will be over. My tears flow as I write at the melancholy idea.

(*L* 6; 14 Jan. 1796)

At this point, Austen's feelings about Tom Lefroy appear to be superficial. Possibly later she made more of them, as one often does in retrospect when no stronger feeling intervenes. Over two years after she had last seen Tom, Austen wrote to Cassandra that Mrs Lefroy had visited,

with whom, in spite of interruptions both from my father and James, I was enough alone to hear all that was interesting, which you will easily credit when I tell you that of her nephew [Tom Lefroy] she said nothing at all, and of her friend [Samuel Blackall, another admirer] very little. She did not once mention the name of the former to *me*, and I was too proud to make any enquiries; but on my father's afterwards asking where he was, I learnt that he was gone back to London in his way to Ireland, where he is called to the Bar and means to practise.

(*L* 27; 17 Nov. 1798)

Austen's tone, though still comic, seems slightly more con-cerned. But too much should not be read into it. She may be reacting uncomfortably to knowledge that Mrs Lefroy was angry at Tom on her behalf,[12] a humiliating position whatever one's own feelings.

Austen's acquaintance with Tom Lefroy when she was 20 offers the only sustained account we have of her behaving as she indulgently said 'young ladies of seventeen ought to do, admired and admiring' (*L* 45; 24 Dec. 1798). Writing to Cassandra, who had apparently scolded her for flirting too openly with Tom Lefroy, Austen clearly preferred to offer a comic version of their acquaintance. This version evaded Cassandra's censorship: she did not destroy these letters, as she evidently did all those that she found too revealing.[13] A comic version of infatuation came easily to Austen, and as a consequence we cannot really know what she felt about Tom Lefroy. All we can be sure of is that Austen never knew Tom well, and in everything she wrote, knowledge is inseparable from genuine affection. Perhaps a year after Tom left, she was to have Elizabeth say of Jane Bennet and Bingley:

> 'As yet, she cannot even be certain of the degree of her own regard, nor of its reasonableness. She has known him only a fortnight. She danced four dances with him at Meryton; she saw him one morning at his own house, and has since dined in company with him four times. This is not quite enough to make her understand his character.'
>
> (*PP* 22)

Although she tended to view infatuation comically, her own and other peoples', as a writer Austen was also interested in exploring its effects on the judgement. She had handled this subject in 'Catharine, or the Bower', written in 1792, but perhaps felt that she had been too quick to expose to the reader Edward Stanley's mischievous motives for flirting with Catharine. Certainly all her subsequent charming deceivers are more ambivalent or mysterious in their behaviour than Stanley. Austen implicates her readers' judgements as well as her heroines' in the deceits of Wickham and Frank Churchill, and creates suspense over Willoughby's and Crawford's conduct. As an author, she acquires the confidence to present these figures obliquely to her readers, suggesting that in late 1796, when she was writing *First Impressions*, she found the problems of judgement that such characters present fascinating but unthreatening. A much greater sense of threat is present in 'Catharine, or the Bower'. The years from 16 to 21 brought Austen many opportunities to meet young men and brought her also the kind of confidence and sophistication in enjoying and estimating them that she shows in all that she writes about Tom Lefroy.

DRAFTING THE EARLY NOVELS

The major events in Austen's literary career between 1796 and 1800 occurred when she produced the first versions of her three early novels. The surviving letters for this period say nothing about the composition of the three novels drafted, according to her sister's memorandum, during that time: *First Impressions* (October 1796–August 1797); *Sense and Sensibility* (begun in November

1797, based on 'Elinor and Marianne'); and *Susan*, the original of *Northanger Abbey* (1798–99).[14] Two letters do mention early readings of *First Impressions*. While in Kent, Cassandra has evidently expressed a wish to reread it, and Austen replies from Steventon, 'I do not wonder at your wanting to read "First Impressions" again, so seldom as you have gone through it, and that so long ago' (*L* 52; 8 Jan. 1799). And Martha Lloyd, visiting later that year at Steventon, must have expressed a similar wish, for Austen writes to Cassandra from Bath:

> I would not let Martha read 'First Impressions' again upon any account, and am very glad that I did not leave it in your power. She is very cunning, but I saw through her design; she means to publish it from memory, and one more perusal must enable her to do it.
>
> (*L* 67; 11 June 1799)

First Impressions was clearly everyone's favourite among Austen's early works. It is the only one for which we have evidence of dissemination beyond Steventon. That is, not merely Cassandra, Martha and George Austen read it – before he offered it to Cadell and Davies – but, as Anna Austen Lefroy has told us, it was read aloud at Deane, perhaps to James as well as Martha on a visit.

Austen's letters during this period do contain one or two remarks that have been thought to illuminate her idea of authorship. The most well known is that 'an artist cannot do anything slovenly', but in context this statement seems very casual, far from a creed, and it refers simply to some drawings:

> I hope George [her nephew, Edward's second son, who was just approaching his third birthday] was pleased with my designs. Perhaps they would have suited him as well had they been less elaborately finished; but an artist cannot do anything slovenly. I suppose baby grows and improves.
>
> (*L* 30; 17 Nov. 1798)

We have to draw on the letters Austen wrote in 1814 to her niece Anna for statements of her commitment to providing realistic detail; nothing in the letters of this period expresses that commitment. One early line does, however, show an amused awareness of contemporary debates on authorship. Cassandra has praised the letter in which Austen details her flirtation with Tom Lefroy, and she responds: 'I am very much flattered by your commendation of my last letter, for I write only for fame, and without any view to pecuniary emolument' (*L* 5; 14 Jan. 1796). As noted earlier, most contemporary women writers excused their publications by alleging destitution in themselves or their dependents, and writing for fame was even worse than writing for profit. Accordingly, her brother's 1818 Memoir asserts that 'Neither the hope of fame nor profit mixed with her early motives' (*NA* 6). Possibly her very earliest motives for writing did not include the hope of making money by it, but certainly she desired fame and praise, even if only within the family. Park Honan has conjectured that Austen decided by the time she was 18 that she would help the family and herself by writing for profit.[15] I believe that she always had publication of some kind in view, but possibilities of profit, while attractive, must have seemed minimal or she would not have accepted £10 for *Susan* in 1803. Henry Austen tells us that she was so sure of losing money on her first novel, that she reserved a sum from her small income against the loss (*NA* 6). After Austen did publish *Sense and Sensibility* successfully, however, she did not give even lip service to the conventional prejudices against profit and fame or praise. She quite sensibly wanted both. She wrote of a projected second edition of *Mansfield Park*:

> People are more ready to borrow & praise, than to buy – which I cannot wonder at; – but tho' I like praise as well as anybody, I like what Edward calls *Pewter* too.
>
> (*L* 419-20; 30 Nov. 1814)

Although they do not tell us much of what we wish to know about her authorship, Austen's letters for 1796–1800 chronicle her everyday life: her visits to London, Kent, Bath and Ibthorpe; her dinners, parties and balls; the activities of brothers, births of nephews, and oddities of neighbours; her impressions of people; and some of her reading. Just before beginning to write *First Impressions* in October 1796, Austen visited London and Kent, where Edward and his family were living at Rowling. She had just finished reading Burney's *Camilla*, published on 12 July, and it was vivid enough in her mind to evoke this allusion when she found herself stranded in Kent (because her brother Henry had unexpectedly decided to go to Yarmouth instead of escorting her home):

> To-morrow I shall be just like Camilla in Mr. Dubster's summer-house; for my Lionel will have taken away the ladder by which I came here, or at least by which I intended to get away, and here I must stay till his return. My situation, however, is somewhat preferable to hers, for I am very happy here, though I should be glad to get home by the end of the month.
>
> (*L* 9; 1 Sep. 1796)

Perhaps some partly-conscious sense of Henry's own scape-grace qualities prompted this parallel to Lionel Tyrold, Camilla's thoughtless brother, though Austen never openly acknowledged such an estimate of Henry. More importantly, reading Burney's work may have inspired Austen to return to third-person narrative for *First Impressions*, a mode that she had last used for 'Catharine, or the Bower' in 1792. Strikingly, all the novels that Austen chooses to commend in *Northanger Abbey*'s defence of fiction use third-person narration: Burney's *Cecilia* and *Camilla*, and Edgeworth's *Belinda*. (That they are all by women is also remarkable.) Austen seems deliberately to exclude epistolary novels like *Evelina* or *Sir Charles Grandison*, both of which she admired, from the canon that she constructs – of works 'in which the greatest powers of the mind are displayed, in which the most thorough knowledge of human nature, the happiest delineation of its varieties, the liveliest effusions of wit and humour are conveyed to the world in the best chosen language' (*NA* 38).

PRIDE AND PREJUDICE, SEXUALITY AND ROMANCE

Most admirers of Austen's works would be inclined to apply this praise of wit, humour and well-chosen language to her own novels, especially to *Pride and Prejudice*, the title that a revised *First Impressions* appeared under in 1813. Exactly how much Austen revised *First Impressions* is unclear. She wrote to Cassandra shortly after *Pride and Prejudice* had been published:

> The second volume is shorter than I could wish, but the difference is not so much in reality as in look, there being a larger proportion of narrative in that part. I have lop't and

crop't so successfully, however, that I imagine it must be rather shorter than S. & S. altogether.

(*L* 298; 29 Jan. 1813)

Austen's remark that she had 'lop't and crop't so successfully' indicates that she must have cut the manuscript extensively. Based on this account, on the evidence compiled in J.F. Burrows' meticulous computer-based analysis of the novels' language, and on other arguments as well, I conclude that Austen's revisions to *First Impressions* consisted largely of cutting: condensing and refining a much longer original.[16] If this view is correct, then it is possible to consider the plot and characters of both versions as fundamentally the same, so that (with a few important exceptions) we can discuss *Pride and Prejudice* as if it were written when Austen was 21.

The wit, humour, and 'best chosen language' of *Pride and Prejudice* have certainly contributed to making it the most generally popular of Austen's works. But possibly even more of its popularity arises from the relationship that the text creates between the central characters, Elizabeth Bennet and Fitzwilliam Darcy. Nothing like that relationship is visible in Austen's earliest works, although otherwise the preoccupations of the most interesting juvenilia anticipate those of *Pride and Prejudice*, such as women's marginality within society or prejudices between classes. Above all, as many critics have noticed, the heroine does figuratively get away with murder. Elizabeth notoriously acts and judges independently and thereby violates many of the norms for proper female behaviour, but instead of finding herself ostracised by society, she becomes mistress of Pemberley, achieving the highest social position and greatest wealth that Austen ever bestows upon any of her heroines.

Elizabeth does not defy authority that she perceives as legitimate, like her father's, although she is quite capable of criticising it, as when she tries to persuade Mr Bennet that he is wrong to allow Lydia to go to Brighton. But Elizabeth does defy Lady Catharine de Bourgh when she visits Longbourn to assert an illegitimate authority, by requiring Elizabeth to promise not to marry Darcy. Elizabeth's powerful declaration of independence to Lady Catharine proclaims the rights of an individual to reject wrongful authority, and thus has political content, as recent critics have argued:

'I am only resolved to act in that manner, which will, in my own opinion, constitute my happiness, without reference to *you*, or to any person so wholly unconnected with me.'

(358)[17]

Elizabeth has always acted according to this principle, and it frequently prompts her to behave impertinently, not just to Lady Catherine at Rosings but to Darcy as well. To be impertinent, the reverse of the compliant and submissive behaviour recommended to young ladies, and not to suffer for it, is figuratively to get away with murder. This is precisely what happens to Elizabeth when she finds at the end of the novel that her impertinence has been transmuted in Darcy's mind to liveliness. She asks:

'Now be sincere; did you admire me for my impertinence?'
'For the liveliness of your mind, I did.'

(380)

This sort of 'reading' or rereading of behaviour and character becomes a theme within the novel, supporting its ironic attack on Elizabeth's and Darcy's pride in their own critical judgements. We see this emphasis on reading most clearly when a rereading of Darcy's letter allows Elizabeth to reinterpret his character. Part of what makes the early exchanges between Elizabeth and Darcy so challenging is that they are 'read' differently by both characters while they occur, Darcy for example believing that Elizabeth's behaviour at Rosings shows her 'to be wishing, expecting my addresses' (369). And they may be 'read' differently by first- and second-time readers of the novel as well. Anyone who on a first reading has missed any of the signs of Elizabeth's blindness, as well as Darcy's vanity and misinterpretation, can, after this explanation from him at the end, return to reread a passage like the following with increased appreciation of its ironies:

More than once did Elizabeth in her ramble within the Park, unexpectedly meet Mr. Darcy. – She felt all the perverseness of the mischance that should bring him where no one else was brought; and to prevent its ever happening again, took care to inform him at first, that it was a favourite haunt of hers. – How it could occur a second time therefore was very odd! – Yet it did, and even a third.

(182)

One of the great triumphs of *Pride and Prejudice* lies in the way that Austen creates conversations that permit characters to expose, beneath the surface restraints of polite, clever talk, their unstated and incongruous or clashing motives, judgements and feelings. The scenes between Darcy and Elizabeth at Netherfield and Rosings have undercurrents of sexual antagonism and attraction not entirely contained by the comedy of misjudgement enacted on the surface, or by the structural irony which allows Elizabeth's and Darcy's misjudgements of each other to be felt again and again throughout the novel. If substantial revisions or alterations *were* made to *First Impressions* when Austen cut it before publishing it in 1813, they may have been to these scenes, which are unlike any in *Sense and Sensibility* or *Northanger Abbey* as we have them. In their complexity, depth and tension, they more closely resemble the scenes that Austen was writing in 1811–13 for *Mansfield Park*.[18]

The process by which Darcy in these scenes at Netherfield and Rosings interprets Elizabeth's provocative, impertinent manner to him as liveliness, misinterprets it as interest, and finds her attractive, is not simply a matter of 'reading', an intellectual exercise. It is a sexual response, in keeping with the open way that sexuality is treated in *Pride and Prejudice*. In her treatment of sexuality, Austen the novelist gets away with murder almost as much as Elizabeth does. Admittedly, Austen attributes the most open sexual responses not to her heroine but to Lydia Bennet, who unabashedly enjoys sex before marriage and initiates a spot of cross-dressing as well, when she and her friends dress an officer in one of Mrs Phillips' gowns:

> 'you cannot imagine how well he looked! When Denny, and Wickham, and Pratt, and two or three more of the men came in, they did not know him in the least. Lord! how I laughed! and so did Mrs Forster. I thought I should have died. And *that* made the men suspect something, and then they soon found out what was the matter.'
>
> (221)

Lydia, of course, is a foil to Elizabeth, an example of unrestrained sexuality and independence. But by allowing her heroine Elizabeth to exhibit such open sexual response to Wickham's charm, Austen is violating some of the rules that govern many women writers in the period. Delicacy and purity were expected of them; even Austen herself expected it to some degree, as is apparent in her comment on Madame de Genlis' beginning her novel *Alphonsine: or Maternal Affection* (1806) with a detailed account of a wife who, refusing to consummate her marriage, takes a lover and is afterwards surprised by her husband in bed with yet another lover, a servant:

> 'Alphonsine' did not do. We were disgusted in twenty pages, as, independent of a bad translation, it has indelicacies which disgrace a pen hitherto so pure.
>
> (*L* 173; 7 Jan. 1807)

Austen's interest lies in portraying not this sort of sensational sexuality, but rather the public sexuality of daily life – attraction, flirtation, infatuation, sexual antagonism and sexual love.[19] As noted earlier, her realistic portraits of women's sexual attraction to men seemed unprecedented to a male reviewer writing a few years after her death. Richard Whately praises Austen's willingness to show that women respond to male beauty and charm, but he unfortunately does so at all women's expense: 'Her heroines are what one knows women must be, though one never can get them to admit it'.[20] Whately does not seem to recognise how stringently women during this period were enjoined not to admit their sexual feelings. He is wrong to blame them for what social mores force upon them, but he is right to notice how different Austen's heroines are. Elizabeth in particular is ready to flirt openly with Wickham, attracted by his looks and manner, and she is equally ready to allow an involuntary sexual response to Darcy's powerful presence to feed the hostility awakened by his insulting refusal to dance with her. That is, she is not attracted to him at first, not even unconsciously, I believe, but there is an edge to her response that derives from sexual energy, not just from wounded vanity. Darcy's response to Elizabeth is more conscious: he gradually becomes attracted by her looks at the same time that he is 'caught' (23) by an intelligence and manner that challenge rather than flatter him – as Elizabeth points out at the end:

> 'The fact is, that you were sick of civility, of deference, of officious attention. You were disgusted with the women who were always speaking and looking, and thinking for *your*

approbation alone. I roused, and interested you, because I was so unlike *them*.'

(380)

It is partly because Darcy and Elizabeth 'rouse' each other and are such powerful and credible sexual antagonists that *Pride and Prejudice* works so well on so many levels. These two opposing central characters who are united at the end seem to many readers to stand for a variety of opposed powers that the plot ultimately reconciles: the individual and society, liveliness and stability, wit and wisdom, sympathy and judgement, feeling and reason, head and heart, even (more recently) liberalism and patriarchy. But none of these powers can be ascribed simply to Elizabeth or to Darcy, any more than 'pride' or 'prejudice' belongs exclusively to either; Austen's treatment is too subtle to permit such simple dichotomies. Similarly, the novel may be read as 'romantic' by some readers, essentially a Cinderella story, and as an attack on romantic expectations by others.[21] Again, Austen's treatment, her double vision, makes it impossible to accept either reading alone. The 'romantic' reading, however, is interesting, not only because so many young readers adopt it when they first read the novel, but because Austen has anticipated, in her plot outline, so many of the elements that have become standard in successful modern romances.

In her sympathetic study of modern women who read romances, Janice A. Radway has inferred these readers' 'ideal romantic plot'. Essential to it is an intelligent, independent, confident heroine whose social position is threatened and who reacts 'antagonistically' at first to a powerful, aristocratic male, who in turn responds to her 'ambiguously'. The resolution of Radway's ideal romantic plot closely reminds us of Austen's novel: having been physically and emotionally separated from the heroine, the hero treats the heroine tenderly, she reinterprets his behaviour, he produces a 'supreme act of tenderness', she responds 'sexually and emotionally to the hero', and her secure social position is confirmed.[22] Darcy's letter, which begins in bitterness but ends in 'charity itself', as Elizabeth notes (368), prompts her to reinterpret his character; their meeting at Pemberley issues in Darcy's arranging Lydia's wedding to Wickham, an act of generosity that moves Elizabeth deeply. According to Radway, reading plots like these allows women who feel powerless within a society that demeans them, and within marriages that oppress them, to deal imaginatively with their powerlessness. Romances allow them to cope with their fears of men by imagining powerful males who in the end actually nurture women.[23]

In a provocative essay, Susan Morgan has analysed the absence of sensational sex in Austen's novels. Arguing that Austen's plots are unique in refusing to base themselves on rape threats and seduction, eighteenth-century conventions for generating plot and introducing sex into the novel Morgan considers the abandonment of these hoary plot devices important because it signals the end of men's control of women's experience. For her, men initiate seduction or rape and are therefore ultimately responsible for a heroine's development. A plot that relies on these elements in charting a 'move from innocence to experience . . . means just one thing for heroines: the loss of virginity.'[24] But Morgan seriously overstates her case. Many eighteenth-century plots define innocence not simply as virginity, experience not merely as its loss. The three novels that Austen cites in her defence of the genre, *Cecilia* (1782), *Camilla* (1796) and *Belinda* (1801), for example, do not depend on rape threats or attempted seductions of the heroines to generate the central action. The heroines' stories arise primarily from misunderstandings, misinterpretations, lack of knowledge of the world and of their own hearts, as Austen's plots do.

Morgan may be obliquely registering, in her inaccurate attempt to attribute 'literary innovation'[25] to Austen's plots, the discomfort that many feminist critics feel with Austen's traditional choice to end her novels with marriage. Accordingly, they try to find some evidence that Austen criticises marriage as well as other institutions, like 'primogeniture, [and] patriarchy – which patently do not serve her heroines well', in the words of one recent critic.[26] They find such evidence because Austen's views are always double; but they often tend to forget that Austen has chosen comedy as her form. Comedy demands marriage. It contains criticism of that social institution, among others, along with affirmation of it. As I have said elsewhere, what is most striking about the marriages that Austen arranges at the close of her novels is how much she insists on disregarding (without denying) the conventions that make wives submissive to husbands. Instead, the endings celebrate an equality as complete as the differences between the characters themselves allow.[27]   Marriage in comedy is always a microcosm of society, and the marriages that Austen arranges for her heroes and heroines represent society as it ought to become: more unconventional, more equal.

Although no letters survive between October 1796, and August 1797, when *First Impressions* was being written, we know of two important events: James married Austen's friend Mary Lloyd in January 1797, and Cassandra's fiancé Tom Fowle died of yellow fever in the West Indies in February 1797. Once Austen had finished *First Impressions* in August 1797, she probably put it aside and revised it before showing it to her father. Her brother Henry tells us that 'though in composition she was equally rapid and correct, yet an invincible distrust of her own judgement induced her to withhold her works from the public, till time and many perusals had satisfied her that the charm of recent composition was dissolved' (*NA* 4). George Austen's decision to submit *First Impressions* for publication in November 1797 must have been flattering, and rejection sight unseen by Cadell and Davies cannot have been too crushing, for Austen began revising *Sense and Sensibility* right away, in the same month. We do not know when she finished her revision, but presumably she had done so before beginning *Northanger Abbey* sometime in 1798.

THE COMMUNITY OF WOMEN IN *SENSE AND SENSIBILITY*

Possibly Cassandra's loss of her fiancé Tom Fowle in 1797 affected the development of both novels that Austen worked on during that year. In the versions of *Sense and Sensibility* and *Pride and Prejudice* that we have, Austen deals with the anguish caused by the apparent loss of a beloved by a resolute, controlled and deeply feeling woman: Elinor Dashwood's loss of Edward Ferrars and Jane Bennet's loss of Charles Bingley. In both cases, the loss seems permanent for a time. Some of Austen's own grief as well as her profound respect for her sister's strength is surely rendered in these portrayals. And her desire to revise 'Elinor and Marianne' as *Sense and Sensibility*, a novel that centres on a community of women, may have stemmed from an increased sense of her own community with her sister. Cassandra was no longer likely to marry and leave Steventon for the distant county of Shropshire – a loss which had until this time seemed certain.[28]

Although it lacks the highly-charged sexual tension of *Pride and Prejudice*, the plot of *Sense and Sensibility* is quite as revolutionary in its departure from contemporary norms. In general, the plot of an eighteenth-century domestic novel divides a heroine from her family, especially her mother. For good reason: in the novels of education and acquired self-knowledge that are best in the period, or even in the sentimental and Gothic novels that are typical, the heroine must be left to her own devices. She must test herself, make her own mistakes and affront her own destiny if the author's didactic purpose is to be served. A good mother, it was felt, would invariably protect the heroine from error and thus from educating herself. As a result, most eighteenth-century heroines have lost their mothers long before the novel opens, like Harriet Byron (of Richardson's *Sir Charles Grandison*), Evelina or Cecilia. If a mother survives, she is foolish or ineffectual like Clarissa's, at a distance like Camilla's, or doomed like Emily St Aubert's in Radcliffe's *The Mysteries of Udolpho* (1794). If a heroine is provided with mother substitutes, they suffer the common fate and die in the first chapter like Mrs B., the 'good lady' of Richardson's heroine Pamela, or are left behind like Evelina's Mr Villars. The heroine then explores London or Bath with a foolish or faulty chaperone: Madame Duval in Burney's *Evelina*, Mrs Delvile in her *Cecilia*, or Lady Delacour in Edgeworth's *Belinda*. In these novels, the substitute mother is a trial rather than a support to the embattled heroine, less supportive to her, finally, than is the hero.

These plot conventions are as visible in Austen's novels as in Richardson's, Burney's or Edgeworth's. Emma Woodhouse and Anne Elliot are motherless; Fanny Price leaves her foolish mother behind in Portsmouth to find a more foolish substitute in Lady Bertram and a more faulty one in Mrs Norris; Catherine Morland leaves her excellent mother behind to visit Bath with the nearly-imbecile Mrs Allen; and Elizabeth Bennet's mother is, of course, unspeakable. This collection of absent or impossible mothers in the novels of Austen and of her predecessors makes the exception more interesting. In Austen's first published novel, *Sense and Sensibility*, the emotional centre is placed on relationships among women in a close, affectionate family. The heroines' mother is not only alive but charming, intelligent and essentially good, though imprudent. She is an important character in her own right. The relations between Elinor and Marianne Dashwood and (to a lesser extent) between both sisters and their mother are more important in working out the novel's themes than are the relations of all three to Edward Ferrars, Willoughby and Colonel Brandon. The courtship plot central to Austen's other novels is peripheral here.

The plot of *Sense and Sensibility* constructs not courtships but elaborate parallels between the experiences of Elinor and Marianne so that their very different responses may be measured and judged. Both Elinor and Marianne endure the unaccountable withdrawal of a lover's attentions and an announcement of his marriage to another woman. These parallel experiences are more important than Edward and Willoughby themselves. As a result, we scarcely see Edward at all, and we have none of the scenes which create attraction and affection between him and Elinor. Willoughby too is more visible through Elinor's and Marianne's eyes than through his own actions, and except for two scenes, he drops out of the novel about halfway through the first volume. Colonel Brandon's presence is even more fitful and more blatantly serves the plot. Many critics have objected that his marriage to Marianne in the last few pages constitutes a great flaw in design, but such readers ignore the clear message of the plot that Austen's interests do not lie in dramatising courtships between men and women. They lie instead, as the last sentence of the novel confirms, in dramatising relationships within a community of women:

> Between Barton [where Mrs Dashwood remains] and Delaford [where Marianne and Elinor are settled] there was that constant communication which strong family affection would naturally dictate; – and among the merits and the happiness of Elinor and Marianne, let it not be ranked as the least considerable, that though sisters, and living almost within sight of each other, they could live without disagreement between themselves, or producing coldness between their husbands.

(380)

Austen's last sentences always bring significant themes to a conclusion. The last sentence in *Sense and Sensibility* focuses not on marriage – a frequent closing theme – but on the continuing relations among Elinor, Marianne and Mrs Dashwood. Although the last word is 'husbands', we are reminded of those appendages only to be informed that their relations to one another depend partly on the relations between Elinor and Marianne. The novel has described a community of women, and its ending necessarily reflects this emphasis.

As the last sentence also reminds us, this community is a family, embodying 'that constant communication which strong family affection would naturally dictate'. But although Austen's vision of human relations does include this strong sense of a good family community, it is never achieved easily. Family feeling, even family affection, is never enough by itself, as the concluding clause implies: 'though sisters, . . . they could live without disagreement between themselves'. The subplot of the novel vividly illustrates the implication that sisters may seldom agree. The careers and characters of Anne and Lucy Steele are designed to parallel those of Marianne and Elinor. The mindless, vapid Jennings sisters – known to us as Charlotte Palmer and Lady Middleton – taken together with their mother provide another disagreeable parody of the Dashwood family. Finally, of course, we have Fanny Dashwood and Mrs Ferrars, monsters of selfishness, who receive in Lucy Steele the very sister- and daughter-in-law they deserve. A kind of climax for parallelism and parody alike occurs in the last chapter, where a description of domestic life in the extended Ferrars family anticipates almost line for line the closing sentence of the novel – but by inversion:

> [The Robert Ferrars] settled in town, received very liberal assistance from Mrs. Ferrars, were on the best terms imaginable with the [John] Dashwoods; and setting aside the jealousies and ill-will continually subsisting between Fanny and Lucy, in which their husbands of course took a part, as well as the frequent domestic disagreements between Robert and Lucy themselves, nothing could exceed the harmony in which they all lived together.
>
> (377)

The good family or the good community of women is surrounded, then, by parodies of itself, largely female also, and acting not merely as foils but as spies. Everyone's conduct and feelings are subject to scrutiny, comment, teasing, prying and conjecture. Mrs Jennings is busiest here, and whether attempting to unearth Colonel Brandon's reasons for leaving Barton so suddenly or whether bestowing on suspected lovers some of that 'ridicule so justly annexed to sensibility' (49), she betrays her citizenship in the community of 'voluntary spies' (Henry Tilney's phrase [*NA* 198]), which surrounds the small, civilised community of good sense, good feeling and good manners eventually established at the emotional centre of every Austen novel. Whatever faults or problems appear within, the good community as a whole is immeasurably superior to the larger social community. In *Sense and Sensibility*, the faults of Marianne and Mrs Dashwood are serious, but their conduct is exemplary by comparison to the monumentally selfish, vain, vulgar, silly, cold-hearted or narrow-minded behaviour of most of the other characters. Just two visits to Barton Cottage assure Willoughby 'of the sense, elegance, mutual affection, and domestic comfort of the family' (46), and although internal reforms are called for, the novel continually reasserts the virtues of this small community of women.

Only Mrs Dashwood and Marianne need reform, however – a disturbing fact to those readers who demand ironic symmetry. Because Marianne's 'sensibility' is shown to need correction, and because she is treated ironically, these readers feel that Elinor's 'sense' should be exposed as equally deficient, in need of parallel correction and reform. Such readers often detect that a middle ground is reached between Elinor and Marianne, usually assuming that Elinor is in some way unfeeling at first and has in the end 'tasted the values of sensibility'.[29] To manufacture this sort of ironic movement in the novel is to overlook the irony with which Elinor's situation is actually treated throughout. Austen is interested in dramatising two ironic perceptions. First, to consider others' feelings is to permit others to be inconsiderate of one's own. Second, excess of sensibility in Marianne and Mrs Dashwood becomes insensibility – insensitivity to and misjudgement of others' feelings. As a result, Elinor is given credit neither for having feelings nor for commanding them. At the same time, however, Austen insists that the consideration and self-command that Elinor shows are not any less required of her for being invariably misunderstood and unrewarded. They remain, absolutely and imperatively, an obligation.

James Edward Austen-Leigh so described his aunts in his *Memoir* that some readers have been inclined to view Cassandra as a model for Elinor. He wrote:

They were not exactly alike. Cassandra's was the colder and calmer disposition; she was always prudent and well judging, but with less outward demonstration of feeling and less sunniness of temper than Jane possessed. It was remarked in her family that 'Cassandra had the *merit* of having her temper always under command, but that Jane had the *happiness* of a temper that never required to be commanded.'[30]

With due scepticism – certainly Austen's temper was frequently under command – we can accept this account. Cassandra apparently did resemble Elinor, while Austen herself was most unlike Marianne. Least excusable in Marianne's behaviour is her injustice to Elinor, her propensity to underestimate and denigrate Elinor's feelings because they are not expressed as her own would be. The real conflict in the novel lies not between sensibility and sense but sensibility and its genuine opposite, sensitivity: the feeling, unselfish behaviour that Elinor consistently shows. The novel explores the sensitive and insensitive behaviour that essentially good, sensible people like Marianne and Mrs Dashwood are capable of. When Marianne recognises this distinction at the end of the novel and criticises both her conduct and her insensitivity, the main plot of *Sense and Sensibility* is resolved, although Mrs Dashwood's parallel recognition scene (prompted by Elinor's sufferings over Edward's supposed marriage to Lucy Steele) is still to come, not to mention Elinor's and Marianne's engagements. The resolution occurs in the earlier scene because there the central relationship is recreated and reaffirmed by Marianne's remorse and by Elinor's supportive response:

> impatient to sooth, though too honest to flatter, [Elinor] gave her instantly that praise and support which her frankness and her contrition so well deserved.

> (347)

The good community of women has been tested, chastened and refined – as every succeeding scene of revelation, support and affection confirms.

This community is present in Austen's other fiction as well. Although she never again will place the relations between a heroine and a good but flawed sister like Marianne or mother like Mrs Dashwood at the centre of a novel, these kinds of relationships are visible, with many variations, between such characters as Jane and Elizabeth Bennet, Emma and Elizabeth Watson, Fanny and Susan Price, Anne Elliot and Lady Russell. Bad relations between mothers, daughters and sisters are so vivid, however – especially between Elizabeth Bennet and her mother, Julia and Maria Bertram, or the Elliot sisters – that Austen's interest and success in dramatising and exploring good ones are generally overlooked or discounted.[31]

Austen was reasonably busy socially during the three years, beginning in October 1796, that she wrote *First Impressions*, *Sense and Sensibility* and *Susan* (or *Northanger Abbey*). She made four visits away from home during these years, two to Bath, one to Godmersham and one to relatives in three different counties. The tour to Bath with Cassandra and her mother occurred almost precisely when she began *Sense and Sensibility*, in November and December of 1797. Possibly this was Austen's first visit to Bath; if so, it must have been useful in drafting the first half of *Susan* during 1798 and 1799. Henry married Eliza de Feuillide at the end of December 1797, perhaps a surprise to the family. Most accounts consider the marriage a happy one, although Austen noted at Eliza's death that Henry was 'so used to be away from her at times, that her Loss is not felt as that of many a beloved wife might be' (*L* 315; 3 July 1813). Austen's two-and-a-half-month visit to Godmersham with her parents and Cassandra coincided with the birth of Edward and Elizabeth's fifth child on 10 October. Cassandra stayed in Kent through till January, but Austen and her parents returned on 24 October. At Steventon, Austen temporarily took over Cassandra's household duties. Mrs Austen had already abdicated hers; a number of references to her poor health punctuate the letters between this time and 1801. By November 1798, the Austens had laid down the carriage that they had kept for less than a year,[32] perhaps because wartime inflation had made the expense prohibitive; Austen comments, 'Our assemblies have very kindly declined ever since we laid down the carriage, so that dis-convenience and dis-inclination to go have kept pace together' (*L* 29; 17 Nov. 1798). She announced the birth on 17 November 1798 of her biographer James Edward Austen-Leigh in a letter to Cassandra and mocked her sister's ingratitude in her next letter: 'I expected to have heard from you this morning, but no letter is come. I shall not take the trouble of announcing to you any more of Mary's children, if, instead of thanking me for the intelligence, you always sit down and write to James' (*L* 30-1; 25 Nov. 1798). Finally, perhaps the most joyful news of the year was written to Cassandra on 28 December: 'Frank is made. – He was yesterday raised to the Rank of Commander & appointed to the Petterel Sloop, now at Gibraltar'. Charles was at the same time removed to a frigate, which he had desired, and Austen herself was invited to Lady Dorchester's ball, 'which tho' an humble Blessing compared with what the last page records, I do not consider as any Calamity' (*L* 47-8; 28 Dec. 1798).

VERSIONS OF *NORTHANGER ABBEY*

Austen visited Bath again in May and June of 1799, this time with Edward, who was ill, his wife and his two eldest children. Possibly she had by this time completed her first draft of *Susan*, later published as *Northanger Abbey*. This work represents a great departure from *Pride and Prejudice* and *Sense and Sensibility*, for in it Austen reverts to the modes of burlesque and parody that she had enjoyed in the juvenilia. Those modes never lost their appeal for her; she adopted them again for her last uncompleted work, *Sanditon*. Perhaps Austen always felt the impulse, after having created large-scale realistic fictions, to relax into a comic re-examination of fiction itself. The parodic elements in *Northanger Abbey* allow Austen to create a central character rather closer to the models in the juvenilia than to her other heroines. Catherine Morland is unique among Austen's heroines in her naïve, unaffected pursuit of the hero, who learns to care for her only because he cannot help perceiving that she prefers him. In this respect, Catharine violates conventional norms for female behaviour even more radically and more successfully than Elizabeth Bennet.

Although I have been considering *Pride and Prejudice* and *Sense and Sensibility* as if they are (except for cuts) virtually identical to the novels that Austen drafted between 1796 and 1798, that view is controversial. *Northanger Abbey*, however, can be accurately dated. Austen's own account in an 'Advertisement' written in 1816 makes it clear that the novel was completed in 1803, but that an earlier version had existed: she writes, 'thirteen years have passed since it was finished, many more since it was begun' (*NA* 12). The version produced in 1798 and 1799, which I will refer to as *Susan*, was probably considerably revised before being sold under

that title to the publisher Crosby in 1803. I take that revised version
to be substantially the same as *Northanger Abbey*.[33] *Northanger Abbey*
can offer us, then, the most reliable view of what kind of writing
and revising Austen produced in her youth.

Stylistic evidence for the kind of revisions that Austen made
to *Susan* can be located in Austen's use of a particular form of
'free indirect speech', a form that is extremely rare in all three
early novels, *Pride and Prejudice, Sense and Sensibility* and *Northanger
Abbey*, but extremely common in the three later novels.[34] This form
is also very conventional in eighteenth-century prose. In it, a
character's thought or speech is conveyed in the third person,
but quotation marks surround the words as though they represent
first-person discourse. Unless otherwise indicated, I will use the
phrase 'free indirect speech' to refer *only* to instances that include
these quotation marks. The technique is ubiquitous; Richardson,
Fielding and Burney use it, among others. When she read Smith's
Emmeline, Austen quite soon encountered the following passage:

> The violent and artless sorrow of a beautiful young woman,
> whose fate seemed to be in his power, affected [Lord
> Montreville].
> He took her hand with kindness, and told her 'he was sorry
> to have said anything that appeared harsh.'
> His Lordship added, 'that he would have her write to Mrs.
> Watkins.'[35]

If Smith had used direct speech, Lord Montreville's words would
have appeared, 'I am sorry to have said any thing that appears
harsh' and 'I would have you write to Mrs. Watkins'. Casting
such direct speech into free indirect speech tends to obscure
the distinction between narrative and dialogue. It permits a
speedier, smoother flow of narrative. And it also distances the
speaker somewhat: he or she almost appears to be speaking in
the third person, causing a slight shift in perspective to any
reader who notices. This shift of person is seldom suffered by a
central character; generally, the speeches of those who address
the central character are affected. The shift thus encourages the
reader to maintain the perspective of the central character, who
alone remains 'I' – the others become 'she' or 'he'.[36]

Austen was familiar with the practice of putting quotation
marks around indirect speech when she wrote her juvenilia.

She followed it twice in 'Love and Freindship' and twice in 'A Collection of Letters'.[37] But curiously enough, the longest and most ambitious of the juvenilia, 'Catharine, or the Bower', contains no example of free indirect speech, though indirect speech without quotation marks is common enough. For example, Mrs Percival:

> could not therefore refrain from saying that for her part, she had lived fifty Years in the world without ever having a correspondent, and did not find herself at all the less respectable for it –.
>
> (*MW* 211)

Quotation marks could have been placed before 'for her part' and at the close of the sentence. Austen seems in 'Catherine' deliberately to avoid using quotation marks around indirect speech to blur the distinction between narration and dialogue, although she had used the device in earlier works. Instead, Austen creates a narrator who knows the characters' speeches and their minds but remains distant from them. Narration and dialogue are kept strictly separate. It is as if the young Austen, in abandoning burlesque, felt that she had to exert tremendous authorial control over her characters. She cannot allow her narrator's voice to blend with theirs, nor can she give her characters the freedom to approach narration. Her characters are free to expose themselves in dialogue but not in narrative, which controls them and comments on them from a distance.

This interest in maintaining separation between dialogue and narrative is also evident in all three of the early novels. By Burrows' reckoning, character narrative – narrative that seems to adopt a particular character's point of view, thus including indirect speech such as Mrs Percival's – is much less common in the three early novels than in the later ones. Character narrative takes up less than 5 per cent of all the narrative in *Sense and Sensibility*, less than 10 per cent of narrative in *Pride and Prejudice*, and about 15 per cent in *Northanger Abbey*; significantly, in *Mansfield Park* and *Emma*, it approaches one-third of the narrative.[38] Furthermore, Austen's use of free indirect speech in her early novels is as sparing as her use there of character narrative. In *Pride and Prejudice*, we find only five instances of free indirect speech; in *Sense and Sensibility* seven, and in *Northanger Abbey* 21.[39] The later novels employ this device so frequently that instances cannot be counted; for example, they occur in the very first chapters of *Mansfield Park* and *Persuasion*. Even *The Watsons* (1804) has eight occurrences in 48 pages.[40] The few instances in the first two novels are remarkable, then, and they may represent additions made by Austen when she prepared fair copies of her early versions for the press.[41]

The examples of free indirect speech in *Northanger Abbey* offer some support to C.S. Emden's notion that Austen wrote the Bath sections first, adding the Abbey sections later, perhaps just before offering the novel for publication in 1803.[42] Certainly by 1804 or so, she was very willing to use the device in drafting *The Watsons*. Only five of the 21 instances in *Northanger Abbey* occur in the Bath section, three of them in an interesting scene in Chapter 13 that might well have been also a later addition. I have argued elsewhere that this scene, in which Catherine resists the entreaties of her brother and the Thorpes to join them on an expedition, then rushes to apologise to the Tilneys, seems redundant at first. An almost precisely parallel sequence has occurred in Chapters 11 and 12. John Thorpe has persuaded Catherine to drive with him in Chapter 11 by lying to her: she is pre-engaged to the Tilneys, but he tells her that he has seen the Tilneys drive out of town. On her drive with Thorpe, Catherine sees the Tilneys walking to meet her; she is horrified, and in Chapter 12 she seizes the first opportunity to apologise to Henry Tilney. In Chapter 13, Catherine is once more engaged to walk with the Tilneys and refuses to drive to Clifton with the Thorpes and her brother. John Thorpe, trying to force Catherine to go, lies to the Tilneys and cancels her date with them, alleging that Catherine has recollected a prior engagement.

The parallelism is almost exact, but Austen's treatment of the two sequences is completely different. The first is purely comic. Catharine's distress is treated lightly, and she herself is treated anti-heroically:

> Feelings rather natural than heroic possessed her; instead of considering her own dignity injured by this ready condemnation – instead of proudly resolving, in conscious innocence, to shew her resentment towards him who could harbour a doubt of it, to leave to him all the trouble of seeking an explanation, and to enlighten him on the past only by avoiding his sight, or flirting with somebody else, she took to herself all the

shame of misconduct, and was only eager for an opportunity of explaining its cause.

(93)

When Catherine does explain herself almost immediately, her determination to do right and her willingness to explain herself are fully demonstrated. The parallel sequence in Chapter 13 does not develop her character, but instead briefly allows her to be a heroine. Her resistance to the Thorpes and her brother causes her distress, and the narrative for once allows her distress, to be felt by the reader as painful (though comical also):

> The three others still continued together, walking in a most uncomfortable manner to poor Catherine; sometimes not a word was said, sometimes she was again attacked with supplications or reproaches, and her arm was still linked within Isabella's, though their hearts were at war. At one moment she was softened, at another irritated; always distressed, but always steady.
>
> (99)

Having treated Catherine's distress wholly comically in Chapters 11 and 12, and having thus convinced her readers that the heroic distress of conventional sentimental novels is not 'natural' in life, or at any rate will not be found in her novel, Austen immediately makes such distress felt by her heroine and by her readers. A comic tone is thoroughly reinstated, however, once Catherine hears that Thorpe has lied to the Tilneys; she determines to run after the Tilneys to explain and apologise, running so fast that she has no breath left to do either.

The three passages of free indirect speech that occur in this sequence suggest that it might have been a later addition.[43] Having burlesqued the conventions that create a sentimental heroine's distress in Chapter 11 and 12, Austen chooses to exploit them in such a way that a reader must acknowledge their power despite having been taught to laugh at them. Austen handles the conventions of Gothic literature in exactly the same way in the Abbey section. First, she mocks those conventions: when Henry Tilney, while driving to Northanger , imagines for Catherine many absurd Gothic adventures to be met with there. Then she uses those conventions to create – very briefly – in Catherine's actual adventures at the Abbey just the sort of Gothic suspense that she has taught the reader to ridicule. Some of the examples of free indirect speech in the second half of *Northanger Abbey* appear in precisely the passages where I feel that Austen is either preparing or executing this scheme: to ridicule Gothic convention and then to make it work effectively.[44] That is, this scheme may have been added in revision.

More interestingly, most of the remaining instances of free indirect speech occur in representing General Tilney. His speeches (sometimes including replies) account for eight examples of free indirect speech, and speeches to or about him account for three others.[45] I suspect that in her revision of 1803, Austen was particularly concerned to make the General's character more plausible – which for her, as she indicated in later advice to her niece Anna, meant hinting at his motivation before revealing it:

> St Julian's History was quite a surprise to me; You had not very long known it yourself I suspect . . . Had not you better give some hint of St. Julian's early history in the beginning of the story?
>
> (*L* 421; 30 Nov. 1814)[46]

The General's reason for pursuing Catherine as a daughter-in-law is revealed at the end: coached by John Thorpe, he thinks her rich, and in particular he expects her to be the Allens' heiress (245–6). Significantly, *all* his references to the Allens are associated with free indirect speech.[47] Possibly, in revising Austen decided to provide these hints to the reader of his motives.

Whether or not it is true that, when she revised *Susan*, Austen thus attempted to foreshadow and motivate the General's disgraceful conduct to Catherine, she certainly used free indirect speech in the Abbey section of the novel far more than she did in the Bath section, and more than she did in *Pride and Prejudice* or *Sense and Sensibility*. My sense is that she worked over *Susan* thoroughly before attempting to publish it in 1803, particularly the Abbey sections. If this is true, *Northanger Abbey* is stylistically a later work than *Sense and Sensibility* or *Pride and Prejudice*, but it seems earlier – to Austen scholars in general and even according to Burrows' computer-based analysis – because in conception it is not as interesting as the two other early novels. It does not deal with characters who develop as Elizabeth Bennet and Marianne Dashwood do, or who suffer and endure as does Elinor Dashwood.[48]

A gap in the letters between June 1799, and October 1800, means that nothing is recorded of Austen's response to the arrest, imprisonment and trial of her aunt, Jane Leigh Perrot, which began with her visit to a lace shop on 7 August 1799, and ended with her triumphant acquittal on 19 March 1800. Mrs Leigh Perrot had spent most of the intervening time with her husband in squalid conditions in a warden's house in Ilchester. Their wealth could purchase better accommodations than a jail but could not get them bail, since Mrs Leigh Perrot had actually been found with the allegedly stolen lace in her possession. Mrs Austen had offered her daughters Jane and Cassandra to be Mrs Leigh Perrot's companions, as a letter from a relation reveals:

> You tell me that your good sister Austen has offered you one, or both, of her Daughters to continue with you during your stay at that vile Place, but you decline the kind offer as you cannot procure them Accommodation in the House with you, and you cannot let those Elegant young Women be your Inmates in a Prison nor be subject to the Inconveniences which you are obliged to put up with.
>
> (11 Jan. 1800)[49]

The trial was reported in many newspapers and became the lead article for the April 1800 edition of the *Lady's Magazine*. All these accounts were favourable to Austen's aunt, though rumours that circulated much later held that she had been guilty.[50] Mrs Leigh Perrot was certainly an unpleasant person, a hypocrite and a miser, a wealthy woman who delighted to proclaim her poverty.[51] She was the sort of whom nasty tales might be told with great satisfaction, but possibly without much truth.

Cassandra made a long visit to Godmersham again in the autumn and winter of 1800–01, and Austen made a short visit to Martha at Ibthorpe. During this visit, George Austen suddenly decided to leave Steventon for Bath. He was known for making impetuous decisions, [52] but it is surprising that, in so affectionate a family, such a momentous change would be determined on while both daughters were away. An Austen descendant has reported that Mrs Austen's ill health had prompted the move, and certainly her maladies for the two prior years, and the very serious illness that she suffered in Bath some years later, lend credence to this notion.[53] Austen learned of the decision when she came home from Ibthorpe in December. If she did faint on this occasion, as tradition has it, we need not be surprised.[54] A removal would be the last thing she could expect. Everything that the Austens had been doing for Steventon in the previous months, from buying furniture to planting trees, gave no indication that a move was intended. Furthermore, Cassandra was absent; Austen had no one to talk with unreservedly.

Leaving Steventon was difficult for Austen not simply because she loved the country and disliked Bath. The decision to leave was completely beyond her control. She must have felt powerless in a way that may have made resignation more difficult. By the beginning of the next January, however, only a month later, she was resigned:

> I get more & more reconciled to the idea of our removal. We have lived long enough in this Neighbourhood, the Basingstoke Balls are certainly on the decline, there is something interesting in the bustle of going away, & the prospect of spending future summers by the Sea or in Wales is very delightful.
>
> (*L* 103, 3 Jan. 1801)

Evidently travel did appeal strongly to Austen, especially travel to the shore.

Austen's response to the move is predictable, then: immediate shock and unhappiness, followed by efforts to find consolation. Less predictable is the absence of any record of writing during the year 1800, before the move was announced. The only possible exception is 'Sir Charles Grandison, or The Happy Man', a rendering of Samuel Richardson's seven-volume novel *Sir Charles Grandison* into a very brief five-act play. Its comedy requires an audience familiar enough with the novel to find this drastic compression funny. The work, only recently attributed to Austen, was probably written for a family production and offers further evidence of her affectionate but amused relation to Richardson's novel. Although the first act of the manuscript appears in Austen's earliest handwriting, from about 1788, the remaining four acts are written in her mature hand and can be dated anywhere between 1800 and 1805.[55] Even if Austen did complete the play in 1800, it is negligible compared to what had come before.

The previous five years had produced, in a great creative surge, *Lady Susan*, 'Elinor and Marianne', *First Impressions*, *Sense and Sensibility* and *Susan* (or *Northanger Abbey*). Not even the productive years 1811–17 can match this record. What made Austen virtually silent in 1800? The question is not answerable, but it does suggest caution in approaching the much more common question, why did Austen write so little between 1800 and 1809?

4

The Unpublished Author,
1801–1809

Most biographers have presented this period of Austen's life, from 1801 to 1809, as a dark one, personally painful and unproductive creatively. The only writing we have consists of the revised version of *Susan*, later retitled *Northanger Abbey*, sold to a publisher in the spring of 1803, and the uncompleted draft of *The Watsons*, usually dated 1804. Sometime after 1805, Austen made a fair copy of *Lady Susan*, and she may have written most of the dramatic version of *Sir Charles Grandison* at this time.[1] This literary activity seems minimal by comparison to the drafting of three novels between 1796 and 1799.

The usual explanation for this relative silence is that Austen was unhappy in Bath and later in Southampton. She managed to sell a novel, but it remained unpublished. She left the country for the city, suffering a kind of rootlessness. She met a man whom she could love, but he died soon after their meeting. Her friend Mrs Lefroy and her father died suddenly, within about five weeks of each other. Above all, she lost her assured position, becoming at her father's death in 1805 a poor dependent rather than a clergyman's daughter. These losses and upheavals – to some extent paralleled in her social world, where inflation and other effects of the Napoleonic Wars were being felt – were responsible for a peripatetic life and straitened circumstances unfavourable to writing.

No doubt this usual view of Austen's life during these eight and a half years is substantially correct. But some qualifications are necessary. Again, Austen apparently wrote nothing after drafting *Northanger Abbey* and before hearing of the move to Bath – a period taking up at least the year 1800 and probably some part of 1799 as well. No obvious explanation for this silence exists. More important, some of the upheavals occasioned by the move to Bath were attractive. As Austen had written, the 'prospect of spending future summers by the Sea or in Wales is very delightful' (*L* 103; 3 Jan. 1801). The prospect was realised. She apparently spent the summer of 1801 in the West Country, probably visiting Colyton and Sidmouth, where she may have fallen in love; the next summer was spent with Charles at Dawlish and probably Teignmouth, Tenby and Barmouth; the summer of 1803 in part at Ramsgate and possibly also at Charmouth, Up Lyme and Pinny; that of 1804 at Lyme, where Henry and Eliza joined them; and although her father died early in 1805, Mrs Austen and her daughters made plans to visit the coast that summer with Edward (*L* 153; 8 Apr. 1805).[2]

In general, Austen travelled more while living at Bath than she had earlier, and not simply in the summers. Using the chronology worked out by Deirdre Le Faye, we can see that during the three years following October 1796, when Austen was drafting *First Impressions*, *Sense and Sensibility* and *Susan*, she spent about six and a half months away from home in four visits, two to Bath and two to relatives in Kent and elsewhere. She seems to have been away from home almost that much – over five months – during 1801 alone, the year she moved to Bath, and during most of her subsequent years at Bath: 1802, 1805, 1806 and perhaps 1803.[3] The only year for which we have little evidence of travel, 1804, is also the year in which Austen is generally thought to have drafted *The Watsons*. Visits to seaside resorts, family and friends are not ordinarily conducive to composition, and the heavy social demands of Austen's world were likely to be increased during visits.

Perhaps the best way to account for Austen's literary career between 1801 and 1809, then, is to take all her movement into account. For example, having moved to Bath and having spent the first year and a half there settling in and visiting, she managed by the spring of 1803 to revise and sell *Northanger Abbey* under the title of *Susan*. She travelled a good deal in the following summer and autumn, visiting Lyme Regis in November of the year (like Anne Elliot in *Persuasion*). Despite the disappointment of not seeing *Susan* in print, she had gathered enough literary momentum to draft *The Watsons* in 1804, stopping after the shock of Mrs Lefroy's death on Austen's birthday, 16 December, in 1804, and her own father's death on 21 January 1805. Sometime in or after 1805, however, she made a fair copy of *Lady Susan*. In the four and a half years after George Austen died, his widow and daughters paid many lengthy visits to family and friends and, more important, moved five times: they took two different sets of lodgings in Bath, followed by lodgings then a house in Southampton, until their final move brought them to Chawton in July 1809. At Chawton, Austen began to publish her earlier works and to write new ones. Once there, she travelled comparatively little until 1813 and 1814, by which time she was so well launched as a writer that she could maintain her writing despite interruptions. In other words, like many writers, Austen may have needed to feel that she had a clear, open expanse of time ahead in order to begin a lengthy work, although once well begun, she could continue to write unless a major shock intervened. Her unsettled, crowded life during her years in Bath and Southampton, coupled with the shock of Mrs Lefroy's and George Austen's deaths, are probably responsible for her comparative unproductivity at Bath and particularly Southampton.

But she was not wholly unproductive. Luckily, Austen did not absolutely need a room of her own to write; she seems always to have shared a room with Cassandra. At Steventon, the two rooms that she and Cassandra used included a 'dressing room' that certainly made it easier for her to draft three novels. Perhaps Austen had just such an arrangement in mind when she wrote to Cassandra of one house that her parents looked at in Green Park Buildings:

> The apartment over the drawing-room pleased me particularly, because it is divided into two, the smaller one a very nice-sized dressing-room, which upon occasion might admit a bed.
>
> (*L* 124; 5 May 1801)

But that house proved damp, and even the large house at 4 Sydney Place that they rented from 1801 to 1804 was unlikely to afford two rooms for the daughters, particularly as the Austens had visits from a number of friends while they lived there. In general, life in Bath seems to have been crowded both indoors and out compared to life at Steventon. Rooms were fewer and perhaps even smaller than they had been at the parsonage. Austen expresses distaste for a house that they examined in King Street:

quite monstrously little; – the best of the sittingrooms not so large as the little parlour at Steventon, and the second room in every floor about capacious enough to admit a very small single bed.

(*L* 132; 21 May 1801)

Social life was more demanding and less rewarding in Bath, at least for the first month. In January 1801 Austen could write comfortably from Steventon that 'Our party yesterday was very quietly pleasant. Today we all attack Ash Park, & tomorrow I dine again at Deane. What an eventful week!' (*L* 114; 21 Jan. 1801). Four months later, her tone is much harsher:

Another stupid party last night; perhaps if larger they might be less intolerable, but here there were only just enough to make one card table, with six people to look on, & talk nonsense to each other. . . . I cannot anyhow continue to find people agreable.

(*L* 128-9; 12 May 1801)

We are to have a tiny party here tonight; I hate tiny parties – they force one into constant exertion.

(*L* 132; 21 May 1801)

Clearly, when she first arrived in Bath, Austen was irritated at constantly having to produce small talk with people she hardly knew. No further letters survive until she wrote to Cassandra more than three years later during her second visit to Lyme. By then her tone is less irritable in describing a new acquaintance:

she is very converseable in a common way; I do not perceive wit or genius, but she has sense and some degree of taste, and her manners are very engaging. She seems to like people rather too easily. She thought the Downes pleasant etc etc.

(*L* 142; 14 Sep. 1804)

At this point, Austen herself evidently does not easily find people agreeable.

LOVE AND MARRIAGE

The three-year hiatus in Austen's letters from Bath is partly caused by Cassandra's having destroyed some. As we will see, one niece saw letters in which Austen accounted for her one-day engagement in 1802; those letters do not survive. Cassandra may also have burnt other letters that referred to the 'nameless and dateless'[4] romance which is likely to have occurred during this period. The most reliable account of this episode derives from Austen's niece Caroline, who obtained it from Cassandra. In Devonshire 'one summer when they were by the sea', the Austens met a man who:

> seemed greatly attracted by my Aunt Jane – I suppose it was an intercourse of some weeks – and that when they had to part (I imagine he was a visitor also, but his family might have lived near) he was urgent to know where they would be the next summer, implying or perhaps saying that he should be there also, wherever it might be. I can only say that the impression left on Aunt Cassandra was that he had fallen in love with her sister, and was quite in earnest. Soon afterwards they heard of his death. . . . I am sure she [Cassandra] thought he was worthy of her sister, from the way in which she recalled his memory, and also that she did not doubt, either, that he would have been a successful suitor.[5]

This account is very far removed from Austen herself, depending not so much on Caroline Austen's memory of facts as on her impressions of Cassandra's impressions. There is, however, no reason to doubt that Austen did meet a man whom she felt that she could love, perhaps on the visit to Sidmouth in 1801, and his loss must have been painful even though the acquaintance had been short.

Although this nameless and dateless romance remains impossible to fix in time with any precision, the date of Austen's one-day engagement to Harris Bigg-Wither is certain. He proposed to her at his father's house on 2 December 1802; she accepted; she changed her mind overnight, told him so in the morning and left immediately. She had been visiting at Manydown, where her friends Catherine and Alethea Bigg lived with their brother Harris, who at 21 was six years younger than Austen and had known her probably since he was in his early teens. She had visited at Manydown frequently to attend Basingstoke balls, so that she had known Harris long if not well. The niece who had evidently been permitted to read some letters that were later destroyed wrote:

> I gathered from the letters that it was in a momentary fit of self-delusion that Aunt Jane accepted Mr. Wither's proposal, and that when it was all settled eventually, and the negative decisively given she was much relieved. I think the affair vexed her a good deal, but I am sure she had no attachment to him.[6]

Caroline Austen wrote more fully of the incident. First, she offered an unattractive description of Bigg-Wither as 'awkward, & even uncouth in manner' though with 'sense in plenty', and continued by offering her own interpretation of Austen's refusal:

> I *conjecture* that the advantages he could offer, & her gratitude for his love, & her long friendship with his family, induced my Aunt to decide that she would marry him *when* he should ask her – but that having accepted him she found she was miserable & that the place & fortune which would certainly be *his*, could not alter the *man*.[7]

If she had been able to read Austen's letters to her niece Fanny Knight, Caroline Austen would have had greater authority for some of her conjectures. Fanny had asked her aunt's advice about John Plumtre, whom Fanny had once fancied herself in love with and to whom she now felt indifferent, although he was at last seriously pursuing her. Austen's response at first is in the young man's favour:

> Oh! my dear Fanny, the more I write about him, the warmer my feelings become, the more strongly I feel the sterling worth of such a young Man & the desirableness of your growing in love with him again. I recommend this most thoroughly. – There *are* such beings in the World perhaps, one in a Thousand, as the Creature You and I should think perfection, Where Grace & Spirit are united to Worth, where the Manners are equal to the Heart & Understanding, but such a person may not come in your way, or if he does, he may not be the eldest son of a Man

of Fortune, the Brother of your particular friend, & belonging
to your own County. – Think of all this Fanny.

(*L* 409–10; 18 Nov. 1814)

Austen proceeds to excuse his major fault – modesty – and to
defend his religious convictions. And then, suddenly, she shifts
ground:

> And now, my dear Fanny, having written so much on one
> side of the question, I shall turn round & entreat you not
> to commit yourself farther, & not to think of accepting him
> unless you really do like him. Anything is to be preferred
> or endured rather than marrying without Affection; and if
> his deficiencies of Manner &c &c strike you more than all
> his good qualities, if you continue to think strongly of them,
> give him up at once.

(*L* 410)

The reason for this shift may be that Austen has recalled the
parallel to her own circumstrances. She too had been asked in
marriage by the eldest son of a man of fortune, the brother of
her particular friends Catherine and Alethea Bigg, who belonged
to her own county of Hampshire – a man of awkward manners
but sensible and respectable. No doubt she had fully considered
all these advantages in her acceptance of Bigg-Wither. We can
sense Austen suddenly remembering her own parallel position
and recalling her refusal in the altered argument, leading to the
often-quoted line, 'Anything is to be preferred or endured rather
than marrying without Affection'. Having made the connection
to her own experience, she no longer argues for the marriage. She
writes in her next letter to Fanny, almost two weeks later, that:

> You will think me perverse perhaps; in my last letter I was
> urging everything in his favour, & now I am inclining the other
> way; but I cannot help it; I am at present more impressed with
> the possible Evil that may arise to *you* from engaging yourself
> to him.

(*L* 417; 30 Nov. 1814)

In her own case, Austen preferred comparative poverty and
dependency to marriage without affection.

On the day that she broke her engagement, 3 December 1802, Austen left for Steventon, returning the following day to Bath, no doubt 'vexed' in spirit (as her niece gathered from the letters that were destroyed). As Austen wrote years later to Fanny Knight, 'The unpleasantness of appearing fickle is certainly great' (*L* 418; 30 Nov. 1814). Disappointing her friends, Catherine and Alethea, must also have been unpleasant, although the friendship remained strong. More important, she was forced to accept that she would probably never be anything but a dependent. Although no one with a brother as rich and affectionate as Edward could fear absolute poverty, Austen faced dispossession and increased powerlessness at her father's death. Dependency even on affectionate brothers would mean living with or near them, relying on them for subsistence and indulgences. She was very unlikely to regret her refusal of a loveless marriage that would make her mistress of an affluent home, but like Fanny Price she may have regretted not having the power and comparative independence of such a position. Longing to help her sister Susan, Fanny considers:

> Were *she* likely to have a home to invite her to, what a blessing it would be! – And had it been possible for her to return Mr. Crawford's regard, the probability of his being very far from objecting to such a measure, would have been the greatest increase of all her own comforts. She thought he was really good-tempered, and could fancy his entering into a plan of that sort, most pleasantly.
>
> (*MP* 419)

Perhaps Austen too wished that she could have returned Harris Bigg-Wither's regard, so that she might offer Cassandra a home once their father died.

Having faced the powerlessness of her future, Austen may have taken up revising *Susan* as a means to exercise some power and control in her life. Whether she began after the proposal or earlier, she submitted the work to the London publisher B. Crosby and Company through Henry's agent Mr Seymour. The novel was accepted and paid for at what was then a low rate of £10[8] by 'the spring of the year 1803', according to Austen's angry letter to the firm six years later (*L* 263; 5 Apr. 1809). Austen adopted the pseudonym 'Mrs Ashton Dennis' for this letter to Crosby, a name which allowed her to sign herself 'M.A.D.'

Austen was angry because Crosby had never published *Susan* although 'an early publication was stipulated for at the time of sale' (*L* 263). Perhaps Henry had suggested including this businesslike detail in the letter, to strengthen Austen's bargaining position. That Crosby chose to purchase *Susan*, to advertise it as in press, but not to publish it is puzzling; surviving publishers' records from the period offer no parallel instance. The firm was an odd choice in any event. It was certainly not as large or as reputable a publishing house as Cadell and Davies, the publishers whom George Austen approached in 1797. It did have one advantage over them: it was prepared to look at and to accept an anonymous work, perhaps because Mr Seymour had some business connection with the firm. But Crosby and Company was not large, nor was it a very notable source for novels. At this time, it tended to produce reliable sellers like reference works, compilations and children's books more than fiction. For example, in 1803 the firm published *Flowers of Literature for 1801 & 1802*, a compilation of essays and short tales generally copied from previously published works – a practice that we would consider plagiarism, but which was acceptable then. In the last two pages of the *Flowers of Literature*, the firm inserted a list of fourteen 'New and Useful Books; Published by B. Crosby & Co', including five novels, and a list of two works 'In the Press': 'Susan; a Novel, in 2 vols.' and 'Dict[ionar]y of Celebrated Women, by Miss Beetham, in one vol.'[9] Only Mary Matilda Betham's work appeared (1804). The firm had traded under the name of Crosby and Letterman between 1799 and 1802.[10] Perhaps the recent dissolution of this partnership caused financial difficulty that magnified the risk of publication. Crosby may have felt that absorbing a £10 loss was preferable to investing the money required to print *Susan*. Advertising the novel in his own publication had cost him nothing, after all, and presumably the advertisement created no demand. Similarly, Crosby may have tried to obtain pre-publication orders from the trade when *Susan* was allegedly 'in press' and met with little interest. Accordingly, he decided against publication. Such a scenario seems more plausible than a theory that Crosby was producing too many Gothic novels to risk publishing a burlesque of such works.[11] Surely this objection would have occurred to Crosby before he paid for *Susan* – unless he paid for it sight unseen, an unlikely contingency.

The novel that Crosby bought I take to be substantially the same as *Northanger Abbey*, primarily on Austen's own evidence, in the short 'Advertisement' that she composed in 1816 for the novel, her only direct address to her readers:

> This little work was finished in the year 1803, and intended for immediate publication. It was disposed of to a bookseller, it was even advertised, and why the business proceeded no farther, the author has never been able to learn. That any bookseller should think it worth while to purchase what he did not think it worth while to publish seems extraordinary. But with this, neither the author nor the public have any other concern than as some observation is necessary upon those parts of the work which thirteen years have made comparatively obsolete. The public are entreated to bear in mind that thirteen years have passed since it was finished, many more since it was begun, and that during that period, places, manners, books, and opinions have undergone considerable changes.
>
> (*NA* 12)

Austen does not speak of herself here as an 'authoress', a term frequently used in a patronising manner, but an author. And typically, she is concerned that thirteen years have rendered the work no longer a faithful representation of places, manners, books and opinions. Austen's commitment to realism motivates this explanation, but the soreness of a slighted author is also strongly evident despite the passage of time.

THE WATSONS

Revising *Susan* or *Northanger Abbey* was for Austen an exercise in control and distance. It permitted her to play with and manipulate her readers at the same time that she both mocked and exploited the conventions of the sentimental and the Gothic novel, the two major genres in contemporary fiction. Given the complexity and abstraction of these aims, that Catherine Morland, Isabella Thorpe and Henry Tilney have as much novelistic life as they do is a triumph for Austen's comic art. Like most writers, Austen must have been exhilarated at finding for the first time that someone was willing to pay for her writing, even though the fee was low. The stipulation for early publication that she mentions in her 1809 letter to Crosby suggests that she may have been willing to

accept a low fee in return for quickly seeing her work in print.
The disappointment created by Crosby's failure to publish a novel
on which so much aesthetic effort had been expended must have
been correspondingly great. But possibly that disappointment
convinced her to abandon burlesque and return to somewhat
more conventional novel-writing in *The Watsons*, an unfinished
work of about 17 500 words.

The Watsons dwells on dispossession, poverty and marginality,
perhaps in part because Austen had confronted the prospect
of both in her own life after refusing Harris Bigg-Wither, and
because the antidote to both – exerting her power as a novelist
– had miscarried. The heroine, Emma Watson, is the youngest of
six children of a poorly-beneficed clergyman. When her father
received the living of Stanton, fourteen years before the novel
begins, Emma was adopted by a childless aunt who was married
to the well-off Mr Turner. Mr Turner treated Emma as a daughter,
but he did not provide for her; his will left all his money to his wife.
After Mr Turner died, Emma remained with her aunt until her
aunt remarried. The second husband, however, an Irish captain,
refused to keep Emma with them when they removed to Ireland:
'It did not suit them, it did not suit Capt. O'brien that I sh^d be
of the party' (*MW* 326). Accordingly, when the novel opens,
Emma has been thrown back on her family. She attends a ball
near Stanton and favourably impresses Lord Osborne, the great
proprietor of the neighbourhood; Mr Howard, Lord Osborne's
former tutor, at present a clergyman residing near Osborne Castle;
Mr Howard's sister Mrs Blake, who lives with her brother; young
Master Charles Blake; and Mrs Edwards, who chaperones Emma
at the ball. Nonetheless, her brother Robert, in his 'Hard-hearted
prosperity' (361), harshly sums up her marginal position:

> To find yourself, instead of heiress of 8 or 9000 £, sent back
> a weight upon your family, without a sixpence. – I hope the
> old woman will smart for it. . . . she has left the pleasure
> of providing for you, to your Father, & without the power.
> – That's the long & the short of the business. After keeping
> you at a distance from your family for such a length of time
> as must do away all natural affection among us & breeding
> you up (I suppose) in a superior stile, you are returned upon
> their hands without a sixpence.

(352)

In short, another novel lies behind *The Watsons*, the story of Emma's progressive loss first of her immediate family, then of a beloved uncle and finally of an aunt and a fortune. The plot of *The Watsons* may have developed from Austen's earliest attempt at a novel, 'Catharine, or the Bower'. That is, Austen may have begun with the germ of the earlier work – the heiress Catharine Percival who suffers deprivation by the loss of her friends the Wynnes and by her aunt's unloving supervision – and decided to deprive her heroine further of her aunt and her money, while retaining a perplexed social position. Catharine, although an heiress, is marginal within her social world because she is not really of the gentry, but a merchant's daughter. Similarly, Emma Watson is marginal because she has the upbringing of a gentry heiress without any means at all. But in choosing to place deprivation, loss and social marginality even more at the centre of *The Watsons* than it was of 'Catharine, or the Bower', Austen also chose to change the heroine's character drastically. Catharine was untried, unsure of herself, undeveloped. Emma Watson is poised and assured in the most trying situations.

In *The Watsons*, then, Austen created a situation of the utmost distress for her heroine, yet granted her almost complete superiority to her circumstances. An outsider in her own family, she acts there rather like an anthropologist, studying interrelationships, uncovering values, recording manners. Although her position is that of a poor dependent, facing even greater poverty once her father dies, she acts with authority, she judges independently. Cassandra revealed to her nieces the shape that the plot was to take:

> Mr. Watson was soon to die; and Emma to become dependent for a home on her narrow-minded sister-in-law and brother. She was to decline an offer of marriage from Lord Osborne, and much of the interest of the tale was to arise from Lady Osborne's love for Mr Howard, and his counter affection for Emma, whom he was finally to marry.[12]

Even in Croydon, patronised and disgusted by the 'low-minded Conceit' and 'Hard-hearted prosperity' of Jane and Robert Watson, we can be sure that Emma will retain her poise, assurance and even independence (361).

James Edward Austen-Leigh implausibly argued when he first printed the fragment in 1871 that Austen had abandoned *The Watsons* because she had placed her heroine in too 'low' a situation; most students now believe that Austen ceased writing the novel when her father died.[13] *The Watsons* as we have it strongly foreshadows Mr Watson's death, and Austen's own father's sudden death must have made it impossible for her to continue writing. Art would be imitating life too closely, a consequence of Austen's having, probably unconsciously, used the plot of *The Watsons* to assert her own superiority to the powerlessness and poverty that threatened her own life. But though George Austen's death is sufficient reason for Austen's interrupting her work on *The Watsons*, it may not fully account for her choosing never to take up the novel again. I would argue that Emma Watson is too triumphant a heroine, rising superior to every occasion in a manner that evidently appealed to Austen when she began the novel, but which prevented her from wishing to resume it.[14] Emma's superiority is most obvious in the well-known incidents that occur when Emma is so much the lady that others are rebuked: when she impulsively offers herself as a partner to little Charles Blake, who has been disappointed by Miss Osborne; and when she tells Lord Osborne, who seeems to feel that she ought to be able to afford a horse:

> 'Female Economy will do a great deal my Lord, but it can-not turn a small income into a large one.' – Ld Osborne was silenced. Her manner had been neither sententious nor sarcastic, but there was a something in it's mild seriousness, as well as in the words themselves which made his Lordship think; – and when he addressed her again, it was with a degree of considerate propriety.
>
> (346)

When Mr Knightley rebukes the ill manners of Mr Elton in *Emma* by asking the slighted Harriet Smith to dance, we see the incident from Emma Woodhouse's point of view, not his, and we are not required to believe that the Eltons are reformed by his action. Emma Watson is a lady as Mr Knightley is a gentleman, but evidently to greater effect. A tribute to female strength and power in adversity, so much so as to be almost incredible, she resembles the embattled Austen heroines who endure more than they change or develop: Elinor Dashwood, Fanny Price and to a lesser extent Anne Elliot. But Emma Watson does not really suffer or struggle as much as they do, although in most respects her position is worse. She is a far more conventionally 'distressed' heroine than they:

> of importance to no one, a burden on those, whose affection she c^d not expect, an addition in an House, already overstocked, surrounded by inferior minds with little chance of domestic comfort, & as little hope of future support.
>
> (362)

But in actuality, she seems less distressed. She remains secure and assured, however marginal she is.

Emma's sisters respond to their marginal and threatened position by relentless pursuit of men – not mindless pursuit, like Kitty and Lydia Bennet's, but shameless, like Charlotte Lucas's. Emma's fretful, petulant, hypocritical, poisonous sister Margaret is pursuing Tom Musgrave; her sister Penelope Watson is in Chichester pursuing 'a rich old Dr Harding' (317); and not even Elizabeth has given up the chase, although she is without an object. Elizabeth eloquently expresses the sisters' position:

> 'you know we must marry. – I could do very well single for my own part – A little Company, & a pleasant Ball now & then, would be enough for me, if one could be young for ever, but my Father cannot provide for us, & it is very bad to grow old & be poor & laughed at.'
>
> (317)

The argument that follows between Emma and Elizabeth over women's limited options for supporting themselves is more direct than anything else that Austen wrote on the subject. Emma avers:

> 'To be so bent on Marriage – to pursue a Man merely for the sake of situation – is a sort of thing that shocks me; I cannot understand it. Poverty is a great Evil, but to a woman of Education & feeling it ought not, it cannot be the greatest. – I would rather be Teacher at a School (and I can think of nothing worse) than marry a Man I did not like.' – 'I would

rather do any thing than be Teacher at a school – said her sister. *I* have been at school, Emma, & know what a Life they lead; *you* never have. – I should not like marrying a disagreable Man any more than yourself, – but I do not think there *are* many very disagreable Men; – I think I could like any good humoured Man with a comfortable Income. – I suppose my Aunt brought you up to be rather refined.'

(318)

One does not feel that Elizabeth's position is entirely to be despised. Interestingly, although most of the manuscript of *The Watsons*, according to R.W. Chapman's edition, is heavily interlineated, erased and corrected, Austen seems to have written out both these passages freely, without any alterations or second thoughts.[15] They came easily.

The world that Austen creates for Emma Watson is rather like that of Elinor Dashwood: it is primarily a world of women in which men, though a possible source of income, are either intrusive (Tom Musgrave, Lord Osborne) or negligible (the bridge-playing, gossiping Mr Edwards, the invalid Mr Watson). Perhaps the most interesting feature of the plot that Cassandra outlined is that Lady Osborne, an attractive woman 'nearly 50' (329), is to love Mr Howard, who is 'a little more than Thirty' (330) – for I cannot accept R.W. Chapman's complacent note that 'Lady Osborne' in Cassandra's account is 'Doubtless a slip for *Miss Osborne*' (*MW* 363). Austen's niece Catherine Hubback followed Cassandra's outline exactly when she completed and published the fragment under the title of *The Younger Sister* (1850). The author of the unconventional portraits of women in the juvenilia would enjoy dramatising the love of a woman in her late 40s for a man in his 30s, and the more mature writer would be unlikely to render that love merely ridiculous. Mr Howard will be the pursued, not the pursuer, for Emma will be at a distance, in Croydon. In short, Austen seems to be forcing her hero into a reversal of roles rather like that portrayed by Charles Adams, the dazzling beauty of the juvenilia. Mr Howard's introduction to Emma is as perfunctory as possible. We hear no conversation between them and have no opportunity to judge him. We take Emma's word for his merit, rather as we must take Elinor's word for Edward Ferrars' virtues for most of *Sense and Sensibility*. In *The Watsons* as we have it, women spend their lives mostly with other women – just as Austen did. Those are the central relationships.

Although Austen did not choose to resume work on *The Watsons* after her father died, she did make a fair copy of *Lady Susan* on paper watermarked 1805 and probably wrote the brief conclusion at the same time. Perhaps she was hoping to publish it. In the early 1790s, when *Lady Susan* had been drafted, novels in letters were still reasonably common, but by 1805, they had declined in popularity. In 1805, however, Maria Edgeworth successfully published *Leonora*, a short epistolary novel in which a passive wife temporarily loses her husband to a disreputable friend – a Susan-like figure but far less entertaining. The success of Edgeworth's work may have inspired Austen to think of publishing *Lady Susan* – to make a fair copy with a conclusion. If so, however, we have no information that she ever offered the work to a publisher. If she was not thinking of publication, she may simply have regained interest in this portrait of a powerful woman whose manoeuvres are largely successful. Lady Susan's daughter Frederica possibly appealed to her as well. Frederica's wretched education and poverty make her marginal, but she is after all able to foil her mother's plan to marry her off to Sir James Martin. In her letter, Frederica reminds us of Emma Watson by asserting that 'I would rather work for my bread than marry' Sir James (*MW* 279; Let. 21). The alternatives facing a single woman without money – uncongenial work or a disagreeable husband – were evidently present to Austen's imagination at this time, although she certainly did not imagine herself forced to embrace either. It is clear, however, that if pressed she would have preferred work.

After her father's death in January 1805, Austen resided in Bath with her mother and sister and later Martha Lloyd for a year and a half, although in fact she probably spent little time in the city. In March 1805, they moved to lodgings at 25 Gay Street, until a round of visits began in June to Steventon, Godmersham and Worthing. They may not have come back to Bath until mid-March 1806, two months after Mrs Austen had returned to take lodgings in Trim Street. They left three and a half months later, on 2 July, 'with what happy feelings of Escape' (*L* 208; 30 June 1808).

The small income that remained to Mrs Austen after her husband's death had been more than doubled by her sons. The optimistic Henry considered that his mother and Cassandra would have £210 between them, that he, Frank and James could each contribute £50 a year, and Edward £100:

> she will be in the receipt of a clear 450 pounds per ann. – She will be very comfortable, & as a smaller establishement will be as agreeable to them, as it cannot but be feasible, I really think that My Mother & sisters will be to the full as rich as ever. They will not only suffer no personal deprivation, but will be able to pay occasional visits of health and pleasure to their friends.[16]

But as usual Henry was too sanguine. In 1820, Mrs Austen wrote that she had only £122 a year, her 'children' (not her sons) supplying the rest of her income.[17] By 1816, neither Frank nor Henry could contribute,[18] and in 1819 James died. Clearly, Mrs Austen was relying on Edward and on Cassandra, who by this time was Austen's heiress as well as Tom Fowle's, to supplement her income. Still, in 1805 Mrs Austen's funds seemed ample, and she managed well during her first two years of widowhood, as Austen reported: 'she began 1806 with 68*l*., she begins 1807 with 99*l*., and this after 32*l*. purchase of stock' (*L* 174; 7 Jan. 1807). Possibly the 'stock' furnished the new lodgings in Southampton, where Mrs Austen arrived in September 1806, after long summer visits with her daughters to relatives at Adlestrop in Gloucestershire (which included a visit at Stoneleigh Abbey) and Hamstall Ridware in Staffordshire.

SOUTHAMPTON

The move to Southampton involved an enlarged household. Martha Lloyd had agreed to live with the Austens after her own mother's death in 1805; she was with them by the following November in Worthing. Furthermore, Frank Austen had married Mary Gibson of Ramsgate in July 1806, and the plan was to take a house in Southampton large enough to accommodate them all. They eventually found one in Castle Square. Austen had possibly seen relatively little of her sailor brother since moving to Bath. He was of course on active service except during the Peace of Amiens, from March 1802 to May 1803. Charles had joined the family at Bath when peace was declared and had therefore been available as an escort for summer travels in 1802, but Frank's whereabouts are unknown. Austen had almost certainly not shared a home with Frank for any length of time since he left

Steventon as a boy for the Royal Naval Academy at Portsmouth in 1786. That she enjoyed the opportunity to live with him in Southampton is implicit in her portrait of Captain Harville in *Persuasion*. Late in life, Frank wrote that 'I rather think parts of Capt. Harville's [character] were drawn from myself. At least some of his domestic habits, tastes and occupations bear a strong resemblance to mine'.[19] Perhaps the pleasure of sharing a home with Frank is also implicit in Austen's criticism of her brother James, whose visit to Southampton was so trying. As she wrote to Cassandra:

> I am sorry & angry that his Visits should not give one more pleasure; the company of so good & so clever a Man ought to be gratifying in itself; – but his Chat seems all forced, his Opinions on many points too much copied from his Wife's, & his time here is spent I think in walking about the House & banging the doors, or ringing the bell for a glass of water.
>
> (*L* 181; 8 Feb. 1807)

The combined household in Castle Square lasted until September 1808, when Frank, Mary and the daughter Mary Jane who had been born there moved to lodgings in Yarmouth, leaving the Austens and Martha Lloyd in possession temporarily. They were in fact looking for lodgings in Alton, a town with several attractions for the Austens. First, it was in Hampshire, their own county, only about 16 miles by carriage roads from Steventon where James still resided, less if one rode cross-country as James did, by 'cross roads & rough lanes inaccessible to wheels which lay between the two places'.[20] Alton was also only a mile or two from Edward's estate at Chawton. Moreover, Henry's London banking firm of Austen and Maunde had in 1806 joined in partnership with an Alton firm, Gray and Vincent; by 1808, the two firms were known as Austen, Maunde and Tilson in London and Austen, Gray and Vincent in Alton.[21] But before any lodgings could be taken, Edward's wife Elizabeth died two weeks after the birth of her eleventh child, on 10 October 1808. Almost immediately, Edward offered his mother the choice of a house near Godmersham or one near his Chawton estate. She chose the latter, Chawton Cottage, although the move was delayed for more than eight months. By then, Mrs Frank Austen was also settled nearby, in lodgings at Alton, to await the birth of her second child while Frank sailed to China. No doubt this drawing together of so many of the family was deliberate. Although at this point Edward did not reside at Chawton Manor – he had leased the property to John Middleton between 1808 and 1812 – he did so intermittently once the lease expired.

The family enclave eventually centred at Chawton was anticipated late in August 1807, when Edward took some of his family to Chawton Manor and invited his mother, his sisters and James and his family to stay with them for about two weeks. Austen's record of her expenditures for this year has survived; a 'Journey' cost her £1.2.10, 'Waterparties & Plays' cost a further 17s9d and 'Servants' another 13s9d (one gave tips or 'vails' to a host's servants when visiting a house, to compensate them for their extra work). These expenses, presumably for the Chawton visit, were minimal compared to the year's expenditure of more than £45 - considerably more than the allowance of £20 a year that she had enjoyed during her father's lifetime. She had extra funds because she and Cassandra had each been left £50 by a Mrs Lillingston (a friend of their aunt Mrs Leigh Perrot) who had died in January 1806.[22] Accordingly, Austen's expenses for 1807 are inflated but still offer a sense of how she apportioned her income. Nearly half went for 'Cloathes & Pocket' (almost £14) and for keeping clothes clean (over £8). Her 'Sittings in Church' cost eleven shillings, presumably in Southampton: a seat or pew or 'sitting' had to be paid for during this period. Charity took about three and a half pounds. Austen also spent over six pounds on presents and nearly four pounds to send parcels and to receive letters (for one paid upon delivery of a letter – a condition that leads Austen occasionally to joke about how much letters are worth). Finally, she spent £2.13.6 to 'Hire Piano Forte' in Southampton, a luxury that perhaps determined her to buy one when she moved to Chawton: 'Yes, yes, we *will* have a pianoforte, as good a one as can be got for thirty guineas' (*L* 243; 27 Dec. 1808); clearly Austen had in mind a much better instrument than the one that sold for eight guineas when she left Steventon (*L* 126; 12 May 1801).

The nearly three years that Austen spent in Southampton were apparently the most unproductive of her literary career. Her silence cannot be blamed on travel. Except for the short visit to Chawton in the summer of 1807, Austen seems to have been with her mother, Frank (when not on active service) and his wife in Southampton from October 1806, until January 1808 – at which point she began about half a year of travel to Steventon,

Manydown, Kintbury, London and Godmersham. But being fixed for over a year in Southampton did not bring Austen uninterrupted leisure. Visitors arrived, and social life was demanding: as Austen wrote to Cassandra, 'Our acquaintance increase too fast' (*L* 174; 7 Jan. 1807).

Probably more disturbing than any of these social demands was the presence of Frank's wife Mary, whose difficult first pregnancy was followed by a painful delivery of a daughter, Mary Jane, on 27 April 1807. Possibly sharing a house with an infant was not conducive to literary activity, and the child's birth was the first of a number of events that brought home to Austen the dangers of motherhood. A year and a half after Mary Jane Austen was born came the death in childbirth of Edward's wife Elizabeth, the first such death that had touched Austen nearly. Six years later, in 1814, another brother's wife died shortly after giving birth: Fanny Palmer, who had married Charles when she was 17 and who died before reaching 25. Many biographers have noted that Austen's letters to Fanny Knight during the last months of her life show an increasing concern, even anger, with the costs to women of multiple pregnancies, in part because her niece Anna Austen Lefroy seemed to be pregnant with a third child after less than two and a half years of marriage. She wrote to Fanny:

> [B]y not beginning the business of Mothering quite so early in life, you will be young in Constitution, spirits, figure & countenance, while Mrs Wm Hammond is growing old by confinements & nursing.
>
> (*L* 483; 13 Mar. 1817)

> Anna has not a chance of escape . . . Poor Animal, she will be worn out before she is thirty. – I am very sorry for her. – Mrs Clement too is in that way again. I am quite tired of so many Children. Mrs Benn has a 13th.
>
> (*L* 488; 23 Mar. 1817)

This concern with the cost of pregnancy may have begun when Austen witnessed Mary Gibson Austen's sufferings. What seems to be the first of her exasperated remarks on the subject occurs 18 months afterward, a few days before Elizabeth's death. Austen had written of Henry's partner's wife, Mrs Tilson, 'poor Woman! how can she be honestly breeding again?' (*L* 210; 1 Oct. 1808).

Two months later, Austen was clearly connecting the ideas of birth and death, although in a different context. On her own 33rd birthday, 16 December 1808, She wrote a poem to the memory of Mrs Lefroy, who had died suddenly on that date four years before:

> The day commemorative of my birth,
>> Bestowing life, and light, and hope to me,
> Brings back the hour which was thy last on earth.
>> O! bitter pang of torturing memory!

(*MW* 440)

Seven months afterward, Austen was able to write from Chawton a quite different sort of poem to Frank, rejoicing in the birth of his second child and also in the 'comforts' of the Chawton home. But even this cheerful poem begins with a reminder of Mary's difficult first pregnancy:

> My dearest Frank, I wish you joy
> Of Mary's safety with a Boy,
> Whose birth has given little pain
> Compared with that of Mary Jane.

(*L* 264; 26 July 1809)

Amusingly, Austen is using here the metre of Walter Scott's popular poem *Marmion*, which she had not particularly liked when her brother James first read it aloud to her at Godmersham, but which she had sent to Charles in January 1809: 'very generous in me, I think' (*L* 197; 20 June 1808; *L* 248; 10 Jan. 1809). Her ear must have retained Scott's rhythms.[23]

One senses a return of literary energy, of purpose, of family harmony and security, in Austen's poetical letter to Frank – the only one we have – and in her decision a few months earlier to enquire into the fate of *Susan*. Perhaps the return of Cassandra in February 1809 after a nearly five months' stay with her bereaved brother Edward was a relief, as was their mother's return to health after a serious illness in March and April. But above all, the prospect and the reality of the move to Chawton was joyful:

> Cassandra's pen will paint our state,
> The many comforts that await

Our Chawton home, how much we find
Already in it, to our mind;
And how convinced, that when complete
It will all other Houses beat
That ever have been made or mended,
With rooms concise, or rooms distended.
You'll find us very snug next year,
Perhaps with Charles & Fanny near,
For now it often does delight us
To fancy them just over-right us.

(*L* 266; 26 July 1809)

Although Charles and Fanny Austen were not to arrive in England until 1811, this picture was otherwise accurate. Comforts, snugness, delight in rooms concise, with family near – this seems to be what Austen required to begin the astonishing eight years of writing and publishing that followed.

5

The Professional Writer, 1809–1817

When Austen arrived in Chawton on 7 July 1809, she was 33 and unpublished, a condition that she was determined to alter. Her enquiry in April to the publisher Crosby and Company testifies to this determination. She had written then that 'from particular circumstances' she would not be able to produce a fair copy of *Susan* until August (*L* 263; 5 Apr. 1809). No doubt she simply meant that she would have no time to make a fair copy until after the move to Chawton. Once settled there, Austen evidently began her efforts to achieve publication by looking over all her extant work. She examined even her longer juvenilia, for she made alterations in Volume the Third, containing 'Evelyn' and 'Catharine, or the Bower', that date from 1809.[1]

Although Austen's preference for writing her drafts on small pieces of paper, approximately four to five inches wide by seven or eight inches long, was probably lifelong, the practice is usually associated with her residence at Chawton. There, she had to write downstairs, in company; at Steventon, she had had somewhat greater privacy. Her nephew James Edward Austen-Leigh noted of her Chawton writing:

> She was careful that her occupation should not be suspected by servants, or visitors, or any persons beyond her own family party. She wrote upon small sheets of paper which could easily be put away, or covered with a piece of blotting paper. There was, between the front door and the offices, a swing door which creaked when it was opened; but she objected to having this little inconvenience remedied, because it gave her notice when anyone was coming.[2]

These 'small sheets of paper' could be stored in Austen's

mahogany writing-desk, possibly a nineteenth-birthday present from her father.[3] Wherever she travelled, she seems to have taken this desk with her, primarily to write letters.[4] It was large enough, however, to hold both the unfinished manuscript of *Sanditon* and the cancelled chapters of *Persuasion* in 'one of the small Drawers'.[5] It had a long drawer as well, which may have contained longer manuscripts and which Austen permitted a child to explore at Southampton in 1807: 'she is now talking away at my side & examining the Treasures of my Writing-desk drawer' (*L* 178; 8 Feb 1807).

Unfortunately, no letters have survived between the time Austen settled at Chawton and her visit to London in March and April 1811, when *Sense and Sensibility* was already in the press. We can know nothing directly about when she decided to work on *Sense and Sensibility* or how much time she spent on it. She was probably fixed at Chawton once she arrived there, although she may have visited Alethea Bigg at Manydown with Cassandra during July and August 1810.[6] Her social life was perhaps more exclusively devoted to her family than at any other time in her life. She shared a home with her mother, Cassandra and Martha Lloyd; Edward and other brothers visited occasionally; and Frank's wife was settled for some time in Alton. According to her niece Caroline Austen, she was 'upon *friendly* but rather *distant* terms, with all' her Chawton neighbours.[7] Eventually, however, she did make new local friends during her residence at Chawton – among them Maria Beckford, Catherine Ann Prowting and her sister Ann Mary (who became Mrs Clement), and a Mrs Barrett.[8] By the time she was in London to correct proofs of *Sense and Sensibility*, she could write of meeting Henry's friends, 'I find all these little parties very pleasant' (*L* 269; 18 Apr. 1811).

But this openness may have been exceptional. At this time, Austen's usual manner to strangers seems to have been very reserved, more so than when she was younger. In Mary Russell Mitford's account (derived from Miss Hinton, a Chawton neighbour), Austen had:

> stiffened into the most perpendicular, precise, taciturn piece of "single blessedness" that ever existed, and that, till 'Pride and Prejudice' showed what a precious gem was hidden in that unbending case, she was no more regarded in society

than a poker or a fire-screen, or any other thin upright piece
of wood or iron that fills its corner in peace and quietness. The
case is very different now; she is still a poker – but a poker of
whom every one is afraid.[9]

Mitford acknowledged that Miss Hinton might not be entirely
reliable, for her family was at law with Austen's brother Edward
for his Chawton estate. A more sympathetic report, however,
mentions the same silence, stiffness and coolness to strangers.
Charlotte Maria Beckford, who was at Chawton House as a
child, wrote:

> She was a most kind and enjoyable person *to Children* but
> somewhat stiff & cold to strangers She used to sit at Table at
> Dinner parties without uttering much . . . her Sister Cassandra
> was very lady-like but *very prim*, but my remembrance of Jane
> is that of her entering into all Childrens Games and liking her
> extremely.[10]

The only authentic portrait of Austen, the rather sharp one by
Cassandra now in the National Portrait Gallery, reinforces this
impression of stiffness and reserve. Deirdre Le Faye conjectures
that it was done at this time, about 1810.[11] In it, Austen appears to
have extremely large, deep-sunk dark eyes, almost no mouth and
an expression that seems alternately pained, critical and aloof.
All verbal portraits of Austen's mature appearance are far more
flattering. Charlotte Maria Beckford recorded her dissatisfaction
with the portrait included in James Edward Austen-Leigh's *Memoir* – one that was based on Cassandra's drawing, but much
prettified:

> Jane's likeness is hardly what I remember there *is* a look, & that
> is all – I remember her as a tall thin *spare* person, with very
> high cheek bones great colour – sparkling Eyes not large but
> joyous and intelligent The face by *no means so broad* & plump
> as represented; perhaps it was taken when very young, but the
> *Cap looks womanly* – her keen sense of humour I quite remember,
> it oozed out very much in Mr. Bennet's Style.[12]

Almost any portrait would probably have been unsatisfying, for those who knew Austen tended to remember her life and energy – her expressiveness rather than her features. Such a description of her in later life comes from Fulwar William Fowle, Eliza Lloyd's son, who was 26 when Austen died and had seen her at various times as he grew up:

> he said she was pretty – certainly pretty – bright & a good deal of color in her face – like a doll – no that wld not give at all the idea for she had so much expression – she was like a child – quite a child very lively & full of humor – most amiable – most beloved.[13]

Cassandra's portrait very closely resembles, however, Sir William Ross's more attractive miniature of Austen's brother Edward, reproduced facing page 208 in Chapman's edition of the *Letters*. The two together probably give the best impression of how Austen appeared to others in her 30s.

FIRST PUBLICATION: THOMAS EGERTON, *SENSE AND SENSIBILITY* AND *PRIDE AND PREJUDICE*

Most biographers infer that Austen attempted to publish *Sense and Sensibility* at this time rather than *Pride and Prejudice* because the latter had been rejected sight unseen by Cadell and Davies. *Sense and Sensibility*, however, had been completed later than *Pride and Prejudice* and may have required less revision. I suspect too that Austen's exasperating experience with Crosby and Company caused her to prefer *Sense and Sensibility*. Despite an unconventional focus upon a community of women, its emphasis upon the importance as well as the costs of self-command made it her most orthodox novel both aesthetically and morally. *Susan* or *Northanger Abbey* constituted a bold experiment in burlesque over which Crosby had clearly vacillated, thinking it a profitable speculation at first and then a poor risk. *Pride and Prejudice* contained an extremely unorthodox heroine, and Austen may have feared either similar vacillation from another publisher, if she succeeded in selling the copyright, or a more ambivalent reception from reviewers and the reading public than *Sense and Sensibility* was likely to obtain. Mary Russell Mitford wrote to a friend in December 1814, for instance, deploring 'the entire want of taste which could produce so pert, so worldly a heroine as the beloved of such a man as Darcy'.[14]

Sense and Sensibility was a safer choice – almost too much so, as Austen jokingly feared when it was in the press. Mary Brunton's improving novel *Self-Control: a Novel* had appeared early in 1811, and Austen wrote in April:

> We have tried to get Self-controul, but in vain. – I *should* like to know what her Estimate is – but am always half afraid of finding a clever novel *too clever* – & of finding my own story and my own people all forestalled.
>
> (L 278; 30 Apr. 1811)

This statement interestingly implies that, for Austen, self-control *was* a theme central to *Sense and Sensibility*. Brunton's novel, however, certainly did not 'forestall' Austen's. Two years later, Austen re-read *Self-Control* with much amusement:

> I am looking over Self Control again, & my opinion is confirmed of its being an excellently-meant, elegantly-written Work, without anything of Nature or Probability in it. I declare I do not know whether Laura's passage down the American River, is not the most natural, possible, everyday thing she ever does.
>
> (L 344; 11 Oct. 1813)

Austen may have approached the publisher Thomas Egerton through Henry, perhaps using his agent Seymour again. Egerton, after all, had sold James's and Henry's *The Loiterer* in his Whitehall shop more than 20 years earlier. We do not know what made Egerton prepared to produce *Sense and Sensibility* on commission. He was not known for bringing out novels, nor did publishing on commission ever prove very remunerative to the publisher. He must have liked the novel well enough to feel that he would gain prestige by being associated with it, and perhaps more important, he must have felt that he could trust Henry Austen, at this time a banker, to settle the bill for costs. Possibly he insisted, unlike some other publishers, on being paid for paper and printing in advance. Certainly Austen herself supposed so (L 368; 3 Nov. 1813).

Once Egerton had agreed to publish the novel, he sent it to the printer Charles Roworth, of Bell Yard, Temple Bar, perhaps in February or March 1811. Roworth was in fact the most frequently employed printer for Austen's works, producing at least 14 of the 27 volumes that were issued through December 1817. Their first association was disappointing to Austen:

> M^rs K[night] regrets in the most flattering manner that she must wait *till* May [for *Sense and Sensibility*], but I have scarcely a hope of its being out in June– Henry does not neglect it; he *has* hurried the Printer. . . .
>
> (*L* 273; 25 Apr. 1811)

The delay was much worse than Austen anticipated; the novel was not advertised until the end of October. She experienced some delay from printers on every novel that she published for herself, though none was as lengthy as this. By contrast, Egerton was able to issue *Pride and Prejudice* within a few months of purchasing it,[15] doubtless because his own profit was at stake. He would earn less than £36 by publishing *Sense and Sensibility* on commission in an edition of 750 copies, by my calculations, whereas Austen herself made £140, as she wrote to her brother Frank (*L* 317; 3 July 1813). It was not worth Egerton's while to hurry the printers.

Although he stood to gain little by agreeing to publish *Sense and Sensibility* on commission, Egerton ran no risk; only the author did. Austen was 'so persuaded . . . that its sale would not repay the expense of publication, that she actually made a reserve from her very moderate income to meet the expected loss' (*NA* 6). At this time, the expenses of publishing 750 copies of the novel would come to about £155, and advertisements would ordinarily take another £24 or so.[16] The novel retailed at 15*s*, but the books were accounted for to the author at the trade price, about a third less than the retail price. If every copy were sold at the trade price of 9*s*6*d*, receipts would be over £356,[17] leaving a maximum profit of about £140 after deducting expenses of £179 and Egerton's ten per cent commission on the sales.

Austen was risking, then, about £180 on the chance of earning £140. In fact, however, her risk was substantially less. The buyer's market for novels was small, but sales to circulating libraries were fairly certain. Even the small circulating library at

Alton purchased *Sense and Sensibility*, Anna Austen Lefroy's daughter amusingly recalled:

> It was in searching this Library that my mother came across a copy of *Sense & Sensibility* which she threw aside with careless contempt, little imagining who had written it, exclaiming to the great amusement of her Aunts who stood by 'Oh that must be rubbish I am sure from the title'.[18]

A novel normally would have to sell between one half and two-thirds of an edition to become profitable. For example, within five months of being issued in February 1810, Maria Benson's *The Wife. A Novel* had sold 275 of the 500 copies printed, and in two more years another 49, realising £7.6.4 to split with Longman, who had agreed to share profits with the author. By June 1812, however, sales had stalled. No more copies were sold until the work was remaindered in April 1813, when 151 were taken at 1s6d each, yielding another £10.11.10 to be split between the author and her publisher. Benson made about £9 finally, as did her publisher, who risked more than £155 to do so.[19]

We can presume that the 275 copies of *The Wife* that were taken right away, however, represent the number that just about any new novel might expect to dispose of on the market. The figure is probably uninflated by sales to family and friends, for Benson took 25 copies for herself to supply that market. (In fact, the copy in the British Library was presented to the Rev. J. Jamison by 'his friend the Author'.) If only 275 copies of *Sense and Sensibility* had sold, Austen would have had £130, less Egerton's ten per cent, to offset her expenses of £179; that is, she would have owed about £62. If the other 475 copies had been remaindered at the same price as Benson's novel, Austen would have received another £32 or so. At worst, then, her loss was unlikely to be more than £30. Although she probably was unable to 'reserve' such a sum from her own 'moderate income', to use Henry's words – for most of her life, her dress allowance had been £20 a year[20] – she could perhaps set aside about half. And every additional copy of her novel that was sold at the full trade price of 9s6d would reduce this possible debt. She would break even once 419 copies were sold, even allowing for Egerton's commission.

In other words, if Austen had been more aware of the economics of publishing for herself, if she had known that even at worst her losses were likely to be manageable, she might have published sooner – perhaps when she inherited £50 in 1807. The women whom she would have considered models, however, Frances Burney, Charlotte Smith, Anne Radcliffe and later Maria Edgeworth, published by selling the copyright of their works. Perhaps because these respected women novelists sold copyright and because doing so entailed no risk to herself, Austen evidently preferred that option until 1811, for otherwise she would not have accepted the offer of £10 for the copyright of *Susan* in 1803. Fortunately, by 1811 Austen was prepared to invest money in herself, in her own authorship.[21]

Austen saw her own words in print for the first time in April 1811 – an exciting experience for any writer – when she was in London and had received the first two 'sheets' of *Sense and Sensibility* to correct. Like almost all novels at this time, it appeared in 'duodecimo': each printed sheet was folded so as to produce 12 leaves or one 'gathering' of 24 pages to the sheet. Printing was charged by the sheet, and one ream of paper was required to print 500 copies of one sheet. The first volume of *Sense and Sensibility* took more than 13 gatherings or sheets. Austen thus replied to Cassandra's query as to the progress of the novel through the press: 'I have had two sheets to correct, but the last only brings us to W[illoughby']s first appearance' (*L* 273; 25 Apr. 1811). She had actually received four gatherings to correct,[22] taking the novel through 96 pages of the first volume and ending with these words in Chapter 9:

> A gentleman carrying a gun, with two pointers playing round him, was passing up the hill and within a few yards of Marianne, when her accident happened. He put down his gun and ran to her assistance. She . . .
>
> (42)

It must have been tantalising to Austen to read so far and no further, especially since she strongly doubted the printer Roworth's reliability.

Although in her works Austen employs similes and metaphors sparingly, in her references to her novels she uses them much more freely. She notoriously referred several times to her novels as her children – but only once she had begun to see them in print. She responds thus to Cassandra's enquiry:

No indeed, I am never too busy to think of S & S. I can no more forget it, than a mother can forget her sucking child; & I am much obliged to you for your enquiries.

(*L* 272–3; 25 Apr. 1811)

She then mentions having the two sheets to correct. Her analogy here is very powerful. Her own mother had suckled eight children, and she herself had recently lived with a mother and her sucking child at Southampton. She knew very well the degree of intense absorption that she was evoking to describe the impossibility of forgetting her first novel. The comparison suggests that, at 35, Austen was happy and proud to feel that she had produced and was nurturing or mothering a book. This maternal pride is evident in the rest of the passage, culminating in the reference to her character as 'my Elinor'. Similar tenderness and pride appear later, when Austen refers to *Pride and Prejudice* as 'my own darling child' (*L* 297; 29 Jan. 1813) and sends a copy of *Emma* to her niece Anna, whose newborn daughter Austen has not yet seen: 'As I wish very much to see *your* Jemima, I am sure you will like to see *my* Emma, & have therefore great pleasure in sending it for your perusal' (*L* 449, Dec. 1815). Austen even permits herself comparable references to her characters, as in *Mansfield Park*: 'My Fanny indeed at this very time, I have the satisfaction of knowing, must have been happy in spite of every thing' (461).

This tendency to refer to books (or characters) as one's offspring should not be regarded too simply as revealing a spinster's wish to be a mother. Had Austen strongly desired children, she would have married Bigg-Wither. Her mature attitudes to actual pregnancy and mothering express a sense of the burdens of these states rather than anything else. And in fact, a maternal metaphor for one's relationship to a book is conventional.[23]

Sense and Sensibility received two favourable reviews, a lengthy one with many long quotations in the *Critical*, and a short one in the *British Critic*. One contemporary comment has been recorded: in a letter postmarked 24 November 1811, Henrietta, Countess of Bessborough, wrote to Lord Granville Leveson Gower, 'Have you read "Sense and Sensibility"? It is a clever novel. They were full of it at Althorp, and tho' it ends stupidly I was much amus'd by it'.[24] (The stupid ending might have been Marianne's marriage.) Althorp in Northamptonshire was the seat of Lady Bessborough's father Lord Spencer; someone in the family had evidently purchased the novel early in November, as soon as it was advertised.

Two good reviews and a steady sale must have been exhilarating to Austen. Her family's immediate response to her publication has not been recorded, but certainly they shared her delight. She visited her brother James and his family at Steventon in November 1811, shortly after the novel came out; possibly the family read it among themselves then. If any of the children were present at such a reading, Austen's authorship was kept a secret, not revealed until a few years later. When he finally learned that his aunt had written two novels, James Edward Austen-Leigh was inspired to versify his amazement:

That you made the Middletons, Dashwoods, and all,
And that you (not young Ferrars) found out that a ball
May be given in cottages, never so small. . . .[25]

No family member or friend seems to have preferred *Sense and Sensibility* to the other novels. James Edward's half sister Anna did like it better than *Mansfield Park* and *Pride and Prejudice*, in that order, but she thought *Emma* equally good (*MW* 431, 438). Only four other 'Opinions' of *Mansfield Park* and *Emma* actually mention *Sense and Sensibility* at all by name or implication, and none rank it clearly in relation to the others, perhaps because it was not fresh enough in anyone's mind. It had been published nearly three years before Austen began to collect opinions – no sooner than May 1814.

Egerton had almost certainly accepted *Sense and Sensibility* by February 1811.[26] This acceptance made Austen optimistic enough about the possibilities of publication to begin her most ambitious novel to date, *Mansfield Park*. According to Cassandra's memorandum, this novel was begun 'somewhere about Feb[y] 1811 – Finished soon after June 1813' (*MW* facing p. 242).[27] No other novel took Austen so long to write. Probably part of the time was spent revising *Pride and Prejudice*, perhaps taken up when she discovered that *Sense and Sensibility* had sold well enough to break even; this point was quite likely to be reached within six months of issue, in May 1812. By the following November, Austen had completed her revisions, made a fair copy and sold the manuscript to Egerton for £110, as she wrote to Martha Lloyd: 'It's being sold will I hope be a great saving of Trouble to Henry, & therefore must be welcome to me. – The Money is to be paid at the end of the twelvemonth' (L 501; 29 Nov. 1812). Austen's unfortunate decision to part with the copyright of *Pride and Prejudice* for less than the £150 she had wished for was made before she could predict that the first edition of *Sense and Sensibility* would sell out and bring her £140. Again, most novels sold best immediately after being published. Egerton is likely to have advised Austen, quite accurately, that publishing a second novel would assist sales of the first. Her acceptance of Egerton's offer may have been influenced by this consideration, not simply by her wish to save Henry the trouble he had evidently undergone in supervising the printing of *Sense and Sensibility* between April and October 1811.

Pride and Prejudice, issued at the end of January 1813, was Austen's most popular novel, both with the public and with her family and friends. Among those who compared *Pride and Prejudice*, *Mansfield Park* and *Emma*, Austen's mother, her nephew Edward, her brother Frank's wife, her friends Ann Sharpe, Alethea Bigg and Fanny Cage, and a Mrs Dickson, liked *Pride and Prejudice* best, and six more preferred it to the only other novel that they mentioned. Both Cassandra and Anna Austen Lefroy, however, liked it less than *Mansfield Park* or *Emma* (MW 431–9). By the spring of 1813, three favourable reviews had appeared. Austen must have been delighted by the reviewers' appreciation of Elizabeth Bennet: the *British Critic* wrote that her character 'is supported with great spirit and consistency throughout; there seems no defect in the portrait'; and the *Critical* wrote that 'Elizabeth's sense and conduct are of a superior order to those of the common heroines of novels'.[28] She was notoriously eager that readers should like her heroine. Besides the most famous reference, quoted below, Austen wrote to Cassandra of her niece Fanny Knight that 'Her liking Darcy & Elizabeth is enough, she might hate all the others if she would', and of the family friend Warren Hastings that, 'I long to have you hear Mr. H.'s opinion of P. and P. His admiring my Elizabeth so much is particularly welcome to me' (L 303; 9 Feb. 1813; L 324; 15 Sep. 1813).

Before May 1813, *Pride and Prejudice* had become the 'fashionable novel', according to Anne Isabella Milbanke, who was to marry Lord Byron. She had been told that the author was a sister of

Charlotte Smith; rumour also assigned the novel to 'Mrs. Dorset, the renowned authoress of *The Peacock at Home*' and to Lady Boringdon, later the same Countess of Morley to whom Austen sent a presentation copy of *Emma*.[29] The popularity of the novel eventually meant the end of Austen's anonymity. By the following September, her authorship was pretty well known, as she wrote to her brother Frank:

> . . . the truth is that the Secret has spread so far as to be scarcely the Shadow of a secret now – & that I beleive whenever the 3^d appears, I shall not even attempt to tell Lies about it. – I shall rather try to make all the Money than all the Mystery I can of it. – People shall pay for their knowledge if I can make them.
>
> (*L* 340; 25 Sep. 1813)

Although Austen joked about both, money was important to her, and anonymity had been so essential that she had had Cassandra write to Godmersham in September 1811, 'to beg we would not mention that Aunt Jane Austen wrote "Sense & Sensibility"'.[30] In this letter, after recounting how Henry 'in the warmth of his Brotherly vanity and Love' has disclosed her authorship 'more than once', she continues, revealing the real strength of her wish for anonymity:

> I know it is all done from affection & partiality – but at the same time, let me here again express to you & Mary my sense of the *superior* kindness which you have shewn on the occasion, in doing what I wished. – I am trying to harden myself. After all, what a trifle it is in all its Bearings, to the really important points of one's existence even in this World!
>
> (*L* 340)

That Austen felt the need to remind herself of religious considerations – for 'this World' evokes the next – shows how little she wished to be known to strangers as a writer. 'If I *am* a wild Beast', she wrote to Cassandra, on hearing that one of Henry's friends wanted to be introduced, 'I cannot help it. It is not my own fault' (*L* 311; 24 May 1813). She notoriously refused an opportunity to meet the literary lion Madame de Staël in London.[31]

Except for this dislike of publicity, Austen responded with delight to the success of *Pride and Prejudice*, so much so that many suppose it to be her favourite novel. I suspect, however, that (like most writers) she preferred her later works to earlier ones. We know more of her delight in this novel than any of the others only because she and Cassandra happened to be separated when it first appeared. No letters survive for the first month of publication for any other Austen novel. Fortunately, Austen's presence in London to read proofs for all the novels that she published for herself – *Sense and Sensibility*, *Mansfield Park* and *Emma* – means that her letters to Cassandra do reveal important details of their publication.

For *Pride and Prejudice*, however, we have Austen's comments on her own and her mother's reading of the novel aloud to a neighbour, Miss Benn, from whom they concealed the authorship. Austen told Cassandra:

> Miss Benn dined with us on the very day of the books coming & in the evening we set fairly at it, and read half the first vol. to her, prefacing that, having intelligence from Henry that such a work would soon appear, we had desired him to send it whenever it came out, and I believe it passed with her unsuspected. She was amused, poor soul! *That* she could not help, you know, with two such people to lead the way, but she really does seem to admire Elizabeth. I must confess that I think her as delightful a creature as ever appeared in print, and how I shall be able to tolerate those who do not like *her* at least I do not know.
>
> (L 297; 29 Jan. 1813)

Austen's next letter rejoices in Cassandra's comments on *Pride and Prejudice*, which she must have re-read with James and Mary Austen at Steventon:

> Your letter was truly welcome, and I am much obliged to you all for your praise; it came at a right time, for I had had some fits of disgust. Our second evening's reading to Miss Benn had not pleased me so well, but I believe something must be attributed to my mother's too rapid way of getting on: and though she perfectly understands the characters herself, she cannot speak as they ought.
>
> (L 299; 4 Feb. 1813)

Austen herself, as Henry tells us, was her own best reader: 'Her own works, probably, were never heard to so much advantage as from her own mouth; for she partook largely in all the best gifts of the comic muse' (*NA* 7). Despite the discomfort of hearing (probably) Mr Collins's splendid speeches in the second half of Volume 1 not rendered to her own taste, Austen continued with her most quoted and ironical remarks upon the novel:

> Upon the whole, however, I am quite vain enough and well satisfied enough. The work is rather too light, and bright, and sparkling; it wants shade; it wants to be stretched out here and there with a long chapter of sense, if it could be had; if not, of solemn specious nonsense, about something unconnected with the story; an essay on writing, a critique on Walter Scott, or the history of Buonaparté, or anything that would form a contrast, and bring the reader with increased delight to the playfulness and epigrammatism of the general style. I doubt your quite agreeing with me here. I know your starched notions.
>
> (*L* 299–300)

Austen clearly had no real wish to intrude essays and critiques into her works, but at this point she was more than halfway through *Mansfield Park*, a novel written in a more serious style. The passage reflects her own sense that her style had changed and deepened since she had first written *Pride and Prejudice* more than 15 years earlier.

Possibly this sense of distance accounts for the frequency with which Austen wrote as if the characters of *Pride and Prejudice* had an existence apart from her. Her criticism to Cassandra that 'There might as well have been no suppers at Longbourn' indicates that she had neglected to alter a detail that would have been acceptable 15 years earlier but would be thought unfashionable now, and the rest of her sentence humourously abdicates responsibility: 'I suppose it was the remains of Mrs. Bennett's old Meryton habits' (*L* 300; 4 Feb. 1813). With similar assumed distance, Austen identified a portrait of Mrs Bingley in a London exhibition; she sought in vain at another for one of Mrs Darcy, adding that she could imagine Mr Darcy having a 'mixture of Love, Pride & Delicacy' that would keep him from allowing Elizabeth's portrait to appear; and she refused to write a letter to her niece Fanny Knight in the style of Georgiana Darcy, saying 'Even had I more time, I should not feel at all sure of the sort of Letter that Miss D. would write' (L 312; 24 May 1813). By contrast, all Austen's comments on events that take place outside her novels indicate enormous intimacy with her characters and stories. These include the information that Anne Steele never married Dr Davies; that Kitty married a clergyman near Pemberley, while Mary was obliged to take one of her uncle Philips' clerks; that the 'considerable sum' Mrs Norris gave to William Price was one pound; that the word Jane Fairfax swept away unread was 'pardon'; that Mr Woodhouse died two years after Emma's marriage; and that Jane Fairfax died nine or ten years after her marriage to Frank Churchill.[32]

Because she had sold the copyright, Austen did not profit from her most popular novel as she should have done. The cautious Egerton probably issued a first edition of 1000 copies of *Pride and Prejudice* and, in the following October, a second edition of perhaps 750, both of which were sold at 18s, a higher price than *Sense and Sensibility*. Had Austen published such editions for herself, she would have made about £475, allowing for Egerton's commission, when they sold out – supposing that Egerton had brought them out as economically for her as he did for himself. Certainly he produced *Pride and Prejudice* more cheaply, using cheaper paper and less of it, even though the novel was longer than *Sense and Sensibility*.[33] And furthermore, he seems to have been guilty of overcharging for *Pride and Prejudice*, which cost three shillings more than *Sense and Sensibility*. The latter had in fact been slightly underpriced: Longman charged 16s6d for a shorter three-volume novel like Benson's *The Wife* early in 1810, and retained that price for *She Thinks For Herself*, which appeared almost exactly when *Pride and Prejudice* did and was of comparable length. Austen seems to have been aware of Egerton's manoeuvrings, for she wrote to Cassandra on 29 January 1813: 'The Advertisement is in our paper to-day for the first time 18s. He shall ask £1.1. for my two next & £1.8 for my stupidest of all' (L 297). For Austen, 'shall' in the second or third person is always emphatic: it 'commands or threatens', to use an eighteenth-century grammarian's formula.[34] By naming sums in excess of one pound – not yet appropriate for a three-volume novel – she jokingly suggests that she will imitate Egerton's sharp business practices. More seriously, she implies that she will not permit him to undercharge

again when her own profit is at stake – and she did not.[35]
The success of *Pride and Prejudice* certainly increased the
demand for *Sense and Sensibility*, which was sold out by 3 July 1813,
according to a letter written on that date to Frank (*L* 317). It had
taken about 20 months to clear the edition. By contrast, *Pride and
Prejudice* was probably sold out before the second edition appeared
on 29 October, nine months after its first appearance. Egerton
may have ordered the reprint of *Pride and Prejudice* before the first
edition was exhausted because a clever publisher who owned the
copyright of a work generally did not allow it to go out of print
while there was still a decent demand. To do otherwise was to
damage the value of the copyright.[36] He advised Austen to reprint
Sense and Sensibility at the same time as he was reprinting *Pride and
Prejudice*: Austen wrote as a postscript to Frank on 25 September
1813 that 'There is to be a 2^d Edition of S. & S. Egerton advises it'
(*L* 341), and both works were advertised together on 29 October.
Egerton may not have suggested an immediate reprint of *Sense and
Sensibility* in July because he judged that a joint publication would
stimulate the sale of both works, or because he calculated that
they could be advertised together (at a slight saving to both). He
was also unconcerned with preserving the value of a copyright
that he did not own. On the whole, however, his advice to
Austen was sound enough. She never lost money by publishing
with Egerton, although she had to wait until 1816 before receiving
profits on the second edition of *Sense and Sensibility*.[37]

POWER AND *MANSFIELD PARK*

In her dealings with Egerton, Austen seems to have learned
quickly that his interests were very different from hers. Her wry
remark on the price that he charged for *Pride and Prejudice* shows
her awareness that he was likely to profit from the novel more
than she had – and more than she had profited from publishing
Sense and Sensibility for herself. After the success of *Pride and
Prejudice*, Egerton certainly offered to purchase the copyright
of Austen's next novel, but she did not accept his offer. It was
no doubt rather low – perhaps £150. She evidently had learned to
prefer her own judgement of the value of her work to Egerton's,
and she was prepared to risk an unfavourable response from the
reading public. In other words, Austen had 'written myself into

£250', as she wrote to her brother Frank, and she chose to invest that money in her own work – wisely, as it happened (*L* 317; 3 July 1813). Publishing *Mansfield Park* for herself would once again give her brother Henry the task of supervising the printers, but Henry probably urged her not to sacrifice her profit to his convenience.

Austen's letters include several details about the writing of *Mansfield Park*, most notoriously the still frequently misunderstood remark that she would write of 'ordination'. As long ago as 1973, F. B. Pinion pointed out that, taken in context, the remark does not refer to writing the novel at all but to writing her letter.[38] Having written to Cassandra at great length about *Pride and Prejudice*, concluding with her supposition that it must be 'rather shorter than S. & S. altogether', Austen continues:

> Now I will try to write of something else, & it shall be a complete change of subject – ordination – I am glad to find your enquiries have ended so well. If you could discover whether Northamptonshire is a country of Hedgerows I should be glad again.
>
> (*L* 298; 29 Jan. 1813)[39]

In context, Austen is telling Cassandra that she will finally change the subject and write no more of *Pride and Prejudice*. Again, her use of 'I will' and 'it shall' always promises, threatens or commands, and here the promise and threat jokingly underline the effort required to get herself off the topic of her novel.[40] Of course, the real joke is that Austen shifts the topic to one involving yet another novel – to the enquiries that she had asked Cassandra to make about ordination, perhaps concerning where and when Edmund Bertram's ordination should take place. In *Mansfield Park* Edmund is ordained at Peterborough 'in the course of the Christmas week' (255). Cassandra was at Steventon and could have asked her brother James whether those details were accurate.

If Austen had brought *Mansfield Park* to Edmund's departure for Peterborough by January 1813, she had reached the 11th chapter of Volume 2 and had thus completed about three-fifths of the whole. Even if her enquiries about ordination predated her writing the chapter, she was still quite far advanced. In an earlier letter to Cassandra she had referred to having to change the Government House at Gibraltar to the Commissioner's, and to the round table at Mrs Grant's, details that occur in the sixth and seventh chapters of the second volume (*L* 292, 294; 24 Jan. 1813). Cassandra must have read at least so far before she left for Steventon early in January. By the time Austen wrote to Frank on 3 July, she had certainly written the Portsmouth section: she tells him that she has mentioned 'the Elephant in it, & two or three other of your old Ships' but will remove these references if Frank objects (*L* 317). Again, Cassandra remembered that *Mansfield Park* had been completed 'soon after June 1813'. In other words, Austen may have written almost half the novel between January and July 1813, despite short visits to London in April and May, the first to attend Henry's wife Eliza in her last illness, and the second perhaps to provide company for Henry in his bereavement.

Austen probably took the finished manuscript with her when she paid her last visit to Godmersham – her first in four years – from September to November 1813. According to Anna Austen Lefroy, Austen was not a favourite with her nieces and nephews at Godmersham:

> They liked her indeed as a playfellow, & as a teller of stories, but they were not really fond of her. I believe that their Mother was not; at least that she very much preferred the elder Sister.[41]

Nonetheless, two of Edward's daughters remembered very similar stories of their aunt's habits of writing, which they may have noticed at this time. Marianne recalled observing, at 12 years of age:

> how Aunt Jane would sit quietly working beside the fire in the library, saying nothing for a good while, and then would suddenly burst out laughing, jump up and run across the room to a table where pens and paper were lying, write something down, and then come back to the fire and go on quietly working as before.

Louisa remembered a similar detail, observed when she was eight: 'She was very absent indeed. She would sit silent awhile, then rub her hands, laugh to herself and run up to her room'.[42] Austen was evidently able to become absorbed in the world of her novels despite an outward show of conventional womanly behaviour: she would have been 'quietly working' at her needle. These anecdotes indicate too that Austen composed in her head, not on the page, a practice evident also in her surviving drafts. These include sentences in which all but a few separated words have been crossed out, showing that Austen had composed her revision completely before she began to make changes.[43]

Louisa Knight is also the source for the notion that Cassandra tried to persuade Austen:

> to alter the end of Mansfield Park and let Mr. Crawford marry Fanny Price. She [Louisa] remembers their arguing the matter but Miss Austen stood firmly and would not allow the change.[44]

It is inconceivable, however, that the 'very prim' Cassandra, who preferred *Mansfield Park* among the novels published in her sister's lifetime, would seriously have argued for such an ending (*MW* 436). She and her sister were almost certainly enjoying a mock argument about the conclusion of the novel, and their eight-year-old niece was understandably baffled by their humour.

Having revised and made a fair copy of *Mansfield Park*, Austen offered it to Egerton perhaps in January 1814. Two to three months seem to have been a reasonable time in which to expect a book to go through the press. If Egerton sent *Mansfield Park* to the printer in January, Austen might expect to see proofs by March. At that time, Henry first began reading the novel as he travelled with his sister to London. If he read it in proof, as Deirdre Le Faye supposes, then the delay of nearly two months before the novel was published on 9 May is difficult to understand. Once proofs were corrected, the copies could be worked off the presses quite soon. Austen herself, however, wrote on 21 March, expecting a delay of at least a month:

> Perhaps before the end of April, *Mansfield Park* by the author of S & S. – P. & P. may be in the world. – Keep the *name* to yourself. I sh[d] not like to have it known beforehand.[45]

Although Egerton apparently did not produce *Mansfield Park* as speedily as he had *Pride and Prejudice*, he seems to have done so quite cheaply, perhaps at Austen's request. The paper is thinner (thus less expensive) than the thin paper used for *Pride and Prejudice*, and because each page contains 25 lines, not 23 as in the earlier novels, further savings on paper were achieved.

R. W. Chapman has conjectured that Egerton printed only 1250 copies; later, Henry Austen reminded John Murray that he himself had 'expressed astonishment that so small an Edit: of such a work should have been sent into the world'.[46] This edition sold out in only six months, more quickly than that of *Pride and Prejudice*, which had been exhausted in eight or nine months despite being almost certainly smaller. Using Chapman's estimate of 1250 copies, we must assume that Egerton produced *Mansfield Park* extremely cheaply indeed, otherwise the figures do not gibe with what we know of Austen's earnings. It exceeded £310, the largest profit that she received during her lifetime for any novel.[47]

If Austen began to write *Mansfield Park* as soon as she had arranged to publish her first novel for herself, that achievement easily accounts for the sense of power evident throughout her most controversial work. Power is central to *Mansfield Park* – domestic power, including what Mary Crawford calls the 'manoeuvring business' of marrying (46). Samuel Johnson recorded of Pope that he 'hardly drank tea without a stratagem',[48] and in *Mansfield Park* too the serving of tea can form part of a courtship strategy, signalling 'approaching relief' for Fanny Price when she is constrained to listen to Henry Crawford's addresses:

> The solemn procession, headed by Baddely, of tea-board, urn, and cake-bearers, made its appearance, and delivered her from a grievous imprisonment of body and mind. Mr. Crawford was obliged to move. She was at liberty, she was busy, she was protected.
>
> (344)

Imprisonment, deliverance, liberty, protection: terms like these and many others that imply the exercise of power – authority, consequence, government, dominion, submission, independence – are continually applied in *Mansfield Park* to the details of domestic life, particularly courtship and marriage.

These concerns reflect an important change from those of the early novels, particularly in the treatment of women. I have argued that in the juvenilia Austen inverts traditional notions of women. She allows them a frequently outrageous assertiveness and power that they are conventionally denied, but she also points to their marginality within society. In *Mansfield Park*, *Emma* and to a lesser extent *Persuasion*, however, Austen is interested in exploring more profoundly the complex power relationships between women and a social world that reduces their options and makes them marginal. She is less interested, in other words, in portraying women like Elizabeth Bennet and Catherine Morland who figuratively get away with murder – who rather easily triumph over their circumstances – than in rendering the way that women are enmeshed in circumstance. Enmeshed, not trapped, for Austen's women can to some extent shape their circumstances to accommodate their desires. Growth, assertion and achievement remain possible. But these possibilities have to be seized within a more fully realised social world, one that is less ready to permit individuals to evade its laws. *Mansfield Park* and *Emma* show women not escaping and evading but working within or re-forming their worlds.

Austen's treatment of courtship and marriage in the three later novels fully reflects her interest in operating within the limits that one's world imposes. The heroines are all well acquainted with the men they marry either before the novels begin or (in *Mansfield Park*) by the end of the second chapter. Emma Woodhouse learns to recognise the love that she already has for Mr Knightley, whereas Fanny Price and Anne Elliot retain their early love for Edmund Bertram and Frederick Wentworth despite the solicitations of other men. Austen's later heroines appreciate what is already there in their lives and manage to secure it. Austen is quite uninterested in creating a heroine who learns to love an interesting stranger, an 'outsider' who will remove her from the world she knows. To that extent, she discounts the processes by which flirtation and infatuation can become love. Emma Woodhouse, for instance, is far more infatuated by Harriet Smith than she ever is by Frank Churchill, but she loves neither. The earlier novels, however, enjoy portraying Elizabeth's infatuation with Wickham, Jane's with Bingley, Marianne's with Willoughby and Catherine's with Henry in some detail, and in the last three cases genuine love develops.

Naturally, Austen never lost interest in the comic possibilities of infatuation, either in life or in literature. Characters like Harriet Smith witness her continuing literary interest. The pleasure that Austen herself had taken in flirtation as a young woman had by middle age been transmuted into enjoyment of more distanced responses, primarily to good writing. Charles Pasley's *Essay on the Military Policy and Institutions of the British Empire* (1810) pleased her so much that she wrote:

> I am as much in love with the author as ever I was with Clarkson or Buchanan, or even the two Mr Smiths of the city – the first soldier I ever sighed for – but he does write with extraordinary force & spirit.
>
> (*L* 292; 24 Jan. 1813)

The Smiths wrote the parodic *Rejected Addresses* (1812), and Clarkson and Buchanan are evidently authors also, though the works that Austen admired have not been clearly identified. More amusingly, Austen responded to George Crabbe's poetry so favourably that she made a running joke to her family of being infatuated with him. She mentioned 'in jest' that 'if she ever married at all, she could fancy being Mrs. Crabbe'.[49] Her letters from London in September 1813 twice mention not seeing Crabbe (*L* 319, 323; 13, 15 Sep. 1813). His wife died shortly afterward, and Austen wrote:

> No; I have never seen the death of Mrs. Crabbe. I have only just been making out from one of his prefaces that he probably was married. It is almost ridiculous. Poor woman! I will comfort *him* as well as I can, but I do not undertake to be good to her children. She had better not leave any.
>
> (*L* 358; 21 Oct. 1813)

Austen's niece Caroline retained a hazy memory of this interest in Crabbe, recalling that:

> she took a keen interest in finding out *who* he was – Other contemporary writers were well-known, but *his* origen having been obscure, his name did not announce *itself* – however by diligent enquiry she was ere long able to inform the rest of the family that he held the Living of Trowbridge, and had recently married a second time – [50]

Literary infatuation amused Austen still, even if the romantic sort did so rather less than it had.

A comparative loss of interest in romantic infatuation permits Austen to take love somewhat for granted in the later novels. She places stress instead on the ways that courtship and marriage operate as social institutions within the constraints of a community. That is, she emphasises not simply the highly comic mixture of sexual and economic motives that prompt courtship and marriage, but the much less comic operations of power – of dominance and submission – that occur within and around both institutions. This emphasis does not affect Austen's willingness to create marriages that suggest a more just, generous and equal society, society as it ought to be. In the later novels, as in the early ones, Austen brings about marriages in which men and women enjoy a nearly ideal equality. Her firm commitment to more equal relations between the sexes is especially evident in the compromise that resolves *Emma*: out of respect for the conditions of Emma's life, Mr Knightley gives up his home to live at Hartfield.

Throughout *Mansfield Park*, Austen exposes the limits of the socially-constructed 'power' allegedly held by women in courtship. Sir Thomas's attempts to manipulate Fanny into marrying Henry underline his power and her comparative powerlessness, and are implicit in the first chapter, from his wish to forward the marriage by giving a ball at Mansfield to his 'medicinal project upon his niece's understanding', to 'teach her the value of a good income' by allowing her to visit her parents in Portsmouth (369). Modern readers are unlikely to accuse Fanny of being self-willed and independent, as Mrs Norris does (323–4), but her attitudes to the sexual and economic politics of courtship and marriage do show some of these qualities. Like other Austen heroines, and like Austen herself, Fanny will not marry without affection no matter what personal, social or financial advantage might accrue to her. But other Austen heroines have a much easier time getting rid of unwanted suitors. Carolyn G. Heilbrun has invited biographers to look for the suppressed anger and pain in women's lives.[51] Austen's comedy transmutes these elements in her own life almost beyond recognition, but in Fanny Price she chose to draw a heroine's pain and anger at being sought by the wrong man and overlooked by the right one quite thoroughly and openly.

In the contests for power that courtships become in *Mansfield Park*, Austen demonstrates that women are the ones who suffer constraint and even imprisonment. Mary Crawford says of Henry that he 'is quite the hero of an old romance, and glories in his chains' (360), but Austen's representation of Henry's courtship makes clear that all real power is on his side. His chains are only figurative; a woman's are not, as Maria Bertram's fate suggests. Maria's encouragement of Henry at Mansfield is succeeded by their mutual seduction at Twickenham, by divorce from Rushworth and cohabitation with Henry in a vain hope to marry him, and finally by her imprisonment with Mrs Norris. Henry might well glory in chains that afford him such freedom. Austen very slightly alludes to the *real* chains of slavery in *Mansfield Park* when she allows Fanny to ask Sir Thomas about the slave trade (198). As the proprietor of an estate in Antigua, Sir Thomas is a slave-owner. We do not hear his answer, and no overt comment is made. Austen leaves us to detect, if we wish, an analogy between a social order that permits human beings to be sold into slavery and one that encourages young women to sell themselves in marriage; but she requires us to register the irony that a generally good man like Sir Thomas will, in the world she describes, participate in both transactions – and will discard the daughter who sold herself when she becomes damaged goods. In this sense, *Mansfield Park* is by implication Austen's most religious book. She exposes the limitations and injustices of this world, 'without presuming to look forward to a juster appointment hereafter' – as the narrator notes of Henry Crawford's unjust immunity from disgrace (468). With her usual tact, Austen leaves that task to her readers.

Part of Austen's purpose in writing *Mansfield Park*, then, is to subject the domesticated social institutions of courtship and marriage to intense ironic scrutiny. Almost everyone agrees that this novel is her most profoundly political work, but so effective is her irony that most readers find the novel difficult. Nonetheless, Austen's family and friends received *Mansfield Park* almost as well as *Pride and Prejudice*. When no review of the novel appeared, Austen evidently decided to record all 'Opinions' that reached her, delighting in praise and apparently entertained by the reverse (*MW* 431-5). After the publication of *Emma* in late December 1815, she also collected opinions of that work. Five of her relatives and friends preferred *Mansfield Park* to *Emma* or *Pride and Prejudice*, including not only Cassandra but Martha Lloyd, Fanny Knight, a clergyman (Mr Sherer), and a friend of Henry's (Mr Sanford); another three acquaintances liked it better than *Pride and Prejudice*, and another better than *Emma*. Yet another, Sir James Langham of Cottesbrooke, whose country house has sometimes been thought the model for Mansfield,[52] thought the novel as good as *Pride and Prejudice* and better than *Emma*. Of the five who preferred *Mansfield Park* to both those works, all but Cassandra also enjoyed *Emma* the least of the three novels, and amusingly enough, Austen incorporated the objections of Fanny Knight, Mr Sherer and Mr Sanford to *Emma* into her satirical 'Plan of a Novel', written after she had collected some 'Opinions' of *Emma* in 1816. Those who preferred *Mansfield Park* evidently did not always do so, in Austen's view, for the best reasons.

A few months after *Mansfield Park* was published in May 1814, Austen's niece Anna at Steventon began a novel and, as she completed each sizeable chunk, sent it to Chawton to be read and criticised. Austen's letters of advice are well known, for they contain almost all her written comments on the art of the novel. She enjoyed her niece's work, encouraged her and clearly expected her to publish it, even advising against including a detail because 'to those who are acquainted with P. & P. it will seem an Imitation' (*L* 394; 10 Aug. 1814). The most familiar advice insists on realism of detail and on probability: the scene should not shift to Ireland where Anna is unfamiliar with manners, for 'You will be in danger of giving false representations' (*L* 395; 10 Aug. 1814); a character should not walk out just after having a broken arm set, even though Anna's father did so, for 'I think it can be so little usual as to *appear* unnatural in a book' (*L* 394; 10 Aug. 1814). Austen is also particularly responsive to language: she enjoys names like Newton Priors and Progillian; she objects to clichés like 'vortex of Dissipation' (*L* 404; 28 Sep. 1814); and she requires conciseness – 'here & there, we have thought the sense might be expressed in fewer words' (*L* 394; 10 Aug. 1814).

But the principal concerns are, always, characterisation and (through it) comedy. Austen frequently wants Anna to develop her characters more: 'I should like to have had more of Devereux. I do not feel enough acquainted with him' (*L* 396; 10 Aug. 1814). She is particularly interested in Anna's use of conversation, for in writing *Emma* Austen was herself perfecting her own skill in using comic dialogue to develop not only characters but themes. Accordingly, she writes to Anna:

Your last chapter is very entertaining – the conversation on

Genius &c. Mr. St. J[ulian] – & Susan both talk in character & very well. – In some former parts, Cecilia is perhaps a little too solemn & good, but upon the whole, her disposition is very well opposed to Susan's – her want of Imagination is very natural. – I wish you could make Mrs. F[orester] talk more, but she must be difficult to manage & make entertaining, because there is so much good common sence & propriety about her that nothing can be very *broad*. Her Economy and her Ambition must not be staring.

(*L* 401–2; 9 Sep. 1814)

This short passage refers to many of Austen's favourite techniques of characterisation: entertaining conversations; characters who talk 'in character'; contrasts between characters; broadly comic characters as well as mixed ones who combine sense and non-sense. And these remarks make clear that for Austen, the object of characterisation is entertainment – comedy, in short.

Anna married Ben Lefroy on 8 November 1814; her first child was born within a year, and she never finished her novel. At about the time of this marriage, Austen was writing very intimately and affectionately on infatuation, love and matrimony to another niece, Fanny Knight, who had encouraged a young man but now found, in Austen's summary, that 'being secure of him (as you say yourself) had made you Indifferent' (*L* 408; 18 Nov. 1814). As I have argued in the third chapter, Austen drew upon her own experience to advise Fanny against marriage to John Plumtre.

SECURITY AND MARGINALITY IN *EMMA*

While Austen was compiling 'Opinions' of *Mansfield Park*, editing Anna's novel, and advising Fanny Knight on courtship, she was busy writing *Emma*, a great departure from the prior work. The intense, perplexed world of *Mansfield Park* is surprisingly isolated. The action is set in Mansfield, Portsmouth, and (offstage) in London, but it is confined to a few families. In Northamptonshire, the action occurs at two houses, Mansfield and the parsonage, with one excursion to Sotherton, and in Portsmouth the confinement to one house and one family is even closer. We are given almost no glimpse of Mansfield village, where Mrs Norris resides in the White House, and none of the villagers themselves. *Emma* is entirely different. Highbury as a community takes centre stage, and the voice of Highbury – its comments on Frank Churchill, Jane Fairfax, Emma Woodhouse herself – is frequently heard.

No doubt Austen's life in Chawton informs her treatment of Highbury to some extent. When she began *Emma* on 21 January 1814, she had been living in a village again for four and a half years, after an eight-year absence, and she was finding the inter-dependency, the intimacy, the tedium and the gossip of village life particularly amusing. These qualities, together with her amuse-ment, are evident in one of the few letters she wrote to Cassandra from Chawton in the year before beginning *Emma*. She jokes about the reading and non-reading of her neighbours, about gossip ('The Coulthards were talked of you may be sure, no end of *them*'), and about visiting the poor with Miss Papillon, the rector's sister:

> *I* had a very agreeable walk, & if *she* had not, more shame for her, for I was quite as entertaining as she was. Dame G[arnet] is pretty well, & we found her surrounded by her well-behaved, healthy, large-eyed children. I took her an old shift, & promised her a set of our Linen, & my companion left some of her Bank Stock with her.
>
> (*L* 295; 24 Jan. 1813)

Except for the outrageous joke about a benefaction of bank stock, this Chawton world is not very different from the world of Highbury that serves as background and occasionally chorus for all the action of *Emma*. Deirdre Le Faye has sugggested that Austen's visit to her cousins the Cookes at Great Bookham at mid-summer in 1814, when she was writing *Emma*, may have allowed her to revisit Leatherhead, supposedly the model for Highbury.[53] Perhaps, but Highbury like all Austen's settings belongs less to the physical world than to the moral. It comes alive through descrip-tion of character and action, not through 'too many particulars of right hand & left', something that at just about this time she per-ceived in her niece Anna's draft of a novel and warned her against (*L* 401; 9 Sep. 1814). Amusingly enough, however, Great Bookham may have offered more immediate inspiration on the claustropho-bia of village life. Cassandra Cooke, author of *Battleridge* and first cousin of Austen's mother, had been something of a bore, at least according to Mrs Lock of Norbury, who wrote thus to her good friend Frances Burney in the summer of 1789:

At six o'clock I was just gone out with my Augusta to enjoy the sweetness of the evening and we were gathering roses from my wall which [i]s covered most luxuriously, when lo, a carriage was heard! A terrific sound: *des visites!*. Augusta, naughty girl, laughing loud enough to be discovered declared she *would* see them and ran to the little gate. I, entreating more caution, prepared to make my escape and burrow – as My Lock calls it – in my wilderness. Down the stairs we went when, alas, a voice called after us and we were compelled to return. Mrs. Cooke and her sister! How few are those one willingly sees. My poor Lock was gone his airing and on returning fell into the jaws of this visit.[54]

We almost hear in these strictures the voice of Emma failing to escape Miss Bates. The point is that in a village, these conjunctions are inescapable.

Notoriously, Austen chose in *Emma* to 'take a heroine whom no one but myself will much like',[55] that is, an assertive, powerful, independent, self-confident woman who is extremely faulty – frequently conceited, blind, snobbish and manipulative. When so described, Emma sounds rather more like Fitzwilliam Darcy before he learns to love Elizabeth Bennet than any other Austen character. This unconventional, almost androgynous, choice of heroine permits Austen a much sharper look at women's options within society than she can take in any other novel. Because her heroine is so secure, nearly as secure as a rich man, Austen is free to explore issues of women's power and marginality more profoundly than she had in earlier novels without destroying a comic tone. As usual, courtship offers a means to approach these issues, and in this novel, courtships are not merely enacted but obsessively discussed. Conversation develops the novel's themes as well as characters. Much more than any other Austen heroine, for example, Emma herself likes to consider and discuss questions of 'female right' (65). Her attitudes are always ironically mistaken, as when her 'woman's friendship' (67) steers Harriet Smith toward Mr Elton and away from Robert Martin, and when she argues with Mr Knightley over Harriet's claims to marry well. Emma is equally wrong when she ignores Jane Fairfax's much better claims and muses on 'the difference of women's destiny' by comparing Mrs Churchill and Jane Fairfax: 'one was every thing, the other nothing' (384). Their destiny is identical, for both acquire Enscombe by marriage.

The comedy of Emma's many blunders about courtship does not entirely obscure a central fact: whenever readers look at almost any woman in *Emma* apart from the heroine, they encounter a sense of threat. They do so even in the first chapter. It is quite surprising, for instance, to notice how much Mr Knightley insists that Miss Taylor needs to be 'settled in a home of her own . . . secure of a comfortable provision' (11). Why is he so insistent? He cannot imagine that the Woodhouses would ever have discarded this 'beloved friend' (6). Before her marriage, Miss Taylor is as secure as any unmarried woman without a fortune can be, but Mr Knightley considers her insecure – as she is. If Mr Woodhouse were to die and Emma were to marry, Anne Taylor would have to leave Hartfield even if the Woodhouses left her an income. Any home that she could then afford would be much inferior, but no doubt she would be in a better position than the other threatened spinsters in the novel, Harriet Smith, Jane Fairfax or Miss Bates. Jane Fairfax is, of course, the worst off, for although she has for the present a home with the Campbells who educated her, that home is so insecure that Jane has resolved to renounce it for work as a governess, the only career possible for her:

> As long as they [the Campbells] lived, no exertions would be necessary, their home might be her's for ever; and for their own comfort they would have retained her wholly; but this would be selfishness: – what must be at last, had better be soon.
>
> (165)

The prospect for Jane of 'penance and mortification for ever' (165) is more immediately threatening than life at Mrs Goddard's for Harriet Smith or Miss Bates's occupation of the 'drawing-room floor' of a house belonging to 'people in business' (155). But in the bleak words of Mr Knightley, Miss Bates 'is poor; she has sunk from the comforts she was born to; and, if she live to old age, must probably sink more' (375). 'Neither young, handsome, rich, nor married', she lost her home when her father, a former vicar of Highbury, died (21). By contrast, the very first sentence of *Emma* assures us that Emma Woodhouse, 'handsome, clever, and rich', possesses among other seemingly 'best blessings of existence', 'a comfortable home'. The importance of a home for a single woman is insisted upon – but its unlikelihood is made clear.

Nonetheless, Emma's home is not entirely comfortable, as the first chapter insists. The position that Emma occupies at Hartfield combines power with constraint. She is constrained by being her father's keeper. 'His spirits required support' (7). She must entertain him, reassure him, humour him. He is 'a valetudinarian . . . a much older man in ways than in years' (7) and at the same time a child in his selfishness and egocentricity (8). Like a mother, Emma must arrange for others to sit with her father if she leaves the house. For these restraints, however, she has great compensation: 'she dearly loved her father' (7) and she is greatly beloved by him. Unlike Fanny Price, loved at Portsmouth only by her brother William and at Mansfield for some time only by Edmund, Emma is surrounded by love – not only her father's, but Miss Taylor's and Mr Knightley's, and at a distance her sister Isabella's. Furthermore, she has power – and not merely 'the power of having rather too much her own way' (3). As Mr Knightley informs us later, 'ever since she was twelve, Emma has been mistress of the house and of you all' (37).

Emma's later abuse of her power over Harriet Smith in persuading her not to marry Robert Martin, and to cut her acquaintance with the entire family, is so glaring that she is seldom given credit for her better management of her father and Hartfield. She has more real work to do than other Austen heroines, and she does it well, almost effortlessly. Her powerful position at Hartfield, together with her father's love, allows Emma to say, as no other Austen heroine does, that she is immune to courtship, to love and marriage. She has 'very little intention of ever marrying at all', partly because:

'I never have been in love; it is not my way, or my nature; and I do not think I ever shall. And, without love, I am sure I should be a fool to change such a situation as mine. Fortune I do not want; employment I do not want; consequence I do not want; I believe few married women are half as much mistress of their husband's house, as I am of Hartfield; and never, never could I expect to be so truly beloved and important; so always first and always right in any man's eyes as I am in my father's'.

(84)

Emma continues by praising her own 'independent resources', which will keep her busy in later life, adding:

'And as for objects of interest, objects for the affections, which is in truth the great point of inferiority, the want of which is really the great evil to be avoided in *not* marrying, I shall be very well off, with all the children of a sister I love so much, to care about.' (85–6)

And amusingly enough, Emma later cites precisely similar motives for Mr Knightley's not marrying:

'Why should he marry? – He is as happy as possible by himself; with his farm, and his sheep, and his library, and all the parish to manage; and he is extremely fond of his brother's children. He has no occasion to marry, either to fill up his time or his heart.'

(225)

All this ignorance and disdain of sexual love is, of course, ironically reversed when 'It darted through her, with the speed of an arrow, that Mr. Knightley must marry no one but herself!' (408). But the reversal does not entirely erase these cheerful images of single blessedness, images that may reflect Austen's own satisfaction at being a single woman in a comfortable home, surrounded by love, employed in exercising her own talent. For Emma, however, these blessings, together with the exercise of her talent for management and mismanagement, are insufficient. She only 'seemed to unite the best blessings of existence' in the first chapter because she did not know herself and was unaware of her own love for Mr Knightley. The dense, perfect construction of *Emma* is evident in every detail, here as elsewhere: Emma knows herself only when she has learned to fear that Harriet will be 'the wife to whom he looked for all the best blessings of existence' (422–3).

Emma was finished in only 14 months, from 21 January 1814 to 29 March 1815. Austen was clearly at the height of her genius. During this time, she also saw *Mansfield Park* through the press, made three visits to Henry in London, and three more to other friends. She was away from home for at least three and a half months altogether.[56] She wrote on 18 November 1814 that the first edition of *Mansfield Park* was sold out, and that her brother wanted her to come to London:

> to settle about a 2ᵈ Edit: – but as I could not very conveniently leave home now, I have written him my Will and pleasure, & unless he still urges it, shall not go. – I am very greedy & want to make the most of it.
>
> (L 411)

She did go, for on 30 November 1814 she wrote:

> it is not settled yet whether I *do* hazard a 2ᵈ Edition. We are to see Egerton today, when it will probably be determined. – People are more ready to borrow & praise, than to buy.
>
> (L 419)

Egerton must already have advised against a second edition. He may have pointed to a falling-off in demand for the first edition before it sold out. Austen had hoped that *Mansfield Park* 'on the credit of P. & P. will sell well, tho' not half so entertaining' (L 317; 3 July 1813). Probably just that happened; the 'Opinions' include a Mrs Dickson's rueful remark, 'I have bought MP. – but it is not equal to P. & P.' (*MW* 434). The second edition was finally issued more than a year later on 19 February 1816, by John Murray, who brought out *Emma* at the end of 1815.

Unfortunately, Egerton's advice turned out to be good. Murray's second edition of *Mansfield Park* lost money. In addition, Murray produced Austen's books more expensively during her lifetime than Egerton had, which reduced her possible profit. Nonetheless, her decision to approach Murray was not, on the face of it, a bad one. Murray's imprint carried much more prestige than Egerton's. By the time Austen submitted *Emma* to him in August or September 1815, he was Lord Byron's publisher and had co-published many of Walter Scott's works, including *Waverley*, an extremely popular novel. As Austen wrote in mock complaint to her niece Anna:

> Walter Scott has no business to write novels, especially good ones. – It is not fair. – He has Fame and Profit enough as a Poet, and should not be taking the bread out of other people's mouths. – I do not like him, & do not mean to like Waverley if I can help it – but fear I must.
>
> (L 404; 28 Sep. 1814)

Furthermore, Murray was reputedly very open-handed to authors, offering large copyright fees. He wrote in 1820 that 'I declare to God it is my first consideration and the chief object of my gratification to recompense those persons for whom I have the honour of being the publisher'.[57] Accordingly, once Murray received a favourable opinion of *Emma* from his editor William Gifford, who wrote that, 'Of "Emma", I have nothing but good to say', Austen might well have expected a generous fee for the copyright.[58] Instead, on 15 October Murray offered the sum of £450 altogether for the copyrights of *Emma*, *Mansfield Park* and *Sense and Sensibility*. Austen commented, accurately enough, 'It will end in my publishing for myself I daresay' (*L* 425; 17 Oct. 1815). Despite illness, Henry dictated early in November an exasperated reply to Murray: 'The terms you offer are so very inferior to what we had expected, that I am apprehensive of having made some great Error in my Arithmetical Calculation'. He went on to point out that his sister had made more than £450 by one small edition of *Sense and Sensibility* and a moderate one of *Mansfield Park*.[59] Henry's illness worsened, and Austen conducted most of the remaining negotiations for herself. In a letter of 3 November, she requested a meeting with Murray, at which time he must have agreed to publish *Emma* on commission, and on 23 November she was already 'vexed' by printers' delays (*L* 431, 432). Murray responded civilly, promising 'no farther cause for dissatisfaction. . . . In short, I am soothed & complimented into tolerable comfort' (*L* 433; 24 Nov. 1815).

Murray's arrangement to publish *Emma* on commission was, in fact, exceptional. His business records show that he published few works by women and very few novels. In his catalogue for May 1817, he lists among more than two hundred publications only five 'novels' apart from Austen's: one by Scott, two by Isaac Disraeli, and two anonymous works.[60] His great admiration for *Pride and Prejudice* probably influenced him. And when he obtained Scott's review of *Emma*, the longest and best that Austen received in her lifetime, Murray did her a favour, since his own profit was not heavily involved. He could make no more than £137.10.0 from *Emma* if every copy were sold.

Hindsight indicates that Murray's offer of £450 for the three copyrights was fair if not generous. Austen would have done well to accept it. First, she would have received that sum within a year. Instead, because losses on the second edition of *Mansfield*

Park were set against the profits of *Emma*, Austen received during her lifetime only £38.18.0 profit on her greatest work.[61] Ultimately, her heirs received a total of about £385 more from the sole edition of *Emma*, from the second of *Mansfield Park* (both of which were remaindered in 1821), and from the sale in 1832 of the copyrights of the three novels for £42 each.[62] In short, Murray's estimate in 1815 of the market value of her copyrights was if anything exaggerated.

Nonetheless, Murray treated Austen rather less generously than other writers. He frequently gave such large payments to his authors that he lost money by their works. For example, he paid £500 for the copyright of John Robison's *A System of Mechanical Philosophy* in 1815; he lost over £800 right away on the four-volume edition, a loss that was finally reduced by remaindering to £258 in 1823. He immediately sustained an even greater loss of over £2400 on a five-volume edition in 1815 of *Modern Costume of Russia, Austria, China, England, and Turkey*. It is tempting to think that such substantial losses prompted the – for him – rather skimpy offer to Austen. But at this time, Murray was still making huge profits from Byron's works, among others, and he was capable of greater generosity to other women writers. For instance, he offered Helen Maria Williams 50 guineas in 1816 for her pamphlet, *Letters on Protestants*; the work sold out, but Murray still realised a loss of £18.2.6. He lost over £68 in the same year on Margaret Holford's poem *Margaret of Anjou*, having paid her £200 for the copyright. His worst loss on a woman's writing apparently came from his £300 payment to Harriet Lee for a reprint of her version of the *Canterbury Tales*; its sale did not cover the expenses of printing, let alone the copyright fee.[63]

Austen's refusal to accept Murray's £450 suggests how highly she valued *Emma* and how willing she was to risk a different valuation from the public. Her recent profit of more than £310 from *Mansfield Park* may have encouraged her to insist that Murray publish the fairly large edition of 2000 copies of *Emma*. Unfortunately, *Emma* was not generally popular with the reading public or her own acquaintance. It received more reviews than any other novel she wrote, most of them favourable, but in the first nine months it had sold only 1248 copies. After four years, the total was 1437, and the rest were remaindered. Although both of her sailor brothers, Frank and Charles, preferred *Emma* to the two preceding novels, and Mrs John Bridges liked it better than 'all the others' many liked it least of all: among others, Mrs and Miss Craven, Mrs Deans Dundas, Mr and Mrs James Austen and Mrs Digweed, who, 'if she had not known the Author, could hardly have got through it' (*MW* 436–9). Perhaps the most interesting remarks came from Alethea Bigg, who liked it less than its two predecessors, but who reread it – as *Emma* requires. At first she had objected 'to the sameness of the subject (Match-making) all through. – Too much of Mr Elton & H. Smith' but found the 'Language superior to the others'. Upon rereading, however, she 'liked Miss Bates much better than at first, & expressed herself as liking all the people of Highbury in general, except Harriet Smith – but c^d not help still thinking *her* too silly in her Loves' (*MW* 436–7).

Ironically enough, at about the same time that Austen was refusing Murray's money and insisting on publishing for herself, she was exposed to her only experience of 'patronage' – the support of polite letters by wealthy patrons. When *Emma* was in the press, the Prince Regent – who admired the novels – apparently learned of Austen's presence in London and sent his librarian to visit her. This officious and rather obtuse character, James Stanier Clarke, invited Austen to visit him at Carlton House and during the course of the visit imparted, in her words, 'the Information of my being at liberty to dedicate any future work to HRH. The P.R. without the necessity of any solicitation on my part'. Austen wished to know 'whether it is incumbent on me to shew my sense of the Honour, by inscribing the Work now in the Press, to H.R.H. – I sh^d be equally concerned to appear either Presumptuous or Ungrateful' (*L* 429; 15 Nov. 1815). The word 'incumbent' suggests her annoyance. She had no admiration for the Regent; less than three years earlier, she had written to Martha Lloyd, jokingly as always, but with an undercurrent of hostility:

> I suppose all the World is sitting in Judgement upon the Princess of Wales's Letter. Poor woman, I shall support her as long as I can, because she *is* a Woman, & because I hate her Husband – but I can hardly forgive her for calling herself 'attached & affectionate' to a Man whom she must detest. . . if I must give up the Princess, I am resolved at least always to think that she would have been respectable, if the Prince had behaved only tolerably by her at first.
>
> (*L* 504; 16 Feb. 1813)

Although Clarke assured Austen in his reply that dedication was not incumbent upon her, her family advised her that she must consider this permission a command.[64] At this point, Austen could choose between hypocrisy and greed. An unctuous dedication in the old eighteenth-century style could perhaps bring her a handsome gift. Henry had, after all, jokingly responded with a cheque for one hundred guineas when Austen dedicated 'Lesley Castle' to him, probably in 1791 (*MW* 110). But a dedication might just as easily bring nothing, or worse, a paltry sum, as it had to Jean Marishall who inscribed her novel *Clarinda Cathcart* (1766) to Queen Charlotte and received ten guineas.[65] Austen's choice was never in doubt. She accordingly wrote the briefest possible dedication to be prefixed to *Emma*, and she was obliged to send an expensively bound copy to the Regent, who took no notice of it or the dedication and certainly sent no money.

This unwilling and unrewarding foray into patronage cost Austen almost two pounds[66] and doubtless considerably more in disgust. Her brother Henry clearly thought more of it than she did, urging her to mention the dedication to Murray as a means to hurry the printers. As she wrote to Cassandra,

> I *did* mention the P. R – in my note to Mr. Murray, it brought me a fine compliment in return; whether it has done any other good I do not know, but Henry thought it worth trying.
>
> (*L* 436; 26 Nov. 1815)

What Austen did obtain from this episode was her 'Plan of a Novel, according to hints from various quarters' written some time after *Emma* was published, probably early in 1816. Clarke had written her several self-centred ideas for plots, which she parodied almost word for word in her 'Plan'. The heroine's clergyman father recounts 'the past events of his Life' for one volume, comprehending:

> his going to sea as Chaplain to a distinguished Naval Character about the Court, his going afterwards to Court himself, which introduced him to a great variety of Characters & involved him in many interesting situations, concluding with his opinion of the Benefits to result from Tythes being done away, & his having buried his own Mother (Heroine's lamented Grandmother) in

consequence of the High Priest of the Parish in which she died, refusing to pay her Remains the respect due to them. The Father to be of a very literary turn, an Enthusiast in Literature, nobody's Enemy but his own –

(*MW* 429)[67]

A marginal note cites 'Mr. Clarke' as the source of this 'hint'. In honour of Fanny Knight, who 'could not bear *Emma* herself' (436), the hero of the 'Plan' is 'all perfection', the heroine accomplished and faultless, enjoying 'elegant Society & living in high style' (430). For Mr Sherer, 'Displeased with my pictures of clergymen' in *Emma* (437), the heroine's father is 'most zealous in the discharge of his Pastoral Duties, the model of an exemplary Parish Priest' (429). Mr Sanford, who evidently objected to the title of *Emma*, will be gratified with one 'of the same sort as S & S. and P & P.'. (430).

The 'Plan' most fully registers, however, Austen's broadly comic response to the most frequent criticism of her work – lack of incident. 'Many critics' suggest changes of scene most unlike *Emma*: 'Heroine & her Father never above a fortnight together in one place' (429); eventually 'hunted out of civilized Society, denied the poor Shelter of the humblest Cottage, they are compelled to retreat into Kamschatka' (430). A more serious response is contained in Austen's last letter to Clarke. He had suggested that she write 'an historical romance, founded on the House of Saxe Cobourg', which she acknowledged 'might be much more to the purpose of profit or popularity than such pictures of domestic life in country villages as I deal in'. But she concluded:

> No, I must keep to my own style and go on in my own way; and though I may never succeed again in that, I am convinced that I should totally fail in any other.

(*L* 452–3; 1 Apr. 1816)

When Austen wrote this letter in April 1816, she had been writing *Persuasion* for nearly eight months, and the phrase 'though I may never succeed again' – though properly modest – may hint at a fear that this novel might fail to earn money, as her second edition of *Mansfield Park* was failing. At this time, 'profit or popularity' was of even more concern to her as a writer than it had been. Her family had suffered financial reverses. Her brother Henry's bank had failed on 15 March 1816; he took orders and became a curate in the Chawton neighbourhood. Austen herself had lost £13.7.0 of profit on *Mansfield Park* that had remained in her account with Henry, but fortunately the bulk of her earnings had been invested in the 'Navy Fives'. Other members of her family were much more seriously affected. Her brother Edward lost £20 000, her uncle James Leigh Perrot £10 000, her brothers James and Frank several hundreds each. As a result, neither Frank nor Henry could afford any longer to contribute to their mother's income.[68] In addition, since 1814 Edward had been at law with claimants to the Chawton estate; if he lost it, he would lose two-thirds of his income and his mother and sisters would lose their home. That threat hung over Austen during the rest of her life, for the suit was not settled until 1818, when Edward paid £15 000 to the claimants.[69]

These losses and threats may have kept Austen from any immediate attempt to publish *Northanger Abbey*, which Henry had probably reclaimed from the London publisher Crosby fairly soon after the publication of *Emma*.[70] In any case, the strain of so many family reverses helped to undermine Austen's own health, evidently first affected when she had nursed Henry through his serious illness in October 1815. Symptoms of Addison's disease, probably the condition that killed her, may have shown them-selves early in 1816.[71] She visited Cheltenham, a spa, in May of that year, and friends whom she saw immediately afterward 'received an impression that her health was failing'.[72] Some time within the following year, she began to feel weak enough to lie down after dinner. A familiar anecdote demonstrates the high degree of mutual thoughtfulness that prevailed in this small household of women. Austen's niece Caroline remembered that:

Aunt Jane laid upon 3 chairs – which she had arranged for herself – I think she had a pillow, but it never looked comfortable – she called it *her* sofa, and even when the other was unoccupied, *she* never took it.

The other sofa was considerately left for Mrs Austen, who in her late 70s also needed to lie down during the day. Austen explained to her niece that Mrs Austen's unselfishness made these arrangements necessary, for 'if she [Austen] ever used the sofa, Grandmama would be leaving it for her, and would not lie down, as she did now, whenever she felt inclined'.[73]

LAST WORKS: *PERSUASION* AND *SANDITON*

Ill health did not, however, prevent Austen's finishing *Persuasion* – three times, in fact. Her first version, completed on 16 July 1816, included the well-known 'cancelled chapter', in which Anne Elliot and Captain Wentworth meet and are reconciled in the Crofts' parlour, and ended with Captain Wentworth's services to Anne's friend Mrs Smith. Two days later, Austen added the extant concluding paragraph on Mrs Smith's resilient happiness, Anne's tenderness, and the navy's 'domestic Virtues' and 'National Importance'.[74] After a few weeks, Austen's dissatisfaction with this ending had prompted her to substitute two new chapters for the original Chapter 10, bringing the Musgroves to Bath, and allowing Anne to be overheard by Captain Wentworth comparing women's constancy to men's. The manuscript of the last chapter (originally Chapter 11, now 12) is the only surviving draft of any part of Austen's completed novels. Her revisions there are seldom studied, but they allow us to come very close to her methods of composition.

The two new chapters improved the structure of *Persuasion* by tying up loose ends, permitting important characters like the Musgroves and Captain Harville to reappear and to comment on the marriages of Louisa and Henrietta Musgrove. In letting us see more of these characters, Austen was also following the good advice on composition that she had given her niece Anna. Other changes to the last chapter show Austen to be deliberately tightening her novel. In an early version of the chapter, for instance, Sir Walter Elliot approves of Captain Wentworth as a son-in-law because '*he* had lost much less of youth & bloom than *she* had, and consequently might now pretend to the best Match of the two'.[75] It was a later version, pasted over this one, that symmetrically permitted Sir Walter 'to prepare his pen with a very good grace for the insertion of the Marriage in the volume of Honour' – the Baronetage with which the novel opens.[76] More interestingly, we see in this draft Austen's customary impatience with the process of concluding her novels. Originally, the first sentence of the last chapter was, 'Who can want to hear anything further?' – as if Austen herself were reluctant to supply it. The rest of the drafted paragraph is almost identical to the printed version, including the reference to a 'bad Morality': young people will overcome opposition to their marrying whether or not they are likely to make each other happy. Further into the chapter, Austen had to confront a more seriously bad morality, Anne's having been a more correct judge than Lady Russell of Captain Wentworth's and Mr Elliot's characters. Precisely this point offended a contemporary reviewer.[77] Perhaps anticipating such objections, Austen allowed herself to lapse into a private joke – referring to her own mother – when first drafting the passage following Lady Russell's admitting herself to be wrong:

> Bad Morality again. A young woman proved to have more Discrimination of Character than her elder – to have seen in two Instances more clearly what a Man was. But on the point of Morality I confess myself almost in despair – after understanding myself to have already given a Mother offense (having already appeared weak exactly in the point where I thought myself most strong) and shall therefore leave the present matter to the mercy of Mothers & Chaperones & Middle-aged Ladies in general.[78]

Austen overwrote this passage almost immediately with the one on 'natural penetration' that appears in the final version (249), but it ironically suggests the source of the impatience that some readers detect in Austen's final chapters. As Carolyn G. Heilbrun summarises, Austen:

> has to tie up the ends to finish her heroines off in the only acceptable way. In the end there is never laughter, but at best contentment, at worst a vague disquiet.

For Heilbrun, who wants closer bonds between women in the novels, Austen's marriages preclude laughter: 'Women laugh together only in freedom, in the recognition of independence'.[79] Although Heilbrun is wrong to detect no female laughter at the end of the novels – Elizabeth Bennet, for instance, compares herself to Jane by saying 'she only smiles, I laugh' (*PP* 383) – there is something like 'vague disquiet' in the conclusions. Not with the marriages themselves, as Heilbrun implies, but with the world that surrounds them. In all her novels, Austen creates marriages that point to a better, more equal social world. In *Persuasion*, that social world is made up of warm-hearted, generous, open men and women like the Crofts and the Harvilles, whose fortunes have come by their own exertions. This world excludes the cold-hearted Elliots and Dalrymples, who inherit, dissipate or marry their money. The Elliots, in fact, represent the social establishment, blazoned in the Baronetage, respected by the world and its chief representative in this novel, Lady Russell. Family tradition indicates that Austen had intended to call the novel *The Elliots*,[80] a title that appropriately reflects the radical criticism of her society that the novel contains. The immense distance between this imagined world and the one that actually exists may have prompted Austen to distance herself to some degree as she was composing her ending. Treatment that may thus seem perfunctory or dismissive actually indicates the depth of her imaginative commitment to a more attractive and equal social world.

Austen's management here of a favourite theme, the importance of a permanent home for a woman, may thus appear perfunctory but is actually sharp and profound. Many critics have noticed that in *Persuasion*, for the first time, the heroine's marriage gives her no home. The text refers to a 'settled life', but we hear only that Anne is 'the mistress of a very pretty landaulette' (251, 250). The carriage rightly suggests Anne Wentworth's mobility; as Mary Musgrove consoles herself, 'Anne had no Uppercross-hall before her, no landed estate, no headship of a family' (250). Anne has, in short, no established position within gentry society, a society too corrupt to contain her. Austen's first impulse in her draft was to make Anne's comparative homelessness even more clear. She wrote first of Captain Wentworth and Anne that 'When they had any home, she [Mrs. Smith] was frequently a' visitor. To imply that the Wentworths seldom had a home apparently was too much. Austen immediately crossed out that sentence and substituted a more ambiguous expression, 'She was one of their first visitors in their settled Life'.[81]

The importance of a settled, permanent home for a woman, paramount in Austen's other Chawton novels, has thus been abandoned for the 'good company' (*P* 150) of an imagined world that cannot be fixed in space or time. Similarly, although the other Chawton novels end with an assertion of perfection, Austen evidently could not conclude *Persuasion* in this way, despite three attempts. The last words of *Emma* refer to the 'perfect happiness of the union' (484) and those of *Mansfield Park* point to Fanny Price's finding everything at Mansfield Parsonage 'as thoroughly perfect in her eyes, as every thing else, within the view and patronage of Mansfield Park, had long been' (473). In her first attempts to finish *Persuasion*, Austen successively wrote (and crossed out) that Captain Wentworth's aid in recovering Mrs Smith's property 'convinced her of his being much nearer Perfection than her intercourse with the World had'; 'And having done so much for her scarcely could his wife even think him nearer perfection'; 'Mrs. Smith's estimate of his Perfections could be surpassed only by that Wife's'.[82] That Austen decided to abandon these attempts to assert perfection at the end of *Persuasion* fully accords with one's sense of its differences from the earlier Chawton novels.

Another significant difference lies in Austen's tendency in *Persuasion* to revert to the comedy of the juvenilia, particularly in rendering sexuality.[83] Captain Wentworth resembles Charles Adams of 'Jack & Alice', so dazzlingly attractive that he finds himself 'accepting the attentions – (for accepting must be the word) of two young women at once', Henrietta and Louisa Musgrove (82). Anne stigmatises this behaviour as 'wrong' not because it reverses traditional courtship roles but because two women are involved – one may be hurt. Otherwise, the Musgroves obtain no criticism for their 'little fever of admiration' for Wentworth (82). Women's pursuit of men seems to receive more approving attention in this novel than in any other; even Anne, the oldest of Austen's heroines, engages in 'a little scheming of her own' to manoeuvre herself near the end of a concert bench to allow Wentworth to approach her (189).

When *Persuasion* was finally completed on 6 August 1816, almost precisely a year after it was begun on 8 August 1815, Austen put it aside for longer than any other novel, perhaps because of the family's financial troubles. In February 1817 she received the first small profits on *Emma*. At this point, she had two completed but unpublished novels on her hands. Possibly she had expected that she could use earnings on *Emma* to underwrite the publication of *Northanger Abbey* or *Persuasion*, or both. Her meagre profit of about £39 probably caused her to write to her niece Fanny Knight on 13 March 1817: 'I have a something ready for Publication, which may perhaps appear about a twelvemonth hence' (*L* 484). Austen may have been hoping that next year's profits would permit the publication of *Persuasion*. In addition, since the failure of Henry's bank, she had been allowing her half-yearly dividends of £15 on the £600 in the

'Navy Fives' to accumulate in a new account at Hoare's bank.[84] She may have planned to draw upon these also, if necessary, to publish *Persuasion* and perhaps *Northanger Abbey* as well. In the same letter, she told Fanny that 'Miss Catherine is put upon the Shelve for the present, and I do not know that she will ever come out' (*L* 484). The phrase 'upon the shelf' is appropriately mercantile, whether applied to an unsuccessful debutante unable to come out into the market or to an unsaleable commodity like *Northanger Abbey*. Austen's mind and language seem to have been particularly attuned to the market after the disappointing failure to earn money from *Emma*.

In any case, Austen did not permit herself to be discouraged from further publication by illness, by having two unpublished manuscripts by her, by the failure of her second edition of *Mansfield Park* or by the relative unpopularity of *Emma*. She was forced to postpone publication, but it remained her goal, as is evident in her decision to begin a new novel, *Sanditon*, on 27 January 1817. Her health had improved slightly, and *Sanditon*, like *Persuasion*, surprisingly harks back to the juvenilia, but to their interest in burlesque rather than in reversing gender roles. Sir Edward Denham, for example, misreads Samuel Richardson's *Clarissa* and determines as a result to be a seducer like Lovelace. He also fancies himself as a literary critic, and Austen permits herself the extremely broad comedy of Sir Edward's inane raptures on the poetry of Scott and Byron. Moreover, *Sanditon* brings to a climax Austen's increasing interest in debility as the inverse of power. In the character of Diana Parker, Austen portrays a woman whose energies, finding no other outlets, make her ill. As Charlotte Heywood concludes:

> The Parkers, were no doubt a family of Imagination & quick feelings – and while the eldest Brother found vent for his superfluity of sensation as a Projector, the Sisters were perhaps driven to dissipate theirs in the invention of odd complaints.
>
> (*MW* 412)

The word 'driven' is revealing. Thomas Parker can expend his energy on turning *Sanditon* into a fashionable spa, but his sister Diana has no such 'vent'. This perception has serious implications for women, glanced at in *Persuasion* when Mrs Croft describes the consequences of being unable to accompany her husband on his ship: she had 'all manner of imaginary complaints from not knowing what to do with myself, or when I should hear from him next' (71). Nonetheless, the comic possibilities of imaginary illness struck Austen with increasing force as she grew more ill herself. Admittedly, serious illness forms part of many novels, from the near deaths of Marianne Dashwood in *Sense and Sensibility* and Tom Bertram in *Mansfield Park* to the constitutional weakness of characters like Fanny Price, Jane Fairfax or Mr Woodhouse. But Mr Woodhouse is also a hypochondriac, like his daughter Isabella and Mary Musgrove in *Persuasion*. Their hypochondria, however, pales beside that of the Parker sisters, who exceed even Mr Woodhouse in their devotion to feebleness and health food. Their tea tray, for instance, 'seemed provided with almost as many Teapots &c as there were persons in company, Miss P. drinking one sort of Herb-Tea & Miss Diana another' (416). Illness is only comic in *Sanditon*, as though Austen has chosen to transmute her own increasing debility into hilarity. Her niece Anna Austen Lefroy believed that the hypochondriacs in this work 'were certainly suggested by conversations between Aunt Jane & me during the time that she was writing this story – Their vagaries do by no means exceed the facts from which they were drawn'.[85] Possibly, but it is more likely that both the conversations and the writing sprang from Austen's comic energy, the talent that drove her to vent whatever pain, anger and fear her illness caused her as comedy.

Austen ceased writing *Sanditon* on 17 March; in seven weeks, she had produced 12 chapters. Returning illness evidently caused some parts of the manuscript to be written first in pencil, then overwritten in ink. When she stopped, she had only four months to live. The progress of her disease was certainly accelerated by yet another financial blow. Mrs Austen's wealthy brother James Leigh Perrot died on 28 March, but he left his sister nothing in his will. Mrs Austen's children were to receive £1000 apiece, but only if they survived Mrs Leigh Perrot. Austen wrote on 6 April to her brother Charles that:

> I am ashamed to say that the shock of my Uncle's Will brought on a relapse, & I was so ill on friday & thought myself so likely to be worse that I could not but press for Cassandra's returning with Frank after the Funeral last night, which she of course did, & either her return, or my having seen Mr Curtis,

or my Disorder's chusing to go away, have made me better this morning. I live upstairs however for the present & am coddled. I am the only one of the Legatees who has been so silly, but a weak Body must excuse weak Nerves.

(*L* 491–2)

If Austen did have Addison's disease, it progressed swiftly afterward, though with intervals of remission. She made her will on 27 April, evidently without telling anyone, for it was unwitnessed. She left everything to Cassandra, apart from legacies of £50 to Henry and to Madame Bigeon, formerly Henry and Eliza's servant, who had lost her savings when the bank failed. On 24 May Austen was taken to lodgings in College Street, Winchester, to consult a good physician there. He let the family know that her case was hopeless early in June.[86] The letters that survive for the last few months of Austen's life are in places as amusing as ever, and she even wrote comic verses on the Winchester races three days before she died. But her letters also contain more serious passages, as Henry's 'Biographical Notice' pointed out. He quoted one letter to a friend:

> I will only say further that my dearest sister, my tender, watchful, indefatigable nurse, has not been made ill by her exertions. As to what I owe to her, and to the anxious affection of all my beloved family on this occasion, I can only cry over it, and pray to God to bless them more and more.

(*NA* 9)

Austen knew that she was dying for some weeks before she actually died, near dawn on 18 July 1817, only 41 years old. Most of the other members of her family survived well into their 70s or 80s; the ailing Mrs Austen was 87 when she died, Cassandra 72. Cassandra's letter to Fanny Knight describing Austen's last hours is enormously painful. Her need to write out such details despite her habitual stoicism reveals the depth of her love and grief. She was to some degree keeping her sister alive by writing this letter – and other less explicit ones to friends and relations, enclosing mementoes of Austen. Later, Cassandra kept her sister's memory alive by arranging for the publication of her two remaining novels and at last by carefully apportioning the letters and manuscripts among the family when she herself was nearing death. Austen's funeral expenses were fairly heavy at about £92; burial within Winchester Cathedral was costly. Cassandra had the will proved on 10 September. After paying burial expenses, £100 in legacies, more than £22 in probate costs, and £25 in debts, Cassandra owed duty on an estate of £561.2.0.[87] Once the estate was settled, Cassandra arranged to publish the two remaining novels with Murray; as a result, she had no duty to pay on those receipts.

Although anxiety about money and ill health had prevented Austen from publishing *Persuasion*, Cassandra was evidently determined to see her sister's last works in print. Possibly the family's financial problems lay behind the apparent insistence that Murray produce *Northanger Abbey* and *Persuasion* as cheaply as possible: only 1750 copies were printed on very inexpensive paper, and they appeared at the end of December 1817. Despite the reception of only two reviews, 1409 copies sold within a year. This four-volume dual publication on commission earned £518.6.5, more than any earlier Austen novel, even though the last 283 copies had to be remaindered at 3s1d each – a far cry from the £1.4.0 retail price.[88] Overall, Cassandra collected £784.11.0 from Murray on this edition and on the final sales of *Emma* and *Mansfield Park*.[89] The sale of the five remaining copyrights to Richard Bentley in 1832 for £210 brought Austen's overall literary earnings to at least £1625, most of which was received after her death.[90]

Austen's gravestone in Winchester Cathedral notoriously makes no mention of her writings. Although she was fortunate enough to live at a time when publishing novels was easier for women than it had been – and perhaps easier than it became, once men had decided that the novel was a legitimate form – it remained suspect. Her own attitudes to her writing became increasingly professional, but conventional attitudes hung on in her family and elsewhere. Even though her brother James does refer to her as a writer in the elegy he wrote on her death, he tends to praise her heart rather than her mind, and he even proffers the conventional defence of a woman author – the assertion that her writing did not interfere with her domestic duties:

> But to her family alone
> Her real, genuine worth was known.
> Yes, they whose lot it was to prove
> Her Sisterly, her filial love,
> They saw her ready still to share

The labours of domestic care,
As if *their* prejudice to shame
Who, jealous of fair female fame,
Maintain that literary taste
In woman's mind is much misplaced,
Inflames their vanity & pride,
And draws from useful works aside.[91]

In James, evidently 'prejudice' against female achievement and pride was not entirely 'shamed'. Only Austen herself could do justice to the multiple ironies of the attitudes implied within this eulogy. Had she lived, no doubt she would eventually have done so.

Notes

Abbreviations appearing among the notes are as follows:

Aspects: Mary Augusta Austen-Leigh, *Personal Aspects of Jane Austen* (New York: E. P. Dutton, 1920).

Austen Papers: R.A. Austen-Leigh, *Austen Papers, 1704–1856* (London: Spottiswoode, Ballantyne, 1942)

Facts: R. W. Chapman, *Jane Austen: Facts and Problems* (Oxford: Clarendon Press, 1948).

Gilson: David Gilson, *A Bibliography of Jane Austen* (Oxford: Clarendon Press, 1982).

Hill: Constance Hill, *Jane Austen: her Homes and her Friends* (London: John Lane, 1904).

Life (1): William and Richard Arthur Austen-Leigh, *Jane Austen, her Life and Letters: a Family Record*, 2nd edn (London: 1913; reissued New York: Russell and Russell, 1965).

Life (2): William and Richard Arthur Austen-Leigh, revised and enlarged by Deirdre Le Faye, *Jane Austen: a Family Record* (London: The British Library, 1989).

Memoir: R. W. Chapman (ed.), James Edward Austen-Leigh, *Memoir of Jane Austen* (1926; rpt. Oxford: Clarendon Press, 1967); the *Memoir* was originally issued in 1870.

Rem-AAL (1): Anna Austen Lefroy, 'Reminiscences of Aunt Jane', in Mary Gaither Marshall (ed.), *Jane Austen's Sanditon* (Chicago: Chiron Press, 1983) pp. 155–76.

Rem-AAL (2): Deirdre Le Faye, 'Anna Austen's Original Memories of Jane Austen', *Review of English Studies*, N. S. 39 (1988), pp. 417–21.

Rem-CA: Caroline Austen, *My Aunt Jane Austen: a Memoir* (London: Spottiswoode, Ballantyne, 1952).

Reports (A): *Annual Reports of the Jane Austen Society*.

Reports (C): *Collected Reports of the Jane Austen Society, 1966–1975* (Folkestone: Wm. Dawson, 1977).

Tucker: George Holbert Tucker, *A Goodly Heritage: a History of Jane Austen's Family* (Manchester: Carcanet New Press, 1983).

1 Conditions of Authorship for Women, 1775–1817

1. Henry Austen's 'Memoir' was printed as an introduction to the posthumous edition of *NA* and *P*; see *NA* pp. 3-9.
2. Rem-CA, p. 10
3. 'Profile of Women Writing in English from 1660 to 1800', in Frederick M. Keener and Susan E. Lorsch (eds), *Eighteenth-Century Women and the Arts* (New York: Greenwood Press, 1988), p. 248.
4. Letter of 18 Mar. 1804; (Margaret Baron-Wilson), *The Life and*

Correspondence of M. G. Lewis, 2 vols (London: Henry Colburn, 1839), 1:278.

5.   *Letters of Lady Louisa Stuart to Miss Louisa Clinton.* Second Series, ed. Hon. James A. Home (Edinburgh: David Douglas, 1903), p. 408.

6.   *Printing Technology, Letters & Samuel Johnson* (Princeton University Press, 1987), p.4.

7.   *Critical Review* 37 (1774), p. 475. Cited by Antonia Forster, '"Women First, Artists Second": Images of Women as Writers and Readers, 1749–1785', unpublished paper read at the American Society for Eighteenth-Century Studies Association meeting in 1988.

8.   Judith Phillips Stanton, 'Charlotte Smith's "Literary Business": Income, Patronage, and Indigence', in Paul J. Korshin (ed.), *The Age of Johnson*, 1 (New York: AMS Press, 1987), pp. 376-7.

9.   Hookham and Carpenter published *The Romance of the Forest*. Their records are located in the Public Record Office, C104/75/1–3; I am very grateful to Ruthe Battestin, whose advice allowed me to discover these records. They comprise three ledgers, the first labelled F (equals 1), the second G (equals 2) and the third Petty Ledger F (equals 3). This information comes from the Petty Ledger, p. 191, where the name is spelled 'Mr Ratcliff'. All subsequent references to the ledgers will be indicated in the text by the alphabetical abbreviation of the ledger followed by page number, for instance: PL/191 for Petty Ledger, p. 191.

10.   Carla Hesse, 'Reading Signatures: Female Authorship and Revolutionary Law in France, 1750–1850', *Eighteenth-Century Studies* 22:3 (1989), p. 486.

11.   *Memoirs of Doctor Burney*, 3 vols (London: Edward Moxon, 1832), 2:145.

12.   *Evelina, or the History of a Young Lady's Entrance into the World*, ed. Edward A. Bloom (London: Oxford University Press, 1982), p. 7.

13.   See also Margaret Anne Doody's compelling analysis of Burney's struggles with 'authority' in the prefatory verses to her father: *Frances Burney: the Life in the Works* (New Brunswick, New Jersey: Rutgers University Press, 1988), pp. 31–2, 37–8.

14.   Rem-CA, p. 7.

15.   Annie Raine Ellis (ed.), *The Early Diary of Frances Burney, 1768–1778*, 2 vols (London: George Bell, 1907), 1:39.

16.   Laetitia-Matilda Hawkins, *Memoirs, Anecdotes, Facts, and Opinions*, 2 vols (London: Longman, Hurst *et al.*, 1824), 1:88–9.

17.   *Memoirs, Anecdotes* 1:157.

18.   See Antonia Forster, 'The Business of Reviewing', read at the South Central Society for Eighteenth-Century Studies meeting, March 1990. See also *Index to Book Reviewing in England, 1749–1774* (Carbondale Ill.: Southern Illinois University Press, 1990).

19.   Serial publication, whereby a large book was issued in small sections, was no longer as popular as it had been in the mid-eighteenth century, and in any case it was generally used for large reference works, Bibles and so forth.

20.   Isobel Grundy emphasises that Hawkins 'belittles' herself and her

efforts in the first sentences of the passage, and I agree; but I think that as a whole the passage allows her to score off publishers a little – their 'sagacious scent', for instance. See Grundy, 'Samuel Johnson as Patron of Women', in Korshin (ed.), *Age of Johnson* 1:61.

21. *Memoirs, Anecdotes*, 1:156.
22. *Memoirs, Anecdotes*, 1:157.
23. Hookham published at least 14 anonymous novels under his own imprint between 1775 and 1791 (that is, he bought the copyrights), according to the Eighteenth-Century Short-Title Catalogue, but Hawkins' work may not be among them: the ESTC, a massive computer data base listing all eighteenth-century materials printed in England that are held by its contributing libraries and institutions, includes only works that survive in libraries.
24. *Memoirs, Anecdotes*, 1:157.
25. *Early Diary*, 2:162.
26. See Tucker, p. 34.
27. Dorothy Blakey, *The Minerva Press* (London: Oxford University Press, 1939), pp. 73-4; Stanton, 'Charlotte Smith's "Literary Business"', p. 388.
28. Tucker, p. 34.
29. *Facts*, p. 43.
30. 'Reading Signatures', p. 469.
31. 'Reading Signatures', p. 473.
32. Bloom, 'Introduction', *Evelina*, pp. xi, xii. Although Bloom gives 800 as the correct number for the first edition, 500 is much more likely. Editions were almost always printed in multiples of 250, and 500 was a common print run for a novel by an unknown writer at this time.
33. Edward A. and Lillian D. Bloom, 'Introduction', *Camilla, or a Picture of Youth* (London: Oxford University Press, 1983), pp. xx, xix; Joyce Hemlow, *The History of Fanny Burney* (Oxford: Clarendon Press, 1958), p. 337.
34. Longman Letter Books, transcribed by Michael Bott and deposited among the Longman archives at the University of Reading, I/100/34, 20 Nov. 1816.
35. Edward A. and Lillian D. Bloom, 'Introduction', *Camilla*, p. xix-xx.
36. *Memoirs of my Life*, ed. Betty Radice (Harmondsworth, Middlesex: Penguin, 1984), p. 159.
37. Jan Fergus and Janice Farrar Thaddeus, 'Women, Publishers, and Money, 1790–1820', *Studies in Eighteenth-Century Culture* 17 (1987), p. 198 and n38, pp. 206–7.
38. Longman Letter Books, I/97/23, 15 Feb. 1811.
39. Archives of John Murray, Commission Ledgers: for *MP*, BB1/242 and for *E*, BB1/228. Copies Ledgers: for *NA* and *P*, B/142. Jane Aiken Hodge has published photographs of BB1/242-3 and 228-9 in *Only a Novel: the Double Life of JA* (New York: Coward, McCann & Geoghegan, 1972); for transcriptions of much of this material, see also Gilson, pp. 59–60, 68-9 and 84–5.

40. Gilson, pp. 59 and 69.
41. For example, Burney is particularly querulous in an 1817 letter to the House of Longman, objecting to their view that sales of *The Wanderer* (1814) had ceased (Letter 1113, 30 Aug. 1817, in Warren Derry (ed.), *The Journals and Letters of Fanny Burney (Madame D'Arblay)* (Oxford: Clarendon Press, 1982) 10: 631–2.
42. Edith J. Morley (ed.), *Edward Young's Conjectures on Original Composition* (Manchester University Press, 1918), p. 24.
43. The date is provided by Deirdre Le Faye, 'JA: Some Letters Redated', *Notes and Queries* (Dec. 1987), p. 479.
44. The records of John, Samuel and Thomas Clay, booksellers in Daventry, Rugby, Lutterworth and Warwick at various times from the 1740s to the 1780s, are on deposit in the Northamptonshire Record Office; those of Timothy Stevens of Cirencester are deposited in the Gloucester City Library and cover the 1780s through to about 1805.
45. Northamptonshire Record Office, ZB 340/6.
46. Samuel Smiles, *A Publisher and his Friends: Memoir and Correspondence of the late John Murray*, 2 vols (London: John Murray, 1891), 1:288.
47. See Jan Fergus and Ruth Portner, 'Provincial Subscribers to the *Monthly* and *Critical Reviews* and their Book Purchasing', in O.M. Brack Jr. (ed.), *Festshrift for William Todd* (New York: AMS Press, 1990).
48. JA's original capitalisation and punctuation have been restored by examination of the copy in the Murray Archives.
49. [Henry Austen], 'Memoir of Miss Austen', in JA, *SS* (London: Richard Bentley, 1833), p. viii.

2 Background and Literary Apprenticeship, 1775–1793

1. Hodge, *The Double Life of JA*; Halperin, *The Life of JA* (Baltimore, Maryland: Johns Hopkins University Press, 1984).
2. See Tucker; Honan, *JA; her Life* (London: Weidenfeld & Nicolson, 1987); and Life (2).
3. Hill, p. 11.
4. *Life* (2), pp. 113–14; Hill's version is slightly different, pp. 91–2.
5. Rem-AAL (1), pp. 155–6. Marshall prints the draft of a letter from Anna Austen Lefroy to her brother James Edward; Deirdre Le Faye has published the somewhat different letter that Anna Austen Lefroy actually sent (Rem-AAL [2]).
6. Hughes, *A London Family, 1870–1900* (London: Oxford University Press, 1946), p. 33.
7. F.C. K[night], 'Aunt Jane', *Cornhill Magazine*, 163 (1947/8), p. 72.
8. Tucker, pp. 27, 30–1.
9. *Life* (2), p. 14.
10. *Life* (2), pp. 23, 69.
11. *Austen Papers*, pp. 23–4.
12. *Austen Papers*, pp. 32–3.

13. The *Memoir* mentions ill-health (possibly owing to a miscarriage) during the move to Steventon 'soon after' July 1768 (*Life* [2], p. 17). The move, something over a mile, took place over 'a mere cart track, so cut up by deep ruts as to be impassable for a light carriage. Mrs Austen, who was not then in strong health, performed the short journey on a feather-bed, placed upon some soft articles of furniture in the waggon which held their household goods' (*Memoir*, p. 9).

14. Deirdre Le Faye, 'Three Austen Family Letters', *Notes and Queries* (1985), p. 329. Henry had been baptised on 8 June.

15. *Memoir*, p. 43.

16. *Austen Papers*, p. 29.

17. *Austen Papers*, pp. 30, 31.

18. *Memoir*, p. 43.

19. Roy Porter, *English Society in the Eighteenth Century* (Harmondsworth, Middlesex: Penguin, 1982), p. 16.

20. Tucker, p. 117.

21. *Life* (1), p. 301.

22. *Life* (2), pp. 44–9.

23. Tucker, p. 151.

24. *Memoir*, p. 16.

25. Honan, *JA*, p. 33.

26. Cassandra may also have had private drawing lessons in 1784; see *Life* (2) p. 47.

27. *Austen Papers*, p. 131.

28. Rem-CA, p. 8.

29. *Life* (2), pp. 39, 68; Honan, *JA*, 18–19. For charades, see *Aspects*, pp. 157–69.

30. R.W. Chapman, 'JA's friend Mrs Barrett', *Nineteenth-Century Fiction* 4 (1949), 172–3. See also *Aspects*, pp. 85–6.

31. Typescript of letters from Frances Fitzwilliam Austen to Mrs J. C. Esten, Bodleian MS Eng Lett d 86/20. Cassandra was born 22 Dec. 1808; her mother had therefore succeeded in teaching her to read two months before she was five.

32. Thomas Dyche, *A Guide to the English Tongue* (London: J. Bruce, D. Burnet, R. Hopper, R. Pennington, L. Martin, 1790), pp. 158, 159.

33. Dyche, *Guide* (London: Sam. Butler, Holbourn, 1710), p. 126. Margaret Weedon has discussed these lines and their many eighteenth-century reprints in '*NA*', *TLS* (26 Nov. 1982), p. 1311.

34. Madame d'Arblay, *Memoirs of Doctor Burney*, 3 vols (London: Edward Moxon, 1832), 2: 123.

35. 'Introduction', in Frances Beer (ed.) *The Juvenilia of JA and Charlotte Brontë* (Harmondsworth, Middlesex: Penguin, 1986), p. 19.

36. The manuscript is in the British Library, Add. Mss. 59874.

37. For extended analyses of JA's reading, see Mary Lascelles' splendid chapter, 'Reading and Response', in *JA and Her Art* (1939; rpt. London: Oxford University Press, 1961), pp. 41–83, and Margaret Anne Doody's excellent 'JA's Reading', in J. David Grey, A. Walton Litz and Brian Southam (eds), *The JA Companion* (New York:

Macmillan, 1986), pp. 347–63.

38. *Reports* (C), p. 257; see also *Reports* (A, 1975).
39. John McAleer has argued that 'Internal evidence enables us to identify more than 50 works familiar to the author of the juvenilia', but he tends to stretch the evidence ('What a Biographer Can Learn about JA from her Juvenilia', in J. David Grey, (ed.), *JA's Beginnings: the Juvenilia and Lady Susan* (Ann Arbor: UMI Research Press, 1989). Grey's collection will hereafter be cited as *JA's Beginnings*.
40. See Gilson, pp. 431–46, for a complete list of surviving books known to be owned by JA.
41. 'Anna Lefroy's Description of Steventon Rectory in the Rev. George Austen's Time', *Reports* (C), p. 246; also *Reports* (A, 1975).
42. Rem-CA, p. 10.
43. Tucker, pp. 100–3, 105.
44. Rem-CA, p. 10.
45. *Memoir*, p. 89.
46. *Aspects*, pp. 26–8, 33.
47. Rem-CA, p. 11.
48. Rem-CA, p. 6.
49. *Life* (2), p. 34; *Austen Papers*, p. 100.
50. *Austen Papers*, p. 148.
51. *Memoir*, p. 157.
52. 'JA and her Hancock Relatives', *Review of English Studies*, N.S. 30 (1979), p. 21.
53. The obituary notes of Mrs Lefroy that, 'At twelve years old she wrote a beautiful hymn, and other small poems; and two or three of her compositions, written nearly thirty years ago, are inserted in the first volume of the "Poetical Register," pp. 32, 36, 112.' But the conventional disclaimer quickly follows: 'possessed of various qualities to please, and capable of delighting by more general and social attractions, she never aspired to the fame of an author. It was only an accidental impulse that occasionally prompted her to seize the pen; when she wrote for private amusement a few glowing and unaffected lines with the same forcible and careless rapidity with which she talked' (*Gentleman's Magazine* [Dec. 1804], p. 1178).
54. *Life* (2), p. 39.
55. Honan, p. 78. Le Faye dates the move to Deane in the spring of 1789 (*Life* [2], p. 64).
56. David Spring, 'Interpreters of JA's Social World', in *JA: New Perspectives, Women & Literature*, N.S. 3 (1983), p. 60.
57. Spring, p. 59.
58. Spring, pp. 60 and 61.
59. Terry Lovell's term 'lesser gentry' to describe the Austen's class seems equally acceptable but does not underline the group's marginality – oddly enough, for Lovell sees the lesser gentry as particularly threatened: 'Squeezed between the rising capitalist tenant-farmer and the upper gentry', 'JA and the Gentry', in Diana Laurenson (ed.), *The Sociology of Literature: Applied Studies* (Keele: Sociological Review Monographs 26, 1978), p. 21.

60. See Diary of John Morley, 1801, deposited in the Warwick County Record Office (hereafter abbreviated WCRO), CR 2486, entry for 2 Feb. Morley had earlier mentioned seeking a place at Guy's for his sister (entry for Thursday 2 Nov. 1797, WCRO Mic 142), and he later mentions her residency there.

61. Robert Bearman, 'Henry Austen and the Cubbington Living', *Persuasions* No. 10 (1988), p. 23.

62. Fanny Catherine Lefroy, in her anonymous article 'Is it Just?' in *Temple Bar* (Feb. 1883), p. 275, quotes Mrs. Austen as writing to 'her wealthy sister-in-law' (presumably Mrs Leigh Perrot), '"One hundred and forty pounds a year . . . is the whole of my own income. My good sons have done all the rest"'. Mrs Austen wrote to Mrs Leigh Perrot on 4 Jan. 1820 that the banker Hoare receives her dividends, 'amounting to not quite £116 a year; this sum, with a little land at Steventon, which I let for £6 a year, is the whole of my own property, my good children having supplied all the rest' (*Austen Papers*, p. 264). The similarity in the two accounts suggests that Lefroy had seen the 4 Jan. 1820 letter but remembered it inaccurately.

63. B.M. Add MSS 38039, f. 184.

64. For George Austen, see Tucker, pp. 25, 27, 31. For Edward, see Tucker, pp. 122–3. For Mrs Austen's connection to the founder of St John's, see Tucker, p. 63. For the value of the Cubbington Living, see Bearman, 'Henry Austen and the Cubbington living', p. 24. For the Leigh Perrots, see Tucker pp. 92–3, 95. For Henry's losses, see Tucker, p. 146, and for the Steventon living, see Maggie Lane, *JA's Family through Five Generations* (London: Robert Hale, 1984), p. 196.

65. 'Aunt Jane', *Cornhill* 163: 72–3.

66. One of the few such dinners on record occurred on 26 March 1799, when Mr and Mrs Chute of the Vyne dined at Steventon; JA dined with them in return on 19 Apr. (*Life* [2], p. 103).

67. Gilson, p. 383.

68. Rem-AAL (1), p. 165.

69. Rem-CA, pp. 5, 10.

70. See especially Litz, *JA: a Study of Her Artistic Development* (London: Oxford University Press, 1965), pp. 14, also 6; Lascelles, *JA and Her Art* (1939; rpt. London: Oxford University Press, 1961), pp. 55, 71–2.

71. I would like to thank Dr Bruce Barker-Benfield, Assistant Librarian, Department of Western Manuscripts, Bodleian Library, for his expert help in examining the manuscript and interpreting changes in ink, pen and handwriting. B. C. Southam has noticed some of the same features of Volume the First, but he infers that JA was creating a 'show-piece', not a book ('The Manuscript of JA's Volume the First', *The Library*, 5th ser., 17 [1962], pp. 232–4, 234).

72. Spacing and changes in ink in the table of contents page of Volume the First make it appear as though JA entered the first 11

tales in four separate groups, and only in the second group, containing the two short tales 'Mr Harley' and 'Sir William Montague', does she write a dedication simultaneously with the tale itself. From this point, all the works in Volume the First, as well as those in Volumes the Second and Third, begin with dedications that are copied down at the same time as the works themselves. Austen then returned to add dedications to four of the five earliest tales (only 'Edgar & Emma' has none). The dedications added later to these four tales point to dates between 1789 and 1790.

73. B. C. Southam dates 'Lesley Castle' in 1792 using the date given for the first letter, 3 Jan. 1792 (*Jane Austen's Literary Manuscripts* [London: Oxford University Press, 1964], p. 15). But 'Lesley Castle' is transcribed between works dated 13 June 1790 and 26 Nov. 1791. Austen may have used the almanac for 1790 or 1791 in composing it; the almanac for 1792 does not work.

74. Southam, *Literary Manuscripts*, p. 17.

75. Sandra M. Gilbert and Susan Gubar, in their influential study *The Madwoman in the Attic* (New Haven: Yale University Press, 1979), argue that the powerful women in JA's juvenilia underscore the limitations women face within society. In my view, the juvenilia as well as the novels explore and celebrate possibility for women (within the constraints of society) rather than confinement.

76. Richard Whately, unsigned review of *NA* and *P*, *Quarterly Review* 24 (1821), pp. 352–76; rpt. B.C. Southam (ed.), *JA: the Critical Heritage* (London: Routledge & Kegan Paul, 1968), p. 101.

77. '"The Kingdom at Sixes and Sevens": Politics and the Juvenilia', in J. David Grey (ed.), *JA's Beginnings*, p. 52.

78. Baron-Wilson, *Life and Correspondence of M. G. Lewis*, 2:241.

79. *Life and Correspondence of M. G. Lewis*, 2: 247–8.

80. 'JA and *The Loiterer*', *Review of English Studies*, N.S. 12 (1961), pp. 253–4. Other critics note verbal parallels. For example, Elizabeth Jenkins points out that in *Loiterer* 58, a character looks triumphant, 'having *pronounced this bitter Philippic*'; in *SS*, Mrs Ferrars 'pronounced in retort this bitter phillippic; "Miss Morton is Lord Morton's daughter"' (235–6); see 'A Footnote to "Sophia Sentiment"', *Reports* (C), p. 13.

81. 'JA and *The Loiterer*', p. 252.

82. *Critical Review* 70 (1790), p. 375.

83. *Critical Review* on *SS*, Feb. 1812, pp.149–57; rpt. *Critical Heritage*, p. 35.

84. John McAleer has suggested that Cassandra may be the author of the letter ('What a Biographer can Learn', *JA's Beginnings*, p. 46). The only argument in favour of this supposition is that the style is not quite like JA's. We have no evidence that Cassandra wrote anything but letters and charades.

85. For accounts of university expenses, see Christopher Wordsworth, *Social Life at the English Universities in the Eighteenth Century* (Cambridge: Deighton, Bell, 1874), p. 414: he quotes a 1760 source that asserts 'that 80*l. per annum* was enough, but a gentleman-commoner spent 200*l*'.

86. For example, one of Austen's favourite poets, George Crabbe, wrote in 1808 that he spent £1300 educating one son at Cambridge and another son for one term there (René Huchon, *George Crabbe and his Times, 1754–1832*, transl. Frederick Clarke [1907; rpt. London: Frank Cass, 1968], pp. 221–2).

87. James became curate of Stoke Charity in June 1789, upon taking orders, then curate of Overton, presumably in 1790, and finally vicar of Sherborne St John in Sep. 1791 (Tucker, pp. 103, 105). Clearly, he almost never was restricted to £50 a year. After his bankruptcy, Henry obtained the curacy of Chawton on 26 Dec. 1816, at a stipend of £54.12.0 (Winifred Midgley, 'The Revd Henry and Mrs Eleanor Austen', *Reports* (A) [1978], pp. 14, 19).

88. After Mr Knight's death, Edward did try to obtain a living for Henry, who requested it even though he was in the militia, but the effort was unsuccessful. See *Life* (2), p. 81.

89. Hill, p. 91.

90. 'Money Talks: JA and the *Lady's Magazine*', in J. David Grey (ed.), *JA's Beginnings*, p. 155.

91. Although JA spells her heroine's name 'Catharine' in the title and on the first page, in other places she spells it 'Catherine' or refers to her as Kitty. Her last name sometimes appears as Peterson, the original version, and more frequently as Percival, the later choice. For the sake of consistency, I will use 'Catharine Percival' and 'Mrs Percival' throughout (except when quoting text directly). The change from a plebeian name like Peterson to Percival is probably significant: JA is lessening the apparent social distance between her heroine and the Stanleys and Dudleys.

92. Johnson, 'Politics', *JA's Beginnings*, pp. 52, 53–4.

93. The best argument for JA's conservative or 'Tory' politics is one of the first: Marilyn Butler's *JA and the War of Ideas* (Oxford: Clarendon Press, 1975). She altered her position slightly in her article 'History, Politics, and Religion' in *The JA Companion*.

94. See especially Claudia L. Johnson, *JA: Women, Politics, and the Novel* (University of Chicago Press, 1988).

3 The Idea of Authorship, 1794–1800

1. Rem-CA, p. 5.

2. Quoted by *Memoir*, p. 209.

3. An exception is Deirdre Le Faye, who dismisses Mrs Mitford's report as prompted by jealousy: 'plain, dumpy' Mrs Mitford, the mother of a 'short fat little girl', was jealous of JA's attractions (*Life* [2], p. 76).

4. 'Is it Just?', *Temple Bar* (Feb. 1883), p. 282.

5. Hill, p. 258; *Life* (2), p. 241.

6. Rem-AAL (1), p. 166. The letter that Anna actually sent to James Edward Austen-Leigh limits the readings at Deane to PP only: 'I have been told that one of her earliest Novels (Pride & Prejudice)

was read aloud (in MS of course) in the Parsonage at Dean' (Rem-AAL [2], p. 418).

7. A. Walton Litz, 'Chronology of Composition', *A JA Companion*, pp. 47, 49.

8. Samuel Richardson, *Clarissa, or the History of a Young Lady*, 4 vols, intro. John Butt (London: Dent's Everyman's Library, 1962), 1: 3-4.

9. *Clarissa*, 2:398.

10. Review in *The Listener* 8 (1933), pp. 799–800, reprinted in 1936 in *Abinger Harvest* (rpt. London: Edward Arnold, 1953), p. 184.

11. *Life* (1), p. 89.

12. Deirdre Le Faye, 'Tom Lefroy and JA', *Reports* (A, 1985), p. 9. JA may also have known that Mr and Mrs Lefroy had sent Tom away from Ashe, fearing 'the idea of an engagement between so youthful and penniless a pair' (*Life* [2], p. 87).

13. Caroline Austen reported: 'her letters to Aunt Cassandra . . . were, I dare say, open and confidential – My Aunt looked them over and burnt the greater part, (as she told me), 2 or 3 years before her own death – She left, or gave some as legacies to the Nieces – but of those that *I* have seen, several had portions cut out – (Rem-CA, p. 10). See also *Life* (2), p. 243.

14. The memorandum is reprinted in *MW*, facing p. 242.

15. Honan, p. 93.

16. Burrows' careful analysis of the common words in JA's novels has established that, by nearly every test, the language of the early novels is separable from that of the 'Chawton' works. As he says, 'It is difficult to conceive of substantial revisions that would not affect the patterning of the very common words' (J. F. Burrows, *Computation into Criticism: a Study of JA's Novels and an Experiment in Method* [Oxford: Clarendon Press, 1987], p. 133 and *passim*). Cutting is the only form of substantial revision that would not affect the patterns he analyses. Admittedly, Cassandra's memorandum mentions that *First Impressions* received 'alterations & contractions' (*MW* facing p. 242) before being published as *PP*. But cutting does always entail some alteration.

    Hitherto, most critics have accepted R.W. Chapman's argument that JA revised *First Impressions* extensively before publishing it as *PP*, using the 1811–1812 calendar. His argument is too detailed to rehearse here. JA would have been much amused by the earnestness of arguments about her use of calendars, for they tend to deny her on the one hand any ability to imagine *anything* without a calendar in hand, and on the other, any liability to errors in consistently applying that calendar. My own feeling is that JA used a calendar in writing *First Impressions*, perhaps that of 1795 as P. B. S. Andrews has argued ('The Date of *PP*', *Notes and Queries* 213 [1968], pp. 338–42), but not very exactly; then in lopping and cropping the novel, she decided to check its chronology against the 1811–12 calendar, but not obsessively.

17. See, among others, Claudia L. Johnson, *JA: Women, Politics, and the Novel*, pp. 86–7.

18. See my discussion in *JA and the Didactic Novel* (London: Macmillan, 1983), pp. 110–18.
19. I have more fully discussed JA's rendering of the sexuality of daily life in 'Sex and Social Life in JA's Novels' in David Monaghan (ed.), *JA in a Social Context* (London: Macmillan, 1981), pp. 66–85.
20. Unsigned review of *NA* and *P*, rpt. Southam, ed., *Critical Heritage*, p. 101.
21. See Mary Poovey's influential *The Proper Lady and the Woman Writer: Ideology as Style in the Works of Mary Wollstonecraft, Mary Shelley, and JA* (University of Chicago Press, 1984), pp. 194–207.
22. Janice A. Radway, *Reading the Romance; Women, Patriarchy, and Popular Literature* (Chapel Hill: University of North Carolina Press, 1984), ch. 4 *passim*, especially pp. 150, 134.
23. Radway, pp. 148–9, 212–13.
24. Susan Morgan, 'Why There's No Sex in JA's Novels', *Studies in the Novel* 19 (1987), p. 351.
25. Morgan, p. 355.
26. Claudia L. Johnson, *Women, Politics*, p. xxiv.
27. 'Sex and Social Life', p. 83.
28. *Austen Papers*, p. 228.
29. Andrew Wright, *JA's Novels; a Study in Structure* (1961; rpt. New York: Oxford University Press, 1967), p. 89.
30. *Memoir*, pp. 17–18.
31. I disagree with those critics who object that JA never considers female friendship as important or sustaining, either as an alternative to marriage within a patriarchal society or as a support to marriage; see Janet M. Todd, *Women's Friendship in Literature* (New York: Columbia University Press, 1980) and Nina Auerbach, *Communities of Women: an Idea in Fiction* (Cambridge: Harvard University Press, 1978). In an ingenious and provocative essay, Ruth Perry answers some of these objections by finding in *E* a subversive message: JA undercuts her marriage plot with an unresolved 'plea for friendship between women' ('Interrupted friendships in JA's *Emma*', *Tulsa Studies in Women's Literature* 5 [1986], p. 200).
32. *Life* (2), pp. 96, 102.
33. Like Burrows, I reject Brian Southam's argument that *NA* was thoroughly revised just before JA's death, made in his article '*Sanditon*: the Seventh Novel', in Juliet McMaster (ed.), *JA's Achievement* (New York: Barnes and Noble, 1976), pp. 3–7.
34. I am indebted to a conversation in 1986 with Kathleen Fowler, a graduate student at New York University, for the germ of this idea. She observed that JA did not use free indirect speech of this particular kind until she wrote *MP*. I found that this observation was mistaken, but it occurred to me afterward that JA's increased use of the form might indicate a later stage in her writing – that is, might be used to identify revised material.
35. Charlotte Smith, *Emmeline, the Orphan of the Castle*, ed. Anne Ehrenpreis (London: Oxford University Press, 1971), p. 27.

36. Norman Page, *The Language of JA* (Oxford: Blackwell, 1972), pp. 123–36, analyses other effects of free indirect speech on JA's narrative.
37. See *MW*, pp. 89, 96 and 151. JA also uses the device in her early letters; she quotes a line from one of Cassandra's letters, but shifts it from the first person to the second although she uses quotation marks (*L* 69; 11 June 1799).
38. Burrows, pp. 166–7. Although in his 'Introduction' Burrows mentions 'free indirect style' as one of the sources of character narrative (p. 10), he also indicates that he has accepted the presence of quotation marks as a signal of dialogue – 'willingly conceding that it is mildly comical to "privilege" inverted commas so highly as this policy entails' (p. 9).
39. *PP* 56, 71, 145, 262, 370; *SS* 5, 62, 126, 143, 214–15, 249, 297; *NA* Bath section, pp. 31, 99, 103, 103, 129–30; *NA* Abbey sections, pp. 156, 160, 165, 166, 167–8, 169, 176–7, 178, 178, 179, 180, 182, 218, 221, 234, 249.
40. See *MW*, pp. 324, 327, 332, 336, 339, 355, 356, 359–60.
41. Some instances point to Austen's revisions: the regret that Mr Bingley expresses at Lambton over not having seen Elizabeth (or Jane) is cast into free indirect speech, followed by a statement in direct speech giving the date of the Netherfield ball as 26 November (*PP* 262). This date is crucial to Chapman's argument that Austen used the calendar of 1811–12 in revising. To me, the insertion suggests that she did use the calendar, but in regularising the novel's chronology, not completely recasting it. Two other instances of free indirect speech in *Pride and Prejudice* occur in scenes between Elizabeth and Darcy, one at Netherfield (56) and the other when they have become engaged (370); I suspect that all scenes between the two were thoroughly gone over by Austen before publication. The most suggestive instance from *Sense and Sensibility* occurs when John Dashwood resolves in Chapter 1 to give his sisters £3000 (5). This resolution (hinting that he might not keep it) might have been added at the same time that the much-admired Chapter 2, in which the money materialises and then melts away, was written. Although Austen could have produced that chapter in the 1790s, she may have been inspired – via ironic contrast – by her brothers' generous behaviour to Mrs Austen after their father's death in 1805.
42. Cecil Stuart Emden, 'The Composition of *NA*', *Review of English Studies* NS 19 (1968), pp. 279–87.
43. See p. 99, ll. 10–13; p. 103, ll. 1–2, 17–19.
44. For example, free indirect speech occurs when Catherine is reacting to Henry's tale of her supposed adventures in the Abbey (160); when she is about to investigate the ebony cabinet (167–8, 169); and when she is inquiring about Mrs Tilney (180) and forming her suspicions of the General (182).
45. Speeches by the General: pp. 103, 156, 165, 166, 176–7, 178, 178, 179; speeches to or about him: 103, 182, 234.

46. The date is supplied by Deirdre Le Faye, 'JA: Some Letters Redated', *Notes and Queries* (Dec. 1987), p. 479.
47. See p. 166, 11. 11–14; p. 178, 11. 17–29, 34–8.
48. For example, Burrows has found that Catherine Morland's use of language (her 'idiolect') is like Mrs Elton's in showing the least change over time compared to the 15 other major 'characters who speak more than six thousand words apiece'; in other words, the other heroines' use of language develops and changes as they do, but Catherine's does not (p. 136).
49. *Austen Papers*, pp. 197–8.
50. See Sidney Ives, *The Trial of Mrs Leigh Perrot* (Boston: Stinehour Press, 1980), pp. 23–4, 34.
51. James Edward Austen-Leigh commented on Mrs Leigh Perrot's hypocrisy and meanness in a letter conjecturally dated 1 May 1818 (*Austen Papers*, p. 259).
52. *Life* (2), p. 113.
53. See Fanny Catherine Lefroy, 'Is It Just?', p. 283; see also *Life* (1), p. 173, and *Life* (2), p. 125, for Mrs Austen's illness in Bath.
54. Hill, p. 91.
55. See Brian Southam, *JA's 'Sir Charles Grandison'* (Oxford: Clarendon Press, 1980), p. 3; *Life* (2), pp. 133–4.

4 The Unpublished Author, 1801–1809

1. Deirdre Le Faye suggests that *Sir Charles Grandison* might have been written on a visit to Godmersham in June 1805: *Life* (2), pp. 133–4.
2. *Life* (2), pp. xix–xx, 124.
3. *Life* (2), pp. xviii–xxi.
4. *Facts*, p. 68.
5. Quoted by *Life* (2), p. 127.
6. *Facts*, p. 62. The writer was Catherine Hubback, one of Frank's daughters.
7. Quoted by *Life* (2), pp. 121–2.
8. Only William Lane of the Minerva Press is known to have offered as little as £5 a volume for novels at this time; see Dorothy Blakey, *The Minerva Press*, pp. 73–4. I have encountered no other equally low copyright fee for a novel in the early 1800s.
9. F. Prevost and F[rancis William] Blagdon, *Flowers of Literature for 1801 & 1802; or Characteristic Sketches of Human Nature and Modern Manners, to which are added a General View of Literature* (London: Crosby, 1803), 1:464. The published works, listed on the previous page, include reference works and compilations like 'Crosby's View of London 1803–4'. 'Beauties of Dr Moore', 'History of Quadrupeds', 'Every Man his own Gardner', as well as five novels: Sophia Woodfall's *Frederick Maltravers, or the Adopted Son* (2 vols); Elisabeth Guenard's *The Three Monks!!!* (2 vols), translated from the French and published by Crosby in conjunction with J. F. Hughes;

Christiana Naubert's *Lindorf and Caroline* (3 vols), translated from the German; and two titles that I cannot identify, listed as 'The Depraved Husband and the Philosophic Wife' (2 vols) and a Mr Lucas's 'Strolling Player' (3 vols).

10. Ian Maxted, *The London Book Trades 1775–1800* (Folkestone, Kent: Dawson, 1977).

11. Suggested by Deirdre Le Faye, *Life* (2), p. 128. Three of the five novels in Crosby's 1803 list can be classified as Gothics, but the other two seem to be a didactic and a picaresque work.

12. *MW*, pp. 362–3; italics omitted.

13. See *Facts*, p. 51, quoted from James Edward Austen-Leigh, *A Memoir of JA* (1871; rpt. London: Macmillan, 1906), p. 296; among others, see Honan, *JA, her Life*, p. 215; *Life* (2), p. 128.

14. One critic considers Emma Watson 'flawless' (Honan, p. 204), but of course she is not; for example, she is slightly ashamed of being interrupted in an early dinner by the fashionable Lord Osborne and Tom Musgrave (*MW* 344–5).

15. See JA, *The Watsons*, ed. R. W. Chapman (Oxford: Clarendon Press, 1927).

16. *Austen Papers*, p. 235.

17. *Austen Papers*, p. 264.

18. *Life* (2), p. 222.

19. *Austen Papers*, p. 303.

20. *Life* (2), p. 156. See also Edward Mogg, *Paterson's Roads* (London: Longman *et al.*, 1824) for the carriage route between Alton and Basingstoke, then Basingstoke toward Overton.

21. Tucker, p. 140; *Life* (2), p. 150.

22. *Life* (2), p. 136.

23. JA later became a splendid reader of the poem. Fulwar William Fowle remembered that, probably in the summer of 1810 on a visit to Steventon, 'She was a very sweet reader. She had just finished the 1st Canto of Marmion, & I was reading the 2nd – when Mr. W. Digweed was announced it was like the interruption of some pleasing dream' (*Life* ([2], pp. 162–3). See *Aspects* for a slightly different version (p. 62).

5 The Professional Writer, 1809–1817

1. JA added letters in 'Evelyn' dated 'Augst 19th 1809' and 'Augst 22^{d}', and in Catharine's reading list in 'Catharine, or the Bower', she substituted Hannah More's heavily didactic novel, *Coelebs in Search of a Wife* (published early in 1809), for Thomas Secker's work on the catechism (*MW* 190–1, 232).

2. *Memoir*, p. 102.

3. *Life* (2), p. 83.

4. For example, she took it on a two-month visit to Godmersham in 1798, and on returning was briefly separated from it and the £7 that she had stowed within; see *L* 21; 24 Oct. 1798.

5. *Life* (2), p. 244.
6. *Life* (2), p. 162.
7. Rem-CA, p. 8.
8. *Life* (2), pp. 155, 209.
9. A. G. L'Estrange, *The Life of Mary Russell Mitford* (London: Richard Bentley, 1870), 1:306.
10. Deirdre Le Faye, 'Recollections of Chawton', *Times Literary Supplement* (3 May 1985), p. 495. The letter is dated only 'Thursday 12 Aug', and Le Faye deduces that it was written not before 1875.
11. *Life* (2), p. 157.
12. 'Recollections of Chawton', p. 495.
13. From a Mrs Harriet Mozeley's letter to a sister, 2 Nov. 1838, after a visit to Fulwar William Fowle in Allington, Wiltshire; see Kathleen Tillotson's letter to the editor of the *TLS* (17 Sep. 1954), p. 591.
14. L'Estrange, *Life*, 1:300.
15. JA wrote to Martha Lloyd on 29 Nov. 1812, that Egerton had paid £110 for the copyright; she writes as if the event were fairly recent (*L* 501). He issued *PP* at the end of Jan. 1813. Egerton allowed Roworth to print the first volume, but employed G. Sidney for the other two, which are 'more carelessly printed', perhaps because he was demanding speed (Gilson, p. 22).
16. I have arrived at these figures by examining the Archives of the House of Longman, microfilmed by Chadwyck-Healey (Cambridge), hereafter cited as Longman. Because my conclusions about JA's early costs, editions and profits differ significantly from other accounts, these notes will document my calculations in detail. The Longman records usefully supplement those of JA's publisher John Murray, which offer no specific information about publishing costs and sales for *any* novels before Dec. 1815, when they begin to record such information for *MP* (2nd edn), *E*, *NA* and *P*. For very different estimates of JA's editions and profits, see (among others) Jane Aiken Hodge, 'JA and her Publishers', in John Halperin (ed.), *JA: Bicentenary Essays* (Cambridge University Press, 1975), pp. 75–85.

Longman brought out 750 copies of a Mrs Hurst's three-volume novel, *She Thinks for Herself*, in Jan. 1813, at a cost for paper and printing of £161.9.3. (Longman reel 1, I/2/230; the novel was published anonymously, but the author's name is given in Longman Letter Books, transcribed by Michael Bott, I/97/377). The cost for printing 750 copies of JA's *SS* over a year earlier is very unlikely to be higher: both required about the same quantity of paper; both were printed in duodecimo, 23 lines to the page; but JA's novel used slightly larger type, which means that composing costs might have been less. Bibliographical analysis shows that *She Thinks for Herself* required about 37 printed sheets; Gilson's analysis of *SS* indicates that it required slightly more, about 38 sheets. Using the best available figures for a printing in 1811, JA's novel may have cost about 31*s* per ream for the 57 reams of paper needed, and probably about 35*s* per sheet to print, yielding costs of £155. Exactly £24.9.2 was spent advertising Maria Benson's novel *The Wife. A Novel*, issued in Feb. 1810; I am assuming about the same for JA's novel (Longman reel 1, *I*/2/156).

17. The trade price to booksellers for a novel expected to retail at 15s would be 9s6d according to Longman's formula as expressed to Mrs Hughes, the author of *She Thinks for Herself*: 'If your work be sold retail at 4/6 Pr. Volume the trade sale price will be 2/10 *in sheets*; and if the price be higher or lower, the trade price will be more or less nearly in that proportion' (Longman Letter Books, *I*/97/381; 26 Nov. 1812). A volume that retailed at 5s would thus be sold to the trade in sheets at 3s2d or 9s6d for 3 vols. Booksellers purchased copies at this discounted price and themselves added cardboard covers ('boards') before selling them. If 750 copies of *SS* were sold at the trade price, receipts would be £356.5.0, and Egerton's 10 per cent commission would come to £35.12.0. Author's copies, if any, would be deducted from the total sold; for every copy JA took, she would lose 9s6d of possible gain. She would pay no commission on such copies, however.

18. Quoted by *Life* (2), pp. 170–1.

19. Longman reel 1, *I*/2/156.

20. JA and her sister seem to have received £5 a quarter during their father's lifetime, and the sum is unlikely to have been increased after his death (*L* 45, 24 Dec. 1798; *L* 47, 28 Dec. 1798).

21. Had JA offered her novels to the House of Longman, she might well have begun her publishing career earlier, for they almost certainly would have offered to share profits with her. A curious reference to JA's work survives in a letter dated 11 Oct. 1813 from one of the Longman partners to Amelia Opie: 'we are particularly interested for the success of the Austen and we sincerely regret that her works have not met with the encouragement we could wish' (Longman Letter Books *I*/98/75). If this reference has been accurately transcribed, it suggests that JA's authorship was indeed widely known, as she acknowledged in a letter of 25 Sep. 1813 (*L* 340). It also suggests that the House of Longman was not impressed by the small editions of her works that Egerton had issued. Second editions of both *SS* and *PP*, however, were to be advertised in a few weeks, on 29 Oct. 1813.

22. The discrepancy can be easily accounted for: the printer might be using larger sheets of paper so as to print two gatherings per 'sheet', a common enough practice in duodecimo printing. Two sheets would thus equal four gatherings of 24 pp. each. Standard printing prices would take this practice into consideration.

23. Maria Benson, for instance, used the metaphor in her preface to *The Wife. A Novel* (London: Longman *et al.*, 1810), p. 4. Even a man could employ it, as did the author and bookseller Robert Dodsley 50 years earlier, when he begged William Shenstone to supply copy for the fifth and sixth volumes of Dodsley's *Collection of Poems by Several Hands*: 'Ah, dear M^r. Shenstone! consider what a sad situation I am in – big with *twins*, at my *full time*, and no hopes

of your assistance to *deliver* me! Was ever *man* in such a situation before?', James E. Tierney (ed.), *The Correspondence of Robert Dodsley 1733–1764* [Cambridge University Press, 1988], pp. 331–2).

24. Quoted by Gilson, p. 9.
25. Quoted by *Life* (2), p. 180; Le Faye conjectures that the lines were written on a visit to Chawton in the summer of 1813.
26. JA's presence in London to read proofs in March along with her hope to see the book before the end of April suggests that Egerton sent *SS* to the printer in late January.
27. I cannot accept Deirdre Le Faye's conjecture that JA could not have begun *MP* at this time because she was busy correcting proofs of *SS* and planning revisions to *PP*; see *Life* (2), p. 176.
28. Reprinted by Southam (ed.), *Critical Heritage*, pp. 41, 46.
29. Gilson, pp. 25, 26, 68.
30. Quoted by *Life* (2), p. 167.
31. Henry Austen, 'Memoir of Miss Austen', *SS* (London: Richard Bentley, 1832), p. ix.
32. See *Life* (1), p. 307 for the last detail, *Memoir*, p. 158, for the rest.
33. These estimations are based upon Gilson's bibliographical analysis of the novel: despite being somewhat longer than *SS*, *PP* was printed in fewer sheets, 36.5 instead of 38, using slightly smaller type in the second and third volumes. With his own profits at stake, Egerton shaved costs. Charges for printing a second edition of 750 copies in Oct. 1813 are unlikely to be more than the £161 charged in Jan. 1813, for 750 copies of *She Thinks for Herself*, printed in 37.5 sheets (Longman, I/2/230) in paper and type similar to that in *PP*, vols 2 and 3. The success of *SS* would probably have encouraged Egerton to bring out a larger first edition of *PP*; printing 1000 copies instead of 750 would have cost perhaps £40 more. The trade price for an 18s novel, 11s6d, would yield receipts of £1006 once 1750 copies were sold. Allowing about £65 altogether for advertisements, and £3.9.0 for six author's copies, both editions would cost about £430, leaving a profit of £475 after deducting Egerton's commission of £100.12.0. More than half the profit would have been made within nine months, by Oct. 1813, when the first edition had sold out. The second edition was exhausted at some point in 1817, for Egerton brought out a third edition in that year.

    Geoffrey Keynes has estimated that the first edition of PP included 1500 copies (Gilson, p. 24); I doubt that Egerton would have risked such a large edition when *SS* had not yet sold out and when recomposing and reprinting was still relatively cheap in relation to the price of paper. If he did print more than 1000 copies, Egerton's profit on the novel would have been proportionally greater.
34. Robert Lowth, *A Short Introduction to English Grammar* (1762), p. 58, quoted by K. C. Phillipps, *JA's English* (London: André Deutsch, 1970), p. 125.
35. The joke becomes more pointed if we suppose Austen's 'stupidest of all' to be, in her own mind, a reclaimed *NA*, much shorter than her other works. More probably, however, she is simply poking fun

at herself by imagining each succeeding novel as worse than the last. Her 'two next' were not yet written although *MP* was nearing completion.

36. The publishing house of Longman wrote to Robert Cruttwell, who owned the copyright of *Cruttwell's Gazetteer*, that 'We consider it justice to the proprietor of the Copyright to inform you that we have but 54 copies remaining, & that if a new edition be not immediately proceeded with the property will suffer most materially' (Longman Letter Books, I/98/123; 27 Jan. 1814).

37. See JA's note of 'Profits of my Novels', reproduced in facsimile in *Plan of a Novel* (Oxford: Clarendon Press, 1926); hereafter cited as 'Note on Profits'.

38. *A JA Companion* (London: Macmillan, 1973), p. 102.

39. Park Honan has pointed out that Chapman's edition of the letters has encouraged misinterpretation by incorrectly transcribing JA's punctuation. The passage should read, 'something else; – it shall be a complete change of subject – Ordination. – I am glad'; see 'Richardson's Influence on JA', in Valerie Grosvenor Myer (ed.), *Samuel Richardson: Passion and Prudence* (London: Vision Press, 1986) p. 169. Honan seems unaware of Pinion's earlier argument. Jo Modert's facsimile edition of JA's letters (1990) should prevent such errors in the future.

40. Phillipps, pp. 125–6.

41. Quoted by *Life* (2), pp. 161–2.

42. Quoted by *Life* (2), p. 184.

43. See, for example, the first sentence of *Sanditon* in the facsimile edition, *Sanditon, an Unfinished Novel by JA*, intro. Brian Southam (Oxford: Clarendon Press, 1975), p. [1].

44. Quoted by *Life* (2), p. 248. The quotation comes from a letter of 26 Mar. 1856 from Lady Campbell, who had just discovered that her acquaintance Louisa, now Lady George Hill, was JA's niece.

45. Sidney Ives, *The Trial of Mrs Leigh Perrot* (Boston: Stinehour Press, 1980), p. iii; Deirdre Le Faye conjectures that this fragment was written to Frank Austen, *Life* (2), p. 188.

46. Bodleian MS Autog d 11/244ʳ; printed in *Life* (1), p. 311.

47. JA must have made over £310 from *MP*, according to the letter from Henry to John Murray that has been cited, for Henry asserts that she received from her small edition of *SS* (£140) and a moderate one of MP more than the £450 Murray had offered for the copyrights of *SS*, *MP* and *E* (Bodleian MS Autog d 11/224ʳ; *Life* (1), pp. 310–11). She also invested the bulk of her profits from her first three novels in £600-worth of 'Navy Fives', according to her own 'Note on Profits'. Scholars have assumed that this £600 represents clear profit, but in fact 'Navy Fives' always sold at a discount during the period when JA could have purchased them. JA's investment cost her less than £600, and her profits were accordingly smaller than has been assumed. Although we cannot calculate her earnings precisely without knowing the date on which she made her purchase, we can nonetheless infer the

size of the first edition of *MP* and arrive at an approximation of JA's profits on it.

Egerton seems to have paid his authors yearly in March. If JA received the money due on *MP* (which had sold out by 18 Nov. 1814) in March 1815 and invested it on 31 March, she would have had to pay only £531 for £600 in the 'Navy Fives', plus perhaps a £1.0.0 commission fee and 2s6d transfer tax (see *Northampton Mercury*, 1 Apr. 1815 for previous day's stock prices of 88.5; see 15 May 1812 receipt to John Plomer Clarke for the sale of £818.19.9 in the 'Navy Fives', Northamptonshire Record Office, Clarke of Welton, Box X5437). Prices fluctuated wildly during 1815, particularly after Napoleon's escape from Elba at the end of Feb. 1815. Between 25 Nov. 1814 and 15 Mar. 1816, 'Navy Fives' were sold at a low of 83.75 (on 18 Aug. 1815) and a high of 97.13 (on 2 Dec. 1814) according to the *Northampton Mercury*, which for most of that time lists only the week's closing prices. JA lost the £13.7.0 of profits on *MP* that remained in Henry's bank when it failed on 15 Mar. 1816; she must have bought the 'Navy Fives' earlier. Accordingly, I calculate that JA earned from £310 on *MP* to a little over £347 (that is, six times the highest price per £100 for 'Navy Fives' plus £1.2.6. commission and tax and the further £13.7.0 that was not invested, less £250 received on *SS* and *PP*).

R. W. Chapman has argued that JA also received about £30 on the second edition of *SS* in 1815 and included this sum in her investment ('JA and her Publishers', *London Mercury* 22 [1930], p. 339). That edition, however, is unlikely to have become profitable before the year 1815; profit would thus have been distributed in 1816. JA's 'Note on Profits' shows that she received a payment of £12.15.0 from Egerton in March 1816. That figure and the one of £19.13.0 for March 1817 suggests a very slow sale – about 39 copies in 1816, despite the appearance of *E*.

JA could have made between £310 and £347 from *MP* only in an edition of 1250 copies. A larger edition of 1500 copies would have generated much more profit when sold out than we can account for – at least £440 even allowing £40 for advertisements, and perhaps more; a sold-out edition of 1000 would have produced a profit of less than £200. These calculations are based upon extant publishing records. John Murray's edition of *MP* (750 copies) required 42.75 printed sheets; Egerton's edition, having the same number of gatherings and similar type, would have required the same number of printed sheets. Murray's edition took 65.5 reams, slightly more than the 64.125 reams that, theoretically, 750 copies of a work of 42.75 sheets would need; 1250 copies would have required at most, then, about 109 reams of paper and perhaps less. Calculations for an edition of 1250 can draw upon the Longman records for a novel that the firm printed fairly cheaply: a translation of Louis Bonaparte's three-volume *Maria, or the Hollanders*, published in Feb. 1815. At 30s per ream, charged for the somewhat better paper in Longman's *Maria*, paper for Egerton's *MP* would come to £163.10.0. Printing for *Maria* was charged at 40*s* per sheet; the type is a bit smaller than that of *MP*, so although *Maria* prints only 24 lines to the page, not 25 as in *MP*, its charges for composing are likely to be a bit higher if anything. Using 40*s* as the base charge, however, printing *MP* would come to £85.10.0 plus an additional 2*s*6*d* per ream or £8.3.9 for all reams 'worked off' beyond the 43.5 required by *Maria* (see Longman, reel 2, I/3/76; also Longman Letter Books, I/97/290, for reference to charges of '2/6 P Rm for the pressing' of a duodecimo work, dated 11 Feb. 1812). At these rates, total expenses for printing *MP* would be £257.3.9. If all 1250 copies sold at the full trade price for an 18*s* novel of 11*s*6*d*, receipts would come to at most £646.17.6 after deducting Egerton's ten per cent. This leaves £389.13.9, a figure that plausibly covers the costs of advertising, further discounts to the trade (for example, the 'quarter book', a free copy sent to trade customers for every 24 books taken), author's copies and a profit for JA of between £310 and £347. I conclude that Chapman is right to infer an edition of 1250 copies.

48. The phrase originally comes from Edward Young's conventional satire on women, *Love of Fame: the Universal Passion, Satire vi, on Women*, 2nd edn (Dublin: George Ewing, 1728), 11. 187–8: 'For her *own* breakfast she'll *project a scheme* / Nor *take* her *tea* without a *stratagem*'. Johnson applied it in his *Life of Pope*, in J. P. Hardy (ed.), *Johnson's Lives of the Poets, a Selection* (Oxford: Clarendon Press, 1971), p. 274.
49. *Memoir*, p. 89.
50. Rem-CA, pp. 8–9.
51. *Writing a Woman's Life* (New York: Ballantine Books, 1988), pp. 12–15.
52. *Facts*, p. 84. See also *TLS* (31 Dec. 1931), *Country Life* (15 Feb. 1936).
53. *Life* (2), p. 191.
54. [Victoria Caetani], Duchess of Sermoneta, *The Locks of Norbury* (London: John Murray, 1940), p. 50.
55. *Memoir*, p. 157.
56. See Deirdre Le Faye's chronology, *Life* (2), p. xxiii.
57. Letter to W. T. Brande, 20 Aug. 1820, Murray Archives, Letter Book, p. 411.
58. Quoted by Gilson, pp. 66–7.
59. Bodleian MS Autog d 11/224[r]; *Life* (1), p. 310.
60. Trade catalogues, Murray Archives.
61. See 'Note on Profits'.
62. Exactly 539 copies of *E* were remaindered at 2*s* apiece on 25 Jan. 1821, 498 copies of *MP* at 2*s*6*d*, and 282 copies of *NA* and *P* at 3*s*1*d* (Murray Archives, BB 1/228–9; BB 1/242–3; BB 2/28–9; Copies Ledger B/151). British Library Add. Mss. 46611, ff. 305, 311, 313 record the sale of JA's copyrights to Richard Bentley. JA and her heirs also received profits on the second edition of *Sense and Sensibility*, which came to about £32 during her lifetime and an unknown

sum afterward; the existence of this edition no doubt helped to lower Murray's offer for the three copyrights.

63. Murray Archives, Copies Ledger (CL)/B/7, 9; Copies Day Book (CB)/B/128; CB/A/134; Letter Book, p. 421 (1 Jan. [1823]).
64. Rem-CA, p. 12.
65. J. M. S. Tompkins, *The Popular Novel in England, 1770–1800* (1932; rpt. London: Constable, 1969), p. 11.
66. The binding was charged at 24s and the copy itself cost JA a further 13s9d in possible receipts; Murray Archives, Ledgers BB1/228.
67. For Clarke's letter, the source of these absurdities, see L 444–5; 21 Dec. 1815.
68. *Life* (2), pp. 211, 222.
69. *Life* (2), p. 195.
70. *Memoir*, p. 138.
71. For this diagnosis, see Zachary Cope, 'Jane Austen's Last Illness', *Reports* (A), 1964, pp. 11–16; rpt. Reports (C), pp. 267-72.
72. *Life* (2), p. 213.
73. Rem-CA, p. 13.
74. British Library Egerton 3038, f. 14.
75. Egerton 3038, f. 10. Here as elsewhere, I transcribe what seems to have been JA's final intention in her first draft. For slightly different readings of the manuscript, see also the notes to R. W. Chapman's *Two Chapters of Persuasion* (Oxford: Clarendon Press, 1926).
76. Egerton 3038, f. 10*.
77. *British Critic*, March 1818; rpt. *Critical Heritage*, p. 84.
78. Egerton 3038, f. 11.
79. *Writing a Woman's Life*, p. 129.
80. *Life* (2), p. 214.
81. Egerton 3038, f. 14.
82. Egerton 3038, f. 14.
83. I have argued in 'Sex and Social Life in JA's Novels' that *P* depicts Anne Elliot's emergence from depression to recover 'bloom' or sexuality (in Monaghan (ed.), *JA in a Social Context*, pp. 75–6).
84. *Reports* (1954).
85. Quoted by *Life* (2), p. 219.
86. *Life* (2), p. 225.
87. *Reports* (1968). Legacy duty came to £16.16.8; see *Life* (2), p. 233.
88. Murray Arhives, Copies Ledger B/142,151.
89. Murray Archives, Customer Ledger D/550. Cassandra withdrew £80 in December, 1817, perhaps to assist in paying legacies or debts.
90. JA had received during her lifetime more than £310 from *MP*, £250 from *SS* and *PP* and £71.6.1 partial profits on *E* and the second edition of *SS*; Cassandra's £784.11.0 from Murray and £210 from Bentley brings the total to £1625.17.1 at least (see British Library Add. Mss. 46611, ff. 305, 311, 313). Some further payments from Egerton for the second edition of *Sense and Sensibility* were certainly also received, and more profit on *MP* is very likely.
91. Quoted by *Life* (2), p. 232.

Index

Main entries in bold